A RESISTANCE HISTORY OF THE UNITED STATES

Tad Stoermer

STEERFORTH PRESS
LEBANON, NEW HAMPSHIRE

Steerforth Press
An imprint of Pushkin Press
254 Plainfield Rd Unit 11, #1063
West Lebanon, NH 03784

Cataloging-in-Publication Data is available from the Library of Congress

www.pushkinpress.com

ISBN 978-1-58642-436-7

Printed in the United States of America

The authorized representative in the EEA is eucomply OÜ, Pärnu mnt. 139b-14, 11317, Tallinn, Estonia, hello@eucompliancepartner.com, +33757690241

1 3 5 7 9 10 8 6 4 2

To Jack and Amy and Peter

Do we call this the land of the free? What is it to be free from King George and continue the slaves of prejudice? What is it to be born free & equal & not to live? What is the value of any political freedom, but as a means to moral freedom? Is it a freedom to be slaves or a freedom to be free, of which we boast?

— Henry David Thoreau, 16 February 1851

Contents

AUTHOR'S NOTE

Why This Book?

The American history you think you know has some pretty big holes in it. Not necessarily because your teachers were malicious, but because the story America likes to tell about itself is often a carefully polished, feel-good narrative. It's the one that glosses over the ugly parts, the brutal truths about how power really works, and conveniently forgets a lot of the people who had the guts to stand up and say, "No more."

This book, *A Resistance History of the United States*, is my shot at dragging some of those inconvenient truths, and those courageous acts of defiance, out into the open. It's not a comprehensive list of every protest — that'd be a library, not a book. It's an argument, a way of looking at our past that shows a pretty consistent, and often infuriating, pattern: real people pushing back hard against abusive power, only to see their efforts get blunted, co-opted, or just plain erased by the very system they're challenging.

I've spent a lifetime immersed in this stuff. My academic trail wound through Johns Hopkins, the University of Virginia, and Harvard, learning from some of the sharpest minds in early American and Atlantic history. They taught me to rip apart national myths, to follow the story wherever it leads, even across oceans, and to understand that history is never simple or heroic in the way the official versions like to pretend.

But I've also spent years as a public historian, out in the real world where history isn't an academic debate; it's about stories, the ones people carry with them, that shape their identity, that get argued over in coffee shops, in living rooms, and on social media. I've seen how Heritage History — that safe, sanitized, often nationalistic version of the past — is usually what's on offer, because it doesn't make target audiences too uncomfortable. My goal is to offer something different, with my version of restorative history. It's not just about digging up forgotten facts; it's about an assertive engagement with the past, one that aims to repair the deliberate distortions and recover the stories, often suppressed, of those who fought back, making their struggles usable for us today.

So this book is driven by that dual vision: the historian's deep dive and the public storyteller's desire to connect. It's about that potent moment when people, driven by their own will, their volition, move beyond just complaining or working within the system and take direct action without asking anyone's permission to demand, even force, fundamental change. And it's about why, in America, that powerful assertion so often gets truncated, cut short before it can achieve lasting, systemic transformation. It's about the myths we tell ourselves and how those myths, even the well-intentioned ones, can end up protecting the very power structures that need challenging.

This book is a journey through some of the most compelling, often overlooked moments when Americans stood up and tried to make this country live up to its supposed ideals — and, along the way, created new ones for us to strive for. Understanding this pattern of courageous, assertive resistance and its all-too-frequent interruption isn't just about knowing the past; it's about understanding why we are where we are now and maybe, just maybe, figuring out how to do things differently.

INTRODUCTION

A Resistance History of the United States

I'm going to tell you something uncomfortable about American history, then spend the rest of this book telling you stories about it: Nearly every significant advance toward justice in American history came from people willing to disrupt, defy, or destroy abusive authority — and nearly every advance was rolled back by mechanisms designed for precisely that purpose.

This isn't the history you learned in school. It's what the evidence shows when you stop asking why the system didn't work better and start asking why it worked exactly as designed.

This is a resistance history of the United States — a history of how people forced change against institutions built to prevent it and how those institutions adapted to contain the changes resisters achieved.

What This Book Is

This book examines nine historical moments, from Bacon's Rebellion in 1676 through Reconstruction in the 1870s. Each chapter presents people who looked at colonial authority, revolutionary settlements, constitutional order, or federal power and concluded: This is wrong, this is illegitimate. Your laws don't deserve obedience. Your property claims don't deserve protection. Your authority doesn't deserve respect.

They were right.

But being right didn't protect them. That's what makes these movements instructive. They reveal how power actually operates — not through the procedural fairness its defenders claim, but through systematic mechanisms that interrupt successful resistance at predictable points.

I study resistance not because resisters were always noble — many weren't — but because their experiences teach more about how American power functions than studying power's own account of itself. The Constitution tells you it established justice. Enslaved people who escaped tell you that it protected slavery by design. Both are historical claims. Only one survives in the national narrative. But only the other one survives empirical scrutiny.

This book takes the side of people who resisted. Not because resistance is always justified — it isn't — but because their choices, their reasoning, and their defeats reveal what nationalist historiography obscures: American institutions were designed to protect property and power; the Constitution was an innovation in abusive authority that constitutionally enshrined exclusion; and progress came not from the system working as intended but from people forcing it to work differently — until the system adapted to contain them.

What Resistance Means

In this book, *resistance* means action outside sanctioned, permitted channels to force abusive power to answer — an escalation that usually follows a sequence. Grievances are voiced. Opposition organizes. Then comes assertion: coordinated, unsanctioned action that compels a response and seeks structural change so the abuse cannot simply resume. It is costly. It is rarely polite. And in the American context, it has been consistently effective in the moment and consistently vulnerable afterward.

Abuse begins when those entrusted with power sever the bond with the governed. When they wield the people's authority for their own interests or for a narrow faction, place themselves beyond accountability, or turn the tools of the state against the public itself. At that moment, the compact is broken, even if the legal scaffolding remains. The language of liberty may still be on the masthead, but the practice of authority has drifted from its source.

The gap created by that break is the ground on which resistance stands.

The First Republic — the constitutional order built in 1787 — announced itself as government by consent, the first state in the world to explicitly draw its authority from the collective will of the governed. That's at least what its leaders said. But from its first breath, that republic mixed the rhetoric of liberty with structures that concentrated power and shielded exploitation, enshrining the abuse of its authority just as it celebrated the source of its authority. That antagonism is why resistance runs like rebar through the nation's story. Again and again, people confronted the distance between the compact as advertised and authority as exercised.

The Structure: Nine Diagnostic Principles

The chapters are organized to teach pattern recognition — how to distinguish genuine resistance from performance, how resistance builds from individual acts to organized networks, how resistance confronts the question of violence, and how — rarely — it seizes power to transform structures.

Chapter 1: Beware False Prophets.

Not every act draped in the language of "the people" counts as resistance. Bacon's war was grievance theater for power, channeling fear and racism into campaigns of extermination against Indigenous peoples. In the same historical moment, Metacomet's coalition in New England was real resistance — protest, organization, and finally assertion against an expanding colonial system intent on erasing his people. This chapter forces a hard test: Whose interests are being served by the defiance you're seeing?

Chapter 2: Take the Weight.

When authority claims the power to define reality itself, your commitment to truth — even at great cost — is the foundation of all resistance. Salem's Unconfessed refused to validate lies that sustained an abusive court, even knowing refusal meant death. Their resistance shrank to a single conscience against the state's demand for complicity. Here the battleground was internal: Would individuals surrender their grip on what they knew to be true?

Chapter 3: My Enemy's Enemy.

Resistance doesn't require morally perfect allies. Nancy Dixon, an enslaved woman in colonial Williamsburg, exploited the divide between British and American interests to seize freedom as a Black loyalist. She didn't trust British intentions; she understood that the British had self-interested reasons for opposing American enslavers, and she leveraged that alignment for concrete results. Strategic pragmatism: Trust interests, not intentions.

Chapter 4: Force the Fight.

The Anti-Federalists lost the ratification battle but forced a compromise that became a tool for future resistance: the Bill of Rights. Don't wait for perfect conditions. Force abusive authority to respond, to pay a price, to make concessions. Even partial victories now can become foundations for total victories later. Organized opposition matters even in defeat.

Chapter 5: Resistance Is a Lifetime, Not a Moment.

Ona Judge escaped George Washington's household and spent fifty years evading recapture. The dramatic act of defiance — her escape — was just the beginning. Real resistance requires persistence to keep pursuing your goal and resilience to withstand inevitable counterattacks without breaking. This is the unglamorous truth: Resistance is mostly endurance.

Chapter 6: Ideas Matter.

Readers might expect Thoreau the wilderness recluse, but they will meet instead Thoreau the diagnostician of American authority. He articulated why resistance is necessary, what makes authority legitimate, and when that legitimacy is forfeited. Resistance without clear ideological foundation is easily redirected or co-opted. You must know what you're fighting for, not just what you're against. Liberty of conscience. Authority in a republic exists only on loan from the governed.

Chapter 7: From Individual Acts to Organized Networks.

The Underground Railroad was a sophisticated infrastructure — specialized roles, compartmentalized knowledge, operational security that remains partially hidden even today. It scaled individual resistance into systematic capacity, moving tens of thousands of people to freedom. But it also revealed limits: You can save individuals without ending the system. Triage in a hemorrhaging nation. The fight would have to come into the light.

Chapter 8: Arming the Hosts of Freedom.

When all peaceful avenues are closed, resistance faces its hardest test: whether to accept violence as necessary, and whether you can carry the permanent moral weight of that choice. The Six — comfortable, establishment abolitionists who enabled John Brown's Harpers Ferry raid — discovered what every resistance movement learns at this interruption point: You either commit completely, accepting the transformation violence brings, or you don't cross the line at all. Half measures don't work. Most couldn't carry the weight.

Chapter 9: Seize the Moment.

When resistance finally achieves power, it must act with ruthless clarity and speed to transform structures that enabled oppression. The Radical Republicans understood that their moment wouldn't last — once Southern states returned, once Northern voters tired of Reconstruction, the window would close. They kept rebellious states out of Congress, forced through constitutional amendments, divided the South into military districts, impeached a president who tried to stop them. This was constitutional hardball that bordered on illegitimate force. They knew it. They did it anyway. And still, they didn't do enough. Redemption followed. The counter-resistance adapted.

The Pattern: Two Interruption Points

Here's what the evidence shows across nine movements spanning two centuries:

American resistance succeeds at assertion more often than nationalist historiography admits. Metacomet's forces controlled New England. Black loyalists established freedom. Ona Judge escaped the most powerful man in the republic. The Underground Railroad moved thousands beyond federal reach. Harpers Ferry sparked the war that ended slavery. Reconstruction briefly established a multiracial democracy.

Then institutional mechanisms and cultural forces interrupted.

These interruptions happen at two predictable points.

The first comes when resistance must move outside legal channels — become "criminal," operate in the "hidden transcript," secret scripts that presume that permitted channels have failed. This is the moment when protesters must acknowledge that petitions won't work, that appeals to authority will be ignored, that the institutions designed to address grievances have been captured by the very forces they're resisting. It requires accepting that the system itself has become the problem, not just the people operating it. Why do so many movements stop here? Because American political culture evolved specifically to preserve the institutions created by the mythologized founders. By the 1820s — shockingly quickly — those accomplishments had been rendered sacred, particularly the Constitution and the governmental structures it created. The founders themselves became objects of reverence rather than historical figures whose choices could be questioned or whose institutions could be reformed or replaced. This creates a profound psychological barrier: To move beyond legal channels means defying not just current law but also the legacy of Washington, Jefferson, Madison — the men whose wisdom Americans are taught to trust implicitly. Many resisters stop here, unwilling to cross that line even when necessity demands it, because doing so feels like — is made to feel like — betraying the nation itself rather than challenging the abusive authority that has captured its institutions.

The second comes when resistance confronts violence — not defensive violence reacting to immediate threat, but strategic violence deliberately initiated to force systemic crisis. Most movements either never reach this point or fracture when they do. Those who cross this threshold discover that it permanently transforms them. The moral weight must be carried for life. This is true everywhere — the decision to kill, to destroy, to initiate force rather than merely respond to it requires accepting a burden that cannot be removed. But American political culture makes this threshold uniquely difficult to cross. In France, active resistance against tyranny is woven into national identity. In America, it's anathema. The same mythology that renders the founders' institutions sacred also renders violence against those institutions unthinkable — not just illegal or immoral but also treasonous to American identity itself. To embrace strategic violence means rejecting the entire national story: that this is a nation founded on liberty, that its institutions are fundamentally good, that the system works if you're patient. The psychological barrier isn't simply moral philosophy. It's that crossing this line means breaking with the myth that gives most Americans their sense of belonging.

Very few American resistance movements have successfully navigated both interruptions. None maintained their gains permanently, because the institutional mechanisms that interrupt resistance are also designed to roll back the changes resistance achieves.

This pattern isn't coincidental. It's how American institutions were designed to function — not through overt suppression, which creates martyrs and legitimizes resistance, but through structures that appear democratic while advantaging power: constitutional federalism that fragments opposition, procedural rights that slow change, property protections that insulate privilege, legal categories that criminalize resistance while sanctifying institutional violence.

The Constitution is the innovation here. It didn't accidentally protect slavery — it did so deliberately, treating humans in bondage as property requiring federal protection. It didn't accidentally fragment democratic power — that was the explicit purpose, described in Federalist 10 as preventing "tyranny of the majority." It didn't accidentally advantage property over people — property was what the founders owned, what their influence derived from, what the constitutional order existed to protect.

What Resistance History Means

Resistance history operates as methodology, not just subject matter. It starts from premises different from nationalist historiography:

Center the excluded. When Frederick Douglass wrote about slavery, he wasn't providing color to an institution historians can understand through slaveholders' ledgers. He was giving evidence about what slavery actually was that other sources concealed. Resistance history privileges voices that experienced power's violence over voices that wielded or justified it — not for political reasons, but because those voices have less reason to lie.

Interrogate legitimacy. The founders claimed to speak for "We the People." Who were those people? Who wasn't included? Who rejected the claim? What does it mean that ratification required coercion, that several states ratified only under threat, that Anti-Federalists predicted exactly the consolidated power that emerged? These aren't rhetorical questions. They're empirical ones with documented answers that indict the founding's legitimacy.

Follow evidence toward uncomfortable conclusions. When evidence shows that the Constitution protected slavery by design, nationalist historiography treats that as a tragic flaw in an otherwise sound system. Resistance history treats it as definitive: A constitutional order built on slavery was illegitimate, and people who resisted it were responding rationally to systematic oppression, not failing to appreciate institutional wisdom.

Take moral stakes seriously. You cannot understand why six hundred thousand Americans died in the Civil War if you treat as an open question what millions experienced as moral certainty: Slavery was evil and worth fighting to end. Demanding "objective distance" from that judgment doesn't produce better history — it makes history that cannot explain its own subject.

Acknowledge position. I think enslaved people were right that bondage was evil, that the Constitution protected slavery by design, that violent resistance was justified, that founders' property claims deserved no respect. These aren't political preferences imposed on the past. They're conclusions reached from evidence — what slavery actually entailed, what the Constitution actually said, what alternatives actually existed, what resisters did and why.

Claiming neutrality on those questions doesn't make you rigorous. It makes you incapable of explaining what happened because you won't grapple with why it mattered.

The Liberal Nationalist Problem

The main obstacle to understanding American resistance isn't conservative triumphalism — few serious historians buy that anymore. It's liberal nationalism: the belief that American institutions are fundamentally legitimate — even when they fail particular groups at particular times.

Liberal nationalists will condemn slavery. They'll admit that the Constitution compromised with it. They'll acknowledge institutional racism. But they won't follow that logic to its conclusion: that a constitutional order built on those compromises, legitimized by founders who enslaved people and conducted genocide, was itself illegitimate.

They condemn John Brown's violence but never question the violence of slave patrols, fugitive-slave commissioners, or federal marshals returning people to bondage. They'll worry about constitutional procedure while people die in chains. They'll defend founding mythology — brilliant founders creating an imperfect but perfectible Union — because to abandon that mythology is to abandon the institutional legitimacy they depend on.

When James Madison told the Virginia ratifying convention that preserving the Union mattered more than ending slavery, he spoke for those who prized stability over justice. Liberal nationalism extends Madison's framework across time: always valuing procedural norms over substantive outcomes, always defending institutions even when institutions enforce evil, always treating challengers as the problem rather than the power they challenge.

This book rejects that framework — not because I have a better ideology to replace it, but because it produces bad history: history that can't explain why people resisted, why they chose their tactics, why institutions failed, and what that failure reveals about American power.

The Counter-Resistance

There is another pattern running alongside resistance that cannot be ignored: American institutions are exceptionally good at containing, absorbing, or erasing the very resistance that forced them to change. Victories are won at high cost, then truncated by courts, legislatures, bureaucracies, and the national habit of turning defiance into patriotic folklore. The memory is polished; the mechanism that made the change possible is blunted.

The consequence is cyclical: New generations are left to refight old battles because the culture and structures that would sustain the gains were never fully remade. For all that the Radical Republicans were able to do in the immediate aftermath of the Civil War, it might not have been enough.

Reconstruction demonstrates this most clearly. Slavery was abolished, Black citizenship established, multiracial democracy briefly achieved — then destroyed by institutional instruments that appeared democratic while reimposing white supremacy. The constitutional amendments that ended slavery contained provisions allowing states to restore it through criminality. The federal government charged with enforcing civil rights abandoned that requirement when it threatened property and position. The revolution was won, then lost through mechanisms the revolution itself created.

This isn't because resisters made mistakes — though they did. It's because American institutions were designed to do precisely this. Understanding this doesn't require cynicism. It requires taking founders at their word about what they built and why. They said they feared that democratic majorities would threaten property. They said they needed to protect slavery to maintain the Union. They said they wanted checks on popular power. They built institutions reflecting those priorities. Those institutions functioned as designed.

Why This Matters Now

I don't write history for moral instruction or political inspiration. I write it because people confronting power need to understand how power actually works — not how it claims to work, but how it actually operates when threatened.

At this very moment in US history, people are asking whether institutional channels can produce necessary change. Whether norms and procedures can constrain authoritarian power. Whether there's a legitimate way to challenge illegitimate authority. Whether violence is ever justified in pursuit of justice.

American resistance movements faced those questions previously. They tried permitted channels. They watched those channels fail or produce change too slowly while people suffered. They chose disruption, confrontation, sometimes violence. Some succeeded temporarily. Most failed. All paid tremendous costs. None maintained gains permanently.

Their experiences teach what works and what doesn't — not because history repeats, but because power operates according to patterns you can learn to recognize:

States protect property and order above procedural rights. Institutions defend their own legitimacy above substantive justice. Procedural norms advantage those who benefit from existing arrangements. Accommodation usually preserves fundamental power structures while appearing to address grievances. Violence is how power responds when seriously threatened, regardless of whether resistance is violent. Disruption is often the only honest response to systematic injustice — and disruption usually fails.

That's what this book provides: usable history. Not inspiration — you don't need to feel inspired by Bacon's genocide or Brown's raid — but instruction, because you need to understand what happens when you challenge power, what the state likely does in response, what those patterns reveal about how institutions actually function versus how they claim to function.

How to Read This Book

Each chapter is structured to teach diagnostic skills: how resistance emerged, what it challenged, what tactics it employed, how power responded, what happened afterward. I'm not asking you to celebrate these movements or condemn them. I'm asking you to understand them — on their terms, in their moment, with their moral stakes — so you can recognize the patterns when they repeat.

Most of these movements failed. But their failures teach more than institutional successes, because they reveal how power actually operates: what it protects, what it crushes, what threatens it enough to provoke massive retaliation, what accommodation it preserves and what it abandons.

You'll notice that I take sides. I think the patriot republicans were wrong to exclude enslaved people from the ideals of the Enlightenment. I think slavery was evil. I think the Constitution protected it by design. I think violent resistance was justified. I think founders' claims to property and moral superiority deserved no respect. These aren't political preferences. They're historical judgments based on evidence. Refusing to make them doesn't produce objectivity — it produces history unable to explain what happened.

The book concludes with a practical chapter: nine principles for recognizing these patterns in contemporary movements. Not because these principles will help resistance succeed — the historical record suggests institutional forces will continue interrupting successful resistance — but because understanding the pattern helps you see through institutional claims about procedural fairness, democratic legitimacy, and why you should accept accommodation.

What You're About to Read

This book argues that American history is a history of effective resistance systematically interrupted by institutional chokepoints and cultural imperatives — not a history of inevitable progress toward justice. The people who fought for change didn't trust the system to deliver it. They forced change by disrupting the system, often temporarily succeeded, then watched American institutions adapt to contain what they'd achieved.

That's not history that makes people comfortable. It's not history that validates American institutions or founding mythology. It's not history that lets you feel good about your country.

But it's what happened. And understanding what happened —

honestly, without the nationalist mythology that obscures it — is the only way to understand how power works, what it takes to challenge it, and why challenging it is so consistently difficult and usually unsuccessful.

This is not a tour of inevitable progress. It is a study of how authority has operated in the United States, how it has been abused, and how people have confronted it — from single lives refusing to yield to coordinated networks that forced the state to move. The aim is to make the past usable: to recover the mechanics of effective resistance, to expose how and why it is so often cut short, and to keep our attention on the central fact that matters across every chapter — authority in a republic exists only on loan from the governed. When it is turned against them, resistance is not a departure from American ideas. It is their defense. And their duty.

That's what this book does. Not to inspire you. To instruct you.

Welcome to resistance history.

Let's begin.

CHAPTER ONE

Beware False Prophets

Bacon's Rebellion That Wasn't

Resistance Principle #1: The banners of resistance and even rebellion are often stolen by those with no aim other than their own share of power.

Two Fires

JAMESTOWN, SEPTEMBER 1676

Imagine the humid Chesapeake air descending like a thick cloak, filled with the acrid bite of burning timber. And the sky, once dark and clear with pinpoints of faraway stars, is now orange, punctuated by sparks. Now add the roar of flames, the crackle of collapsing houses, the shouts of men high on rum and grievance. Nathaniel Bacon — thirty-something, Cambridge educated, a privileged but dangerously disaffected planter — grimly watches it all, surveying his handiwork, as the capital of the first English representative government in North America caves in on itself. Just a week earlier, he had chased the royal governor, the aging Sir William Berkeley, a man drunk on his own claims to power, across the bay. Now Bacon was making sure that Berkeley could never return to what he once ruled — because it would no longer be there.

NINE MONTHS EARLIER, THE GREAT SWAMP, DECEMBER 1675

More flames. More screams. More destruction. A much different kind of smell. More than homes were burning — so were children. And their mothers. And their fathers. Old and young. The Puritan "gospel of terror" in full, bloody swing, the instruments of God, the king, and the authority of the New England colonies. And what was the crime that had yielded such a horrible sentence? Resistance. The Narragansett, caught up in Metacomet's Wampanoag rebellion against the English, chose sides. They were harboring resistance fighters in their winter stronghold in Rhode Island. As far as the English were concerned, that made the Narragansett — every last one of them — as evil as the warriors they were trying to shield, turning toddlers into legitimate targets. So the English set the palisades ablaze and cut down everyone trying to escape. This was not some disaffected, privileged planter torching the symbols of his own government in a battle over his share of it. It was the brutal weight of abusive colonial authority, bent on exterminating a people who had become a threat when they fought to exist and, therefore, to resist.

Two fires. Nine months and more than five hundred miles apart. But also not even in the same universe. Historians have turned Bacon's Rebellion into a principled uprising of freedom-seeking settlers while erasing the effort by Indigenous people to defend themselves and their way of life as just another episode in a long train of conflict that threatened the progress of civilization and betterment in the New World. Nathaniel Bacon, though, was a false prophet, employing the trappings of resistance to further his own claims to authority. His legacy has been aided and abetted by generations of storytellers. Metacomet, however, was the real thing, leading his people in a last attempt to push back power when there was nothing left to lose.

Grievance: A Cover for Conquest

Bacon had arrived in Virginia just a few years before with a massive land grant, a seat on the governing council, and a cousin — Frances Culpeper — married to the royal governor. He was handed a share of Virginia's rule when he stepped onto the shores of the Chesapeake. But he also arrived in the middle of an English war with the Dutch that had tanked the tobacco trade. Dutch fleets were burning whole tobacco fleets right in the James River, almost at will. Planters, large and small, were uneasy and looking for an outlet for their increasing disaffection and, of course, someone to blame for it.

They found both in the Indigenous people, who dared to survive while the new Virginians wanted to settle and trade. The hostilities began in June 1675 when Thomas Mathew, a small planter in the Northern Neck, decided not to pay for goods he'd taken from the neighboring Doeg tribe. The Doeg retaliated, raiding Mathew's farm. The colonials had to strike back — but they messed up and attacked the wrong tribe, hitting the Susquehannock. On a second mistaken foray, in September, John Washington, a former mate on a tobacco trade ship, led a force against a Susquehannock fort in Maryland, and when the chiefs came out to surrender? Washington and the colonials killed them. For that act, the tribes gave Washington a new name: Conotocarious. Town Destroyer. (His great-grandson George Washington would earn the same name.)

The fight then began in earnest, from the Potomac River to the Falls of the James, threatening the safety and stability of the entire colony, forcing Virginia's governor to act.

The seventy-something Sir William Berkeley was entering his thirty-fifth year as royal governor of Virginia. It had not been an easy tenure. He was sent by Charles I to bring an end to an era of "tyranny, extortion, and the most cruel oppressions" in the colony. But the king ran into his own problems in 1642 when Parliament rose against him. After he was executed in 1649, "Un-king-ship" was declared in London, and a commonwealth established. Oliver Cromwell's authority reached Virginia soon after, and Berkeley, always able to read the direction of the wind, surrendered Virginia to Parliament in 1652, entering into an early retirement on his wife's property. So tactfully had Berkeley managed his retreat that he was restored as governor by Charles II in 1660, just in time for another war with the Dutch to begin. But Berkeley weathered that storm, too.

He had never, though, faced the likes of Nathaniel Bacon, someone so full of ambition and animus. When Berkeley pledged restraint and called for a negotiated settlement with the tribes, one that would leverage native allies against tribes hostile to the colonials and build a ring of defensive forts, Bacon called Berkeley a coward and promptly kidnapped several members of the Appomattox. Berkeley reprimanded Bacon and then worked with the Virginia assembly to raise taxes to pay for the military and create a new system of trade with the native peoples — a regulated trade that left out Bacon and, it seemed, everyone but Berkeley's friends.

That was enough for Bacon. The native peoples needed to be exterminated, not coddled. Trade terms should be dictated, not negotiated. And he, not the weak-willed gentlemen in charge, should be the one taking the fight to them. So Bacon spun what mainly had begun as a personal quarrel into a vendetta that engulfed the colony. When Bacon demanded a commission from Berkeley to wage total war against the tribes, Berkeley and the council refused, so Bacon created his own militia and arranged to be elected its general. Bacon then slaughtered a friendly tribe. In May 1676, he lured the Occaneechee to guide him and his men against a camp of Susquehannock. Together, they raised their glasses to celebrate the joint victory. Then, in the night, Bacon and his men fell on the Occaneechee — men, women, and children — leaving none alive. The next day, Bacon collected their beaver pelts and carried those home as a symbol of his superiority.

In the wake of this slaughter, and an assembly session that expanded voting rights in the colony, Bacon issued his own declaration of independence, complete with a bill of indictment against Berkeley that listed the governor's offenses. The assembly, of course, had dramatically reformed Virginia politics without Bacon's influence or even his presence (although he had been elected to the session), in ways that gave "the people" much more say in their government. His *Declaration in the Name of the People*, issued in July 1676, was starkly racist and mostly fictional but also, like the later declaration that Jefferson would draft, a masterstroke in how to shape a historical narrative in real time. Berkeley had "betrayed and sold his Majesty's Country and the lives of his loyal subjects, to the barbarous heathen." The governor protected the tribes exactly when "we might with ease have destroyed them." And he had violated his duties to the people by raising "great unjust taxes upon the Commonalty for the advancement of private favourites and other sinister ends." Bacon became the tribune of the many against the corrupt, tyrannical authority of the few. As the historian Robert Beverley observed, only a few decades later, this was pure Bacon: He was "of a Temper Robust and Haughty, and had a Pompous and prevalent Eloquence, extremely taken with the Common People." Still, Bacon had his priorities: destroy the tribes and make genocide *look* like principled resistance.

Bacon's militia raged, virtually unchecked, across the Tidewater over the next few months, targeting Indigenous people — regardless of their allegiance — wherever they could find and then destroy them. It was one of the most pronounced campaigns of genocide in America's colonial history, permanently erasing a meaningful native presence in eastern Virginia. *Decimation* is too weak a term for what happened that summer. Doeg, Susquehannock, Nottoway — names largely erased from the map of Virginia — were villainized indiscriminately by Bacon. What's more, there was an additional target: All English colonials who weren't with him were against him, implicit supporters of Berkeley's corrupt regime, so their persons and property were fair game, too. The smoke that covered the Tidewater sky from looted plantations and gutted encampments defined that summer of '76.

And on September 19, Bacon's militia torched Jamestown.

That would be the high-water mark for Bacon. Five weeks later, he was dead. Without heroism, without ceremony, without even dignity, his body riddled with "lousy disease" and the "bloody flux," his rebellion — always a matter of personal grievance — died with him. His followers — a coalition of disaffected planters who saw Bacon as an opportunity to gain their share of the spoils, indentured and convict servants, and enslaved men hoping for freedom — quickly faded away, just as Berkeley, with a force that mirrored Bacon's, with servants and enslaved men serving under his banner, finally mounted a response, arresting as many of Bacon's supporters as he could find. They were then court-martialed, and many of them (including my ninth great-grandfather William Rookings) were sentenced "to be carried to the gallows, there to be hanged by the neck."

Bacon's Rebellion is an old and tired story of one man's thirst for a greater share of the power that he already held, fueled by hatred, fear, and racism that he could deploy to enlist the support of others who wanted their piece of that power, too.

The Real Resistance: Metacomet's War of Survival

Now shift your gaze north, just a year earlier, to New England. Here, another conflict was raging, but one with a profoundly different character: Metacomet's War. This was no grab for power by an ambitious chancer like Bacon, eager to expand a system of abusive authority that he didn't think was abusive enough. This was the culmination of a decades-long process of Indigenous resistance against the relentless pressure of English settler colonialism, a brutal, tragic, and existentially necessary fight for survival.

Metacomet, a sachem of the Wampanoag, inherited a world his father, Massasoit, had tried to navigate through an alliance with the Plymouth settlers, the Separatists of Scrooby, who are consigned to history as the Pilgrims. By Metacomet's time, that initial accommodation had curdled. For years, as English encroachment on Wampanoag land accelerated, the Wampanoag and their Algonquian neighbors attempted to play by English rules, protesting their plight through the permitted legal routes that Bacon derided. Summoned before Plymouth authorities in 1671 to challenge his management of property exchanges, Metacomet pointedly observed that "the English press upon us too sore; we have no more land to sell." English cattle trampled their corn. Colonial courts persistently ruled against them. Proselytizing missionaries siphoned off their people into "praying towns" that disciplined their faith and their bodies, turning them into the only kind of Wampanoag that seemed acceptable to the English: docile and controlled.

But Metacomet knew this was not the work of one leader. The invasion of their way of life was not driven by a single individual, no matter how often they invoked the name of a distant king. His people were opposed by an entire system of abusive authority, reinforced pervasively across southern New England. It recognized property deeds that snatched native land under duress or through misunderstanding. Its courts invaded their internal affairs, presuming jurisdiction over Wampanoag affairs. Metacomet and his supporters attempted to work within the channels established by the English, using the tools of diplomacy and negotiation to articulate their grievances in terms that the English might understand, deferring to English sensibilities and perceptions of acceptable opposition, drawing clear lines that might stem the tide of dispossession. But that form of protest, depending on not only dialogue but also a commitment to listening, and hearing, requires good-faith actors on both sides. The English, however, were not showing up to the table.

So Metacomet and his people were not heard, forcing them to take the next step: organize a more vigorous opposition, one that would be much harder for the English to dismiss. If they wouldn't listen to one person or one tribe, they couldn't close their ears to twenty, speaking with one voice. Metacomet, wary and alarmed, worked tirelessly to build a pan-Indian alliance, a coalition of peoples facing a common existential threat. By 1674, he had beaten a well-worn path from Narragansett country to the Connecticut Valley, stitching together a defensive league of Algonquian peoples. This wasn't the act of a rash aggressor but rather one of a leader desperately trying to consolidate his people and their neighbors to resist further cultural annihilation. He and other sachems engaged in tense diplomacy, trying to make the English understand the severity of their actions, all while the colonial system, with its praying towns designed to convert and control, and its growing, land-hungry population, pressed ever inward.

But all resistance efforts have their tipping points, when resisters recognize that protest and organized opposition are not enough, that the abuses of authority will not stop, so they must be stopped.

Enter John Sassamon, a Massachusett close to the Wampanoag. He had taught Metacomet and his brother, Wamsutta, and was an interpreter and scribe for their father. Then he fell prey to the missionaries and was drawn into one of the English praying towns, converting to Christianity with fervor, becoming a minister and working to translate the Bible into Massachusett to bolster their proselytizing campaign. Remaining connected to the Wampanoag, Sassamon knew that his people and their allies had had enough. They were done with the polite language and posturing of protest and organized opposition. Acting for years within the permitted channels had availed them nothing, and the time wasted had cost them dearly. If the English wouldn't hear their reasoned arguments, maybe they would attend to messages delivered with a sharper tone — by their weapons. But Sassamon's allegiance was no longer to his native community. Along with his faith, he had converted his identity. So he told Plymouth Governor Josiah Winslow that Metacomet was done with trying to be heard; he was focused on making the English feel the consequences of ignoring his alliance's demands. When summoned before the governor, Metacomet denied it but discovered where the information came from.

Sassamon disappeared a week later. A few weeks after that, his body was found under the ice in a frozen Massachusetts pond. His fishing gear was on the shore, suggesting that he had simply fallen and drowned, an accident. But his neck was broken and his face badly bruised, injuries not usually associated with accidental drowning.

Although Wampanoag justice rarely disguised its sentences — one tends to miss the message that way — a colonial investigation, drawing on some questionable witness accounts, fingered three Wampanoag men with murdering Sassamon and pushing his body under the ice to make it look like an accident. That was sufficient for the court. Casting aside due process, the colonial authorities arrested the three Wampanoag, who included one of Metacomet's advisers, tried them, quickly found them guilty, and executed them in June 1675.

This was what the years of protest and opposition had come to: an authority that appeared to be acting out of fear to stop resistance before it began. The English had succeeded in co-opting many native peoples, defanging the threat before it could emerge. That's how they were warned about Metacomet's plan in the first place (from Sassamon), how they found some less-than-credible witnesses to his murder (from other natives-turned-Christians), and how they convicted the accused (with a jury partly consisting of "Praying Indians"). But complicity only aggravated the situation by creating an illusion of stability through control.

The execution of the three Wampanoag men was the final spark to light Wampanoag resistance. Clearly, a more assertive opposition was all that the English would listen to. Abusive authority, now using the guise of the official legal channels to unfairly take lives, had become authoritarian. This was no longer about lodging clearly defined complaints or attempting to negotiate on the now laughable terms of equals. Any presumption that the tribes would be heard, or even that the English were listening, had evaporated. In its place was a forceful, desperate declaration that the Wampanoag and their allies would not be, could not be, passively erased. They were acting to force a reckoning.

With little left to lose and everything to gain, Metacomet acted with a desperation that overcame his reluctance. On June 24, 1675, at about the same time as the Doeg raided Thomas Mathew's farm in Virginia, Wampanoag warriors struck the English settlement at Swansea, near the mouth of the Taunton River, during a prayer service. They burned the town to the ground, killing eight people. The attack lit a fire under the Narragansett, the Nipmuc, the Pocumtuc, and many Pequot, who rushed to join Metacomet. His rebellion, an active resistance in its most violent form, came to be called King Philip's War by an English community that could never bear to use native names when they could exert control by expropriating them and twisting them in their image — yet another example of abusive authority.

During the same months that Bacon rampaged across the Virginia Tidewater, Metacomet's war of survival engaged in coordinated attacks up and down southern New England, torching dozens of settlements, reconfiguring the colonial map as one town after another disappeared from it. This was Indigenous warfare born of something common to all resistance movements under duress: a powerful nexus of expertise and desperation, leveraging knowledge of the mental and physical terrain with a fierce determination not to lose everything. The English response, in turn, was brutal and total and in no way surprising, targeting not just warriors but entire communities. In December 1675, colonial troops assembled at Smith's Castle near Wickford, Rhode Island, dragged cannon through waist-deep snow, and annihilated the Narragansett settlement at Great Swamp — the souls of its people escaping only as ash and smoke.

But no resistance movement, no matter how clearly articulated, effectively organized, or passionately pursued, can succeed in holding gains — even if that gain is a pause in the abuse of power — over the long term without external help, without the aid of another authority to back them. Persistence and resilience are essential for maintaining resistance, but they cannot endure indefinitely on their own. Under the weight of the sheer numbers, resources, and utter ruthlessness of the English, and suffering losses to death and slavery that the Wampanoag alliance could not withstand, Metacomet's coalition unraveled. In August 1676, as Bacon marched on Jamestown, Metacomet himself was finally cornered, in Misery Swamp, at a point almost overlooking his Narragansett Bay near Bristol, Rhode Island. Unlike Bacon, Metacomet went down fighting, finally shot by — who else?— a "Praying Indian" allied with the colonials. The civilized English mutilated his body: beheaded, quartered, displayed (his head was on a pole in Plymouth for decades to come). His wife and nine-year-old son were captured and sold into New World slavery.

In the end, Metacomet's resistance for survival, and the subsequent English response to it, wiped out 40 to 60 percent of the native population in southern New England. It was also, proportionally, the deadliest war in American history for the colonials; it bankrupted the economy, shattered the inland trade, and contributed to the revocation of the charter of Massachusetts Bay in the 1680s — a reminder that the effectiveness of resistance must be measured in the long view:

Metacomet's resistance might have lost on the ground, but it forced concessions in English domination. If nothing else, Metacomet made the English pay dearly for every inch of Indigenous land they held on to, a lesson the colonials would not soon forget.

The authority Metacomet confronted was the expanding machinery of settler colonialism, which sought Indigenous displacement or subjugation. The Wampanoag alliance's armed resistance, their assertion of their right to exist on their own land, was a direct response to this existential threat from an authority that, from their perspective, was inherently abusive in its relentless expansionism, bent on consuming all before it. Metacomet's fight was never about acquiring more; it was about not losing everything.

The contrast couldn't be starker. Bacon sought to usurp and expand a colonial authority that he felt wasn't aggressive enough. Metacomet and his allies made an assertion against the very existence of that encroaching colonial authority on their lands, moving through every stage of genuine resistance, from protest against injustices and organized opposition to a desperate, assertive war for survival. This was the resistance that mattered, the one that truly challenged the colonial project, and precisely the kind that American mythmaking would later seek to bury or distort.

Why Bacon Still Matters: The Seduction of the False Prophet

So why does the myth of Bacon as a populist hero persist, often overshadowing the genuine resistance of figures like Metacomet? Because it feeds into a comfortable, self-serving narrative: the rugged individualist challenging a corrupt elite, a champion of the common man (a "common man" being implicitly understood by white historians and their white readers as, well, white).

The first draft of Bacon's reputation, drawing on people who knew him and had lived through his rebellion, was ugly. Berkeley's allies called his followers "giddy people." Robert Beverley, Virginia's first historian, was born right before Bacon's rebellion. His father, a supporter of Berkeley's, had known Bacon well. Writing his *History and Present State of Virginia* in 1705, Beverley painted Bacon as a "seditious" figure with a "powerful Elocution," well suited to duping the "poorer sort" and leading an "unthinking Multitude" for his own ambitious ends — no noble hero there.

But a century later, the new United States needed heroes, and it demanded ones of a particular sort. To justify claims that American independence was of its own making, divorced from Old World influence, and that a new, special people had emerged in a unique way from its own particular history, the mythmakers of the First Republic needed to cobble together a set of origin stories that made the American path practically inevitable. They rediscovered Bacon and found in his exploits a narrative that could fuel a nationalist mythology.

Enter Thomas Jefferson.

Looking for early sparks of his particular vision of American resistance that emerged after the French Revolution and his own election to the presidency in 1800, and ones that were part of his own vision of Virginia as representative of the new country's true spirit, Jefferson championed Bacon as a forerunner to the spirit of '76. He eagerly copied and sought publication of an eyewitness account of the event because "the rebellion of Bacon has been little understood, it's cause & course being imperfectly explained by any authentic materials hitherto possessed." So Jefferson encouraged writers (not, it must be said, historians) like John Daly Burk and his successor, Louis Hue Girardin, in their influential early-nineteenth-century *History of Virginia*. Together they eagerly recast Bacon as an "amiable and popular" youth, a shining talent fighting an anti-democratic, even authoritarian Berkeley. In their eyes, Bacon became nothing less than a homegrown martyr to Old World tyranny. It was here, in the fervent nationalistic glow of the early Republic — several generations removed from Bacon's march on Jamestown — that Bacon's messy, violent gambit was thoroughly laundered and reframed: Now it was a principled "popular uprising" for the people against entrenched elites, a clear foreshadowing of the righteous break from Britain a century later, complete with matching declarations of independence.

This heroic interpretation only deepened throughout the nineteenth century. Bacon was romanticized in fiction and lionized, particularly in the South, as a chivalrous rebel, his image conveniently fitting into the Lost Cause narrative after the Civil War. Even laws passed by an assembly Bacon didn't attend, and in no way influenced, were repackaged as "Bacon's Laws" to bolster the fairy tale of him as a populist reformer. The malicious truth — the raw ambition, the calculated exploitation of frontier fear, the indiscriminate slaughter of native peoples — was purposefully erased.

With the turn of the new century, this version of Bacon dug in even deeper. Early-twentieth-century historians, such as Thomas Wertenbaker, kept that flame alive, casting Bacon once more as the leader of a popular, almost democratic revolt against an aristocratic Virginia — a clear clash between the common man and the entrenched elite. But by the midcentury, scholars like Wilcomb Washburn, in his 1957 reassessment, began to reexamine the evidence and highlight Bacon's brutal aggression against Native Americans. The fairy tale started to fade.

Yet as one myth began to unravel, another powerful and also astonishingly misleading academic narrative arose to take its place — spinning every undergraduate syllabus into an ahistorical vortex from which they have not yet emerged. Edmund S. Morgan, in his widely influential 1975 synthesis, *American Slavery, American Freedom*, offered up what remains the definitive interpretation: Bacon's Rebellion, with its threatening alliance of white indentured servants and enslaved Africans, so panicked Virginia's ruling class that they consciously accelerated the shift to a hardened, race-based slave system. The goal, according to Morgan, was to permanently divide the laboring classes along racial lines, securing elite white dominance. That story, importing the language of class and a "bottom-up" approach to history, framed the rebellion as a crucial turning point in the legal codification of American racism and slavery, became a dominant interpretation in academia for decades, and remains the single most significant influence on its public history. While appearing to offer a sophisticated, critical lens, this view itself has become a kind of origin myth, one that missed the actual interplay of race and power — and the absence of class distinctions, as modern readers understand them — in seventeenth-century Virginia and ultimately constructed its own set of historical distortions that need dismantling. Unraveling these layers of myth — from the heroic patriot to the unwitting catalyst for racialized slavery — is essential to grasping the real and far more instructive lessons of Bacon's destructive ambitions.

Metacomet's reputation followed the opposite path: demonized, diminished, pitied, and ultimately erased. While Bacon was slowly being laundered into a premature patriot, his America had little room for an Indigenous leader who dared to mount a ferocious, principled defense of his people's land and way of life.

In the immediate aftermath of Metacomet's War, the contemporary accounts of it were a cliché of history-as-victor's-justice: drenched in blood, fear, and religious fervor. Increase Mather's *A Brief History of the Warr with the Indians in New-England* (1676) and William Hubbard's *A Narrative of the Troubles with the Indians in New-England* (1677), both written when Metacomet's blood was barely cold, portrayed the Wampanoag sachem as "King Philip," immediately stripping him of his native identity, colonizing his memory. To them, he was no resistance leader defending his homeland but instead "that barbarous Heathen, a tool of Satan." Metacomet was a savage, perfidious instigator of barbaric violence sent to test God's chosen people in the wilderness. His refusal to submit to the saintly people of New England was proof of inherent Indigenous treachery, justifying their brutal suppression and dispossession. Mary Rowlandson's immensely popular captivity narrative from the war further cemented this image of savage brutality, luridly multiplying the tales of native cruelty, deeply ingraining it in the New England colonial psyche.

As the centuries turned and the American mythology project gained momentum, the initial, damning portrait of Metacomet held firm, but, like almost all nineteenth-century narratives, it acquired some romantic flourishes. As Jefferson and his followers were busy transforming Bacon into an early American hero fighting for individual rights, Metacomet, when remembered at all, was often cast in the tragic, but still threatening, mold of the "noble savage" — a doomed figure whose resistance, however brave, was ultimately nothing more than symbol, a rage against the dying of the light, because his world was an obstacle to the inevitable march of American expansion. Washington Irving's story about "Philip of Pokanoket" (1819) and plays such as *Metamora; or, The Last of the Wampanoags* (1829) might acknowledge his prowess or even his people's plight, but always from a perspective that implicitly legitimized colonial triumph — they were always doomed, their resistance tragic because inevitably futile. Thus, his place in American resistance history was diminished to the weakest form of protest — that of doomed, moral symbolism in the dying gasps of a superseded people. The American narrative conveniently erased the fact that Metacomet's fight against colonial authority was a profound act of assertive resistance to protect an existing way of life from an abusive, encroaching power — precisely the kind of resistance the new nation claimed to champion, but only when waged by those it could define as their kind of American, and being white was a prerequisite.

It wasn't until the latter half of the twentieth century, spurred by a broader reckoning with civil rights and a critical reexamination of colonial history, that Metacomet's story was clawed back from the demonizers and the romanticizers. Francis Jennings, in his *The Invasion of America* (1975), showed the colonialist "savage war" narrative for what it was: a ruthless English conquest fired by a greed for land and a venomous hatred for Indigenous populations. Jennings and others finally began to center the Indigenous experience, recovering Metacomet as a leader grappling with impossible choices in the face of relentless colonial pressure, his war a desperate coalition effort to preserve sovereignty and survival. More recently, trenchant scholars like Jill Lepore in *The Name of War* (1998) explored how the act of writing the war's history was itself an act of appropriation and justification by the colonials, further burying the Indigenous experience and the true nature of their resistance under layers of self-serving exceptionalist prose. More recent work by Lisa Brooks and Christine DeLucia has pushed further, reading against the grain of colonialist archives.

So while the mythmakers were busy polishing Bacon into the avatar of the principled fighter for the people — a fantasy that conveniently ignored his own brutalities and served to define resistance in narrow, racially exclusive terms — the genuine, existentially desperate resistance of Metacomet was erased, demonized, or neutralized. Understanding this dual process — this selective inflation of a false prophet and the simultaneous suppression of a true resister — is key to unmasking how the American Patriot Myth was constructed and who it was built to serve.

This chapter, contrasting Bacon's self-serving war with Metacomet's genuine resistance, is a foundational lesson in discernment. True resistance, the kind of assertion against abusive authority that this book explores, demands that we scrutinize who is claiming to challenge power and, crucially, on whose behalf and to what end. Many who wrap themselves in the flag of the people are simply new aspirants to power, eager to redirect popular anger for their own gain, often by targeting scapegoats.

So the real legacy of Bacon is his role as an archetype in our nationalist narrative: grievance theater masquerading as edgy rebellion. Metacomet's resistance, though, hurt the imperial project. It forced the colonials to bleed treasure and reconsider their approach to almost everything, from government to defense to, as we will see in the next chapter on Salem, the role of the Devil in New England society. Metacomet showed how resistance might fail on the battlefield but still raise the cost of oppression, which perhaps buys time for the oppressed. This is the first critical step in writing — and reading — a true resistance history.

The distinction is essential, because if we can't tell the difference between a self-serving false prophet who manipulates and uses the people and a resistance leader who represents them and their interests, we're doomed to fall for the same deadly tricks generation after generation. As you go through the chapters ahead, ask what is truly being risked by those who challenge authority, and whose power expands if they prevail. History often answers with ash, bone, and sometimes, when the challenge is truly an act of resistance, hard-won freedom.

CHAPTER TWO

The Weight of Truth

Resisting Salem's Reign of Lies

Resistance History Principle #2: In a system sustained by state-sponsored lies, the most fundamental act of resistance is the refusal to validate the falsehood. The simple, steadfast, and public assertion of truth, even at immense personal cost, is a direct assault on the legitimacy of abusive authority.

Manufacturing Terror

The year was 1692. Salem Village, Massachusetts Bay Colony. What unfolded in that small Puritan community was not a "witch hunt" in the way popular culture has fantasized about it. It was a meticulously constructed nightmare. What came to be known as the Salem Witch Trials (despite the absence of actual witches) was a chilling demonstration of how abusive authority, a diabolical partnership of the twisted twin powers of church and state, can manufacture terror and sustain itself on lies.

In a community already steeped in anxiety — a contested, confused new colonial charter, the very real specter of wars with Indigenous peoples cast as satanic agents — a few young women faced a confrontation with the Devil's earthly agents. The diagnosis was almost preordained: bewitchment. That constructed fiction, the big lie of 1692, became a diabolical pretext for a devastating assault on truth. And while the net was cast wide, it fell with a particular, suffocating weight upon women — those who, by their independence, their age, or their words, already stood on the precarious margins of Puritan society. It set the stage for extraordinary acts of resistance from those who refused to yield.

Governor William Phips, urged by influential magistrates and ministers like Cotton Mather, hastily convened a special Court of Oyer and Terminer, a tribunal unlike any seen before or since in American history. The very engine of its injustice was its fatal flaw: the admission of "spectral evidence" — the accusers' claims of being tormented by apparitions of the accused, invisible to all others. This evidence was, by its nature, irrefutable. With it, the floodgates of orchestrated oppression opened up. Lieutenant Governor William Stoughton, the court's unbending chief magistrate, prosecuted with a terrifying certainty that equated doubt with heresy and accusation with guilt. But lies that big, the myths that drive power, must have a history, no matter how invented or intellectually bankrupt they may be. And Salem had that in Mather, the man who provided the theological and legal scaffolding for terror, one on which fantasy was hung to look like reality, and compelled conformity and complicity when demands for them fell short.

The story of Salem, the one that needs rescuing from centuries of myth and distortion, is about a state that demanded its citizens validate its lies and the profound courage of those who, at the cost of their lives, refused and, in doing so, resisted.

Coerced Complicity

The machinery of this terror was greased by coerced confessions. The choice offered to the accused was stark: admit to witchcraft, name others, and live (for a time, under a cloud of infamy), or maintain innocence and face the gallows. Tituba, an enslaved woman in the Reverend Samuel Parris's household, was among the first to confess. Her terrifying accounts of diabolical meetings, extracted under duress and shaped by her interrogators' expectations, served a crucial purpose for the authorities: They validated the court's existence and the reality of the demonic plot. Each subsequent confession became another brick in the wall of lies. But while they might have spared individuals, they also emboldened an abusive authority, legitimizing its methods and expanding its reach, expanding its capacity to devour more lives. They made the steadfast denials of the Unconfessed seem like hardened, wicked obstinacy rather than principled stands for truth. Those who confessed, in saying the court's lies were true — yes, they were witches; yes, spectral evidence was legitimate — made things worse, tightening the snare around those who would not break.

The Weight of the Unconfessed

Against this coercive power, against the weight of these state-driven lies, stood the Unconfessed. Their resistance was not an organized rebellion; the structure of the court and the nature of the accusations made that virtually impossible. Their protest was their plea of innocence, an articulation of their truth within a system designed to crush it. Their opposition was limited to their steadfastness during brutal examinations. Their final, powerful act of resistance — their assertion of truth against lies — was made on the gallows or in the shadow of certain death.

Bridget Bishop, a woman who had long been on the wrong side of the wrong people in Salem, was the first to be taken to Proctor's Ledge to hang at noon on June 10, maintaining her innocence until the end. The "afflicted" girls claimed that Bishop had brought the Devil's book for them to sign. Several witnesses testified, under oath, that Bishop, in her spectral form, had attacked them. One, John Louder, insisted that his body was "pricked as with pins . . . and also seized, & choked, so as that I have been under great misery." And the macabre theater didn't end there. The official court records note, with striking temerity, that Bishop looked at the accusing girls, and "when she did but cast her eye on them they were presently struck down." Bishop, though, held firm to the truth. "I am innocent, I know nothing of it, I am clear," she said. Samuel Sewall, one of the judges, recorded in his diary that she remained true to the last: "She said she was no witch."

Rebecca Nurse could be considered the opposite of Bridget Bishop. She was a widely respected church member. The accusations against her shocked many, and a petition was quickly circulated to attest to her good faith and fine character. And she was at first found not guilty by her jury, a brief acknowledgment of the absurdity of the charges, but it was momentary. Right away, "all the accusers in the place were grievously distressed, crying out." Lieutenant Governor Stoughton and the other judges, enraged by the acquittal, sent the jury back. Stoughton himself pressed the case against Nurse to the jury members, pushing other ostensibly damning statements before them. Coerced into complicity, no one should have been surprised when they changed their verdict to guilty, condemning her to death. But Governor Phips was. He granted her a reprieve from execution, the second pause in Nurse's march to the gallows. Stoughton was furious. Nurse was a witch. She used her invisible powers to attack the girls in their very courtroom. Couldn't Phips see that? So Stoughton threatened to ignore the reprieve unless Phips gave in to the judicial murder of the woman who had once been an honor to her church and town. Faced with a choice between the court's legitimacy or one person's life, Phips chose to perpetuate the abuse. Nurse mounted the gallows with five other women on July 19. She maintained her quiet dignity and unwavering insistence on her innocence, even as she was led to her death.

The Reverend George Burroughs, a former minister of Salem Village, had a contentious personal history with the community that made him a target for suspicion. The authorities painted him as the diabolical ringleader, a man of preternatural strength gifted by the Devil. But on the gallows, he became something else entirely. As described by both his chief accuser, Mather, and his defender, Robert Calef, Burroughs stood on the ladder and delivered a powerful speech. Then he did the impossible: He recited the Lord's Prayer from start to finish, perfectly — a feat believed to be beyond any witch's power. It was "so well worded, and uttered with such composedness . . . as was very Affecting, and drew Tears from many."

A silent wave washed over the weeping crowd on Proctor's Ledge.

Generated by this singular act of resistance, a ripple of doubt threatened to halt the entire proceeding. But the state, in the person of Mather himself, mounted on horseback, intervened to reinforce the fictions that his authority relied on (as Stoughton had done twice with Rebecca Nurse). Mather reminded the people of Salem that Burroughs was no longer an ordained minister and that the Devil himself could appear as an "Angel of Light." The lie was reinforced, the moment was contained, and Burroughs dropped with the rope. Calef adds a final, brutal detail that underscores the authorities' contempt: After he was cut down, Burroughs's body was dragged by a halter, stripped of its clothes, and crammed into a shallow grave with another victim, "one of his Hands, and his Chin, and a Foot of one of them, was left uncovered." Even in death, his defiant humanity was denied.

Then, there was Martha Corey, who had mocked the proceedings from the start. Her crime was skepticism; she saw the lies for what they were and was not quiet about it. "We must not believe all that these distracted children say," she insisted during her examination, a direct challenge to the court's pretended authority. For this, she was condemned and, refusing to confess, hanged on September 22.

Her husband, Giles Corey, an eighty-one-year-old farmer, took resistance to its most extreme conclusion. Understanding that the court was a machine designed only to convict, he refused to engage with it at all. There was nothing legitimate about it in the eyes of justice or God, so he would not endorse its foundational lies. But by "standing mute" when asked to accept a trial "by the country," he could not be tried legally. The court, led by the merciless Stoughton, retaliated with the archaic and brutal punishment of *peine forte et dure* — pressing by stones. On September 19, in a field near the jail on Federal Street, he was staked to the ground as heavy stones were piled upon a board on his chest. His death was a slow, torturous spectacle designed to force his validation of the court's authority. Calef noted the horrific detail that as Corey's tongue was forced out by the pressure, "the Sheriff with his Cane forced it in again." Much later, it was reported that he responded to the magistrates' demands with a guttural demand:

"More weight." He chose an agonizing death, sacrificing his body to preserve his final, silent truth — a rational act of resistance that also ensured that his property passed to his heirs rather than being seized by a corrupt state. His silence, his final, crushing burden, was a thunderous denunciation of the court's power to compel falsehood.

These men and women, and the others — nineteen in all — who chose death over a lie, were the true line of resistance in Salem. Their commitment to truth was the only thing that could, eventually, begin to counteract the court's authority, which was built entirely on the acceptance of spectral lies and coerced confessions. Each principled stand, each refusal to confess, however isolated, added to a collective weight of truth that the system could not indefinitely bear.

Salem Retold

So why isn't *this* story — the story of these individuals' courageous, truth-based resistance against a lying, abusive state — the story of Salem we know today? Because from the very beginning, as with Bacon's story, generations of storytelling, mythmaking, and even well-intentioned historical interpretation have often buried or distorted it.

Understanding the courageous defiance of those who resisted this machinery requires first confronting how their stories, and the very nature of their stand, were almost immediately obscured. The telling of the Salem story became a battleground from its inception, with concerted efforts to control the narrative, justify the authorities, and diminish or distort the principled actions of the Unconfessed. This avalanche of fiction and misdirection makes recovering their true weight, even centuries later, a continuous act of restorative history.

The first coat of obscuring narrative paint was applied by those most invested in the prosecutions. Cotton Mather's *Wonders of the Invisible World* (1693) was a defense of the authorities and an affirmation of the diabolical plot. The steadfast denials of the Unconfessed were not evidence of their integrity or the court's error but further proof of their satanic hardness of heart. Their voices, insisting on truth against a system demanding lies, were immediately reframed as the deceitful whispers of the damned.

The orthodox narrative, though, did not go unchallenged, even in its own time. Calef, a Boston merchant, mounted a counterassault against Mather and other Salem apologists in his *More Wonders of the Invisible World* (eventually published in London in 1700 after being suppressed in Massachusetts). Calef meticulously documented the trial excesses, championed the innocence and principled stands of Nurse and Burroughs, and exposed the absurdity of spectral evidence. His work stands as an early, vital piece of restorative history, an attempt to preserve the truth against overwhelming official pressure. Yet despite Calef's efforts and the eventual muted repentance of figures like Judge Samuel Sewall, the dominant colonial impulse leaned toward burying the affair. The apologies and meager financial compensations offered by the Massachusetts General Court (beginning in 1711 with the reversal of some sentences) were more about closing a shameful chapter than fully reckoning with the state's lethal delusions or the profound moral courage of those who had refused to yield to them. The weight of the Unconfessed was already being lightened by a collective amnesia and official downplaying.

Victorian Myth Builders

Throughout the nineteenth century, while Salem remained a fixture in the American imagination, its story was often further bent to different purposes. Historian Charles W. Upham's exhaustive *Salem Witchcraft* (1867) detailed local factions as a cause, but the era's literary figures — Nathaniel Hawthorne, Henry Wadsworth Longfellow, John Greenleaf Whittier — transformed Salem's trauma into symbols of Puritan intolerance or mass hysteria. While powerful, they twisted the Unconfessed into allegorical figures rather than living, breathing men and women who made agonizing choices in the face of a very real, very specific terror. Longfellow's play *Giles Corey of the Salem Farms* (1868) shrouded the real man under a cloak of nineteenth-century romanticism, transforming Corey into a noble, tragic hero whose defiance served the era's need for pathos rather than historical truth. Hawthorne, famously haunted by his own ancestor, Judge John Hathorne, used the specter of Salem as a brooding, atmospheric backdrop for his personal, although timeless, explorations of inherited guilt and hidden sin in works like *The House of the Seven Gables* (1851) and the short story "Young Goodman Brown." Whittier highlighted the injustices of the trials with his poetry and 1885 inscription on Rebecca Nurse's memorial — "O, Christian martyr! who for truth could die, / When all about thee Owned the hideous lie! / The world, redeemed from superstition's sway, / Is breathing freer for thy sake today" — but focused blame on the mistaken belief in witches, drawing a parallel to his own time's acceptance of slavery, casting the Unconfessed in the role of persecuted abolitionists. In such talented hands, the reasoned, individual acts of defiance of the Unconfessed were lost in the grander, more abstract stories of a dark stain on the New England past that reflected forces in their nineteenth-century present.

Perhaps no single story demonstrates this process of mythmaking — and the simultaneous recovery of a core truth — better than that of Giles Corey's last words. "More weight" has become the iconic motto of Salem resistance, a concise distillation of defiance. But its journey into our historical consciousness reveals how memory is shaped. The earliest primary sources, such as Sewall's diary, document Corey's death for "standing mute." Calef provides the gruesome details of the torture. Yet neither of these contemporaneous writers explicitly records the two-word phrase "More weight."

The line entered the historical record through oral tradition that was solidified in later narrative accounts. By the mid-nineteenth century, in works like Upham's *Salem Witchcraft*, the legend — like so much else in the Victorian assault on authentic history — is presented as fact. It was then immortalized in the twentieth century by Arthur Miller's *The Crucible*, which seared the phrase into the American consciousness. Does the potential lack of direct, contemporaneous attribution make the line historically worthless? No. It represents a distilled truth — a phrase that so perfectly summarizes the *spirit* and documented reality of Corey's action that it is, to me, inseparable from the event itself. Corey's entire purpose in enduring that torture was to refuse the court; his actions screamed for more weight because yielding, not dying, was the only outcome he sought to avoid. The line's evolution is a case study of how posterity crafts language to give an almost unbearable act of resistance a memorable human voice.

Busting Myths, Making More

This tendency to generalize or explain away the core issue of individual confrontation with abusive authority persisted even as twentieth-century scholarship saw the event through fresh lenses. Sociological explanations, such as those offered by Paul Boyer and Stephen Nissenbaum in *Salem Possessed* (1974), illuminated the socioeconomic fault lines within the community. Psychological and anthropological frameworks, like those in John Demos's *Entertaining Satan* (1982), provided invaluable context for understanding why the crisis might have occurred. But their focus on the causes of the outbreak continued to overshadow the responses of the Unconfessed as acts of conscious resistance, or of the confessed as acts of compelled complicity, decentering the raw, ethical decisions and the direct, perilous stands made by all of the accused themselves when faced with one awful demand: to lie or die.

More recent scholarship by historians like Carol Karlsen, Bernard Rosenthal, Mary Beth Norton, and Emerson Baker has done crucial work in recovering the experiences of the accused, highlighting gender dynamics and the effect of trauma from Metacomet's War as well as, crucially, recognizing the principled, active resistance of the Unconfessed in their refusal to exchange the truth for their lives.

Yet as academic history paints a fuller, more authentic picture of

1692, the popular perception of the Salem Witch Trials has unmoored the event from reality. In our media-saturated twenty-first century, Salem is a fairy-tale landscape where the real people and their actual, agonizing experiences are lost. They range from the ridiculous (a far-fetched theory that ergot poisoning from infected grain caused the afflicted girls' hysteria) to the absurd (the town of Salem today officially refers to itself as Witch City), as films, movies, and digital media insist on centering witches in any story about Salem, endorsing, however implicitly, the impossible possibility that witches (at least of the supernatural variety conjured by Mather) were in any way real. The actual terror of a theocratic state demanding conformity to demonstrable lies has given way to fantasy horrors that erase the profound weight of the Unconfessed's choice to die for the truth.

Other creators have legitimately mined Salem to explore other historical moments of persecution and trauma, spotlighting authentic historical dynamics. *The Crucible* dives into the toxic interplay of fear and intolerance in 1692 as an avenue for exploring the anti-communist hysteria of America in the 1950s. But its power as a brilliant work of cultural invention, like Hawthorne's a century earlier, misleads audiences into thinking that they are witnessing history, that Miller's story is a faithful reflection of the Salem experience, and into accepting it and its fictions as more or less a complete representation. More recently, though, Kimberly Belflower's play *John Proctor Is the Villain* sets the narrative down a more reliable path, even though it is framed by Miller's fictional relationship between John Proctor, one of the Unconfessed, executed in 1692, and Abigail Williams, the leading accuser among the afflicted girls. The play explores that relationship in a modern context, along with the implications of what generations of American high school literature classes have done with *The Crucible*. But crucially, it shines a spotlight on a key aspect of the trials that cannot be ignored: It was a woman hunt, not a witch hunt. The exploitation of women, especially young women, by men who use them as both tools and objects of their abusive authority, is the beating heart of the historical Salem experience.

"That Sad Time of Darkness"

The Unconfessed of Salem paid the ultimate price, but their collective insistence on truth was not symbolic — it was substantive. It was their "more weight." Each refusal to confess, each defiant speech from the gallows, each silent endurance of torture added to a moral pressure that the abusive authorities could not indefinitely bear. This growing weight, coupled with accusations that reached the highest levels of Massachusetts society, exploited cracks in the foundation of lies. In October 1692, Governor Phips halted the proceedings of the special court, and spectral evidence was later disallowed. The machine shuddered to a stop, choked on the very truths it had tried to crush.

The story of the Unconfessed during what Elizabeth Proctor later called "that sad time of darkness" that took her husband, John, offers a stark, foundational lesson, a resistance history principle that echoes from the seventeenth century straight into the heart of our own modern struggles with disinformation and authoritarian narratives.

The Unconfessed could not form a militia or publish a manifesto. Their entire battleground was the space between their conscience and the state's demand for a lie. By choosing truth, they demonstrated that authority built on myths is inherently fragile. It relies on our complicity, our fear, and our silence. Their legacy, the weight they ask us to bear today, is the understanding that power can command obedience; it can never command belief. And in that gap, resistance finds its voice.

CHAPTER THREE

A Declaration of Their Own

Resistance Principle #3: The enemy of my enemy.

AUGUST 21, 1783

A sweltering Saturday on a wharf in New York City. The docks bristled with masts, thick with the stench of salt, rope, and sweat. British troops crowded the streets, loyalists called out for boarding passes and transport, and carts rattled past with last-minute provisions. For most, this was the end of a war. But for Nancy Dixon, it was a beginning.

She stood among three dozen Black faces. Most of them had once been enslaved; some of them still were. That contrast — a status not divided by skin color — might have made her draw her six-year-old daughter closer. They were waiting to board the *Nautilus*, a transport bound for Abaco in the Bahamas. There was no fanfare, no music, no victory parade. This personal triumph was quiet — and powerful. Like the others waiting on the docks that day, this group came from up and down the Atlantic seaboard, from cities and plantations. Nancy was a mother born into slavery, leaving a republic that refused her humanity, and boarding a ship on her terms. She had not been returned to the person who owned her under the law, even though patriots who had supported independence from British rule demanded it. She had not been reclaimed, even when enslavers came looking. Her freedom had been certified by the defeated British, who were still in the process of evacuating loyalists through New York, the last British port in its former colonies. She carried the paper with her, and now she was leaving under that authority's protection, not just by its permission.

So there was reason for celebration, or maybe just intense relief. After three years of uncertainty, of instability, of escaping from bondage in Virginia to negotiating a tenuous liberty in New York City, surviving the collapse of one order and the creation of another.

But they were free. And that fact — that outcome, the result of her personal resistance — is what this chapter is about.

In a larger sense, for Nancy Dixon — and thousands like her — it marked the dividing line between two regimes. The British colonial order that had enslaved her was dead. But what replaced it was not freedom. The First Republic, born out of this moment of nationalist triumph, would reconstitute power around exclusion and racial hierarchy. It would declare liberty while denying it to those who had claimed it on their own terms.

Nancy Dixon's journey was not an accident of war or an incidental by-product of the Founding Fathers' fight for their freedom. It is a case study in resistance, one rooted in strategic pragmatism: a clear-eyed, action-oriented approach that prioritized real-world outcomes and seized opportunities rather than relying on abstract ideals or moral appeals. She didn't rely on patriot promises or Enlightenment morality. She relied on what she had seen, what she had learned, what she had calculated. She didn't write a pamphlet or sign a declaration about rights. She lived them. Her presence on the *Nautilus* was her declaration of independence — made not on parchment but in action.

Return to Williamsburg

To understand how Nancy Dixon and her daughter reached the deck of the *Nautilus*, we have to return to Williamsburg, Virginia, where the rhetoric of freedom rang loudly — and the machinery of slavery ground on.

By 1753, when Nancy was born, Williamsburg was two towns occupying the same space. It was a diverse British colonial world that the people of Salem in 1692 would not have recognized. Free, white Williamsburg, less than half of the town's population, dominated the public spaces: the long, undulating Duke of Gloucester Street; the broad, dusty Palace Street; the newly rebuilt capitol; the Governor's Palace, and all the taverns and shops. In the 1750s, Williamsburg's white residents were concerned about the stagnant tobacco trade, worried over "the Illegality of laying Taxes upon the People without Law," and wondered what the French were doing in the West, on the Ohio River.

Black Williamsburg, the majority of the town, controlled its own spaces: the backyards, the wash yards, the alleys, and the side streets. Most enslaved people in that part of Virginia's Tidewater were heading into their third and fourth generation in bondage, evolving into their own Creole Atlantic culture. Still, the nature of their peculiar experience became clear as the racial complexion of the enslaved community emerged — the closer one worked to a house, the greater the likelihood of sexual violence and its inevitable consequence: lighter-skinned children. In a town like Williamsburg, as much as half of the enslaved population may have been mixed race. They were also increasingly influenced by a vernacular version of the Great Awakening, with an evangelical message that stressed equality in the Lord's eyes. But standing in stark contrast with their experience were the waves of newly enslaved Africans, with a kaleidoscope of unfamiliar languages and beliefs: Igbo, Akan, Bambara, Mande. They all stopped in the Tidewater town on their way to meet the demand for enslaved people on the Piedmont.

We don't know anything about Nancy's young life. As a girl in Williamsburg, her enslaver, printer John Dixon, likely saw her as more of a burden than an asset, something to be managed until she could be of actual use. However, her young fingers might have been valuable in separating and sorting the type he and his apprentices used to publish *The Virginia Gazette* every week. She also would have hauled water and tended to fires as soon as she could lift a bucket or stoke cinders, before dawn and long after the sun set. Depending on Dixon's demands, her mother might have had time on Sundays to take her to Bruton Parish Church, to sit in a gallery built especially for enslaved people, or even to a hidden yard to hear a free Black or enslaved preacher explore the Gospel.

As a young woman, Nancy lived at the center of a revolutionary world: the print shop and household of Dixon. His shop was more than a publishing house; it was a hub that sold ink, paper, pamphlets, and books from around the British Atlantic world.

Nancy might have spent long nights cleaning the molasses-like blend of lampblack and varnish that made up eighteenth-century ink from his clothes, or separating the broadsheets to dry on the print shop's lines, or maybe just emptying Dixon's chamber pots. But she also saw and heard everything. Rousseau, Montesquieu, Hume, and Burke. The broad Enlightenment ran through the spaces she occupied, infusing them with ideas. What was a man? What was liberty? And how did slavery fit into any of that?

She wasn't on the edges of the patriot revolution — she was embedded in it, pressed against its hypocrisies every day. The rhythmic thump of the press, the oily tang of ink, the sharp clink of the type — these were the sounds of her world. Her sweat made possible the very operation that declared that men were born free while refusing to see her as human. Those words, printed in that sticky black, were her constant companions.

Nancy also knew the men behind those declarations. Dixon had married into the printing dynasty created by William Hunter, Sr., a close friend of Benjamin Franklin. When Hunter, Sr., died, Franklin raised his ten-year-old son, William "Billy" Hunter, Jr., in his Philadelphia home. In 1767, the now seventeen-year-old Billy, born the same year as Nancy, returned to Williamsburg to apprentice under Dixon and share her roof.

Names like Jefferson, Henry, and Washington were not just impressions on paper; they were faces in Dixon and Hunter's bookshop. She would have known them, their words, and what they truly meant by them. The titles on the shelves would have been part of her world, too: Phillis Wheatley's poems, Thomas Paine's pamphlets, Laurence Sterne's novels.

In those years, the divisions in American society ran through the middle of the print shop. While Billy had learned about printing from Benjamin Franklin, he had learned about the British world from Franklin's son, William, the royal governor of New Jersey. He bristled when Dixon began to align their newspaper with the patriots. For Billy, Nancy might have heard, the press wasn't for Dixon's politics. Nancy, in turn, might have told him how other local presses were being pressured to support the radicals. Billy didn't care. A press must be open to all, he insisted.

As America separated, so did Dixon and Hunter. Nancy watched as Dixon became a patriot colonel and then Williamsburg's mayor. Billy was bewildered. The patriots claimed that King George III was a tyrant bent on enslaving Americans. Billy knew this wasn't true. Nancy and every enslaved person knew it was a lie.

A key principle of the Enlightenment was that all men were born free and equal. Did Nancy roll her eyes whenever it came up? Watching enslavers walk through the shop door every day, Nancy would have agreed with the English writer Samuel Johnson's question in 1775: "How is it that we hear the loudest yelps for liberty among the drivers of Negroes?" The patriots insisted on a clear distinction between their imagined political slavery and her very real bondage — one that compelled them to act, and her to submit. It seemed like everyone in Nancy's world talked about freedom while defending, and engaging in, slavery. The patriots' abusive authority, which deprived enslaved people of their freedom, demanded resistance. And yet resistance seemed futile. Maybe the backyard preachers were right — the only liberty would come in the next life. There they would all be free.

By 1777, the year Nancy's daughter was born, the divided print shop could stand no more. Hunter, "firmly attached to the British Constitution," found that he could no longer work with Dixon. One of his warehouses had already burned down in a mysterious blaze, while Dixon leaned into the patriot cause. Hunter lowered his profile and bided his time.

And Nancy saw it all. The betrayals, the conflict, the rhetoric. She read the propaganda. She heard the lies and tracked the truth. She was part of a community of enslaved people who were watching, recording, and remembering who did what, and why. Perhaps something would break their way.

The Landscape of Possibility

It took another few years for Nancy and so many other enslaved people in Virginia and across the Southern colonies to act. By then, she had already observed a decade of warning signs — and opportunities.

In 1772, news from London sent waves of panic through Williamsburg's white community and of hope through its Black community. The story, which Nancy would have seen and heard discussed daily as it unfolded in *The Virginia Gazette*, concerned an enslaved man named James Somerset. His enslaver, a Virginia customs collector named Charles Stewart, had taken Somerset from Norfolk, Virginia, to England, where he then tried to ship him to the sugar plantations of Jamaica — a death sentence. But Somerset refused and, with the help of friends, used English law to challenge his enslaver's authority.

The very idea was revolutionary. Since when did an enslaved man have rights in any court? Not in Virginia, certainly. There, they were property, subject to the law's penalties but not deserving of its protections. Yet in England, the case was proceeding to the highest court, before Lord Chief Justice William Murray, Baron (later Earl) of Mansfield. For the legions of Stewart's allies among Virginia's enslavers, the prospect of Somerset prevailing was terrifying. For Nancy and her community, it suggested possibilities they had never been allowed to entertain.

The question before Lord Mansfield was simple: Could an enslaved person be forcibly removed from England? Did Virginia law, which made a man property, apply on English soil? The arguments boiled down to a fundamental conflict: Was Somerset a person with rights or a thing to be moved and sold? What Nancy's community would not have known was that for Lord Mansfield, this was no mere abstraction; he was raising his mixed-race great-niece, Dido Elizabeth Belle, in his own home. He had already decided she was a person, not property. And as for the case, Mansfield was ready for the impact. "Let justice be done," he told the opposing lawyers, "whatever the consequences may be."

A month later, the verdict arrived in Williamsburg, likely set in type on John Dixon's press. Mansfield's ruling was narrow, but its substance was monumental. "The state of slavery is . . . so odious, that nothing can be suffered to support it, but positive law," he declared. Since Virginia law could not apply in England, and finding no such law on the books there, he ruled that Stewart had no authority to compel Somerset. He was free to go.

The news was interpreted in two starkly different ways, drawing a sharp line between the two worlds that Nancy inhabited. In London, the free Black community held a party to toast Lord Mansfield. Inspired by the news, other enslaved people in England simply walked away from their masters and took their freedom.

Virginia's enslavers were incandescent with rage. They saw the *Somerset* decision as another act of tyranny by a British government that had no respect for their property rights. As one patriot put it, without irony, "who are Slaves but those, who . . . can have no Property."

For people in bondage, the message was clear and consistent with their own common sense. A correspondent's report printed on Dixon's press put it in universal terms: "All Mankind, as they are born, ought to live, equally free." The highest justice in England had recognized an enslaved man as a person with rights. In England, Black people could be heard. In England, they could refuse.

Patriots like Dixon began to tighten their hold over their property in people, their authority becoming even more brutal now that resistance had been given a legal foundation. For Nancy, the landscape of possibility had fundamentally, and irrevocably, changed.

A Choice of Enemies

After the *Somerset* decision, the idea of freedom was no longer just a hope; it had a legal rationale and a destination. Enslaved people who took their liberty were no longer just running from the whip; they were running *to* the promise of English law, to the principle that people could not be property. It wasn't long before Nancy saw those sparks of resistance erupt into flame on her doorstep, stoked by Virginia's last royal governor, John Murray, the Earl of Dunmore.

Dunmore, an aristocratic, irascible Scot with a keen sense of his personal interests, arrived in Williamsburg in 1771 and quickly came to understand a key vulnerability of the patriot planters: They were terrified of the people they enslaved. Dunmore had observed that the only way to control them was with "the most exemplary punishment." As tensions neared a boiling point with his patriot enemies, Dunmore began to wield that fear as a weapon. James Madison noted that the governor was "tampering with the Slaves," planning to "make great Use of them in case of a civil war." Madison further observed, "That is the only part in which this Colony is vulnerable."

Nancy witnessed this strategy explode into the open in June 1775. Inventing a threat of insurrection by enslaved people, Dunmore seized the town's gunpowder supply. The patriots, in a rage, claimed that *they* needed the gunpowder to defend themselves from that very same quarter. Nancy and hundreds of other enslaved people watched as the two white authorities faced off, each twisting the Black experience into a lie that suited their purpose. Dunmore then crossed a line, threatening to "declare Freedom to the Slaves, and reduce the City of Williamsburg to Ashes" if the patriots harmed him.

That one phrase — *freedom to the slaves* — sparked immediate action. Enslaved men and women descended on the Governor's Palace, hoping to claim the offer, only to be turned away; Dunmore had fled to a warship. The patriots responded with brutal clarity, publicly executing two enslaved men charged with conspiracy. The message was clear: This is what happens to those who look to the British for freedom.

On November 7, 1775, the threat became official. From his warship, Dunmore issued a proclamation declaring "all indented servants, negroes, or other (appertaining to rebels) free, that are able and willing to bear arms." The effect was electric. An enslaver wrote the very next day that his "very shrewd, sensible fellow" had taken off, inspired by a "determined resolution to get liberty . . . by flying to lord Dunmore."

The patriots were terrified. They rushed to Dixon's press to control the narrative, publishing broadsides that Nancy would have seen, and perhaps even handled. They decried Dunmore's "Damned, infernal, Diabolical proclamation" and revealed the brutally racist limits of their republican ideals. In long articles, they made it clear that the American Revolution had nothing to do with enslaved people; it wasn't their fight. They painted Dunmore's offer as a trick and chillingly described the violent fate that awaited the women, children, and elderly who would be left behind. For anyone in Nancy's position, the patriot message could not have been clearer: A lifetime in brutal bondage for Black people was not only consistent with their vision of liberty, it was necessary to it.

But the resistance continued, fueled by the actions of enslaved people themselves. They renegotiated Dunmore's terms in the moment. The proclamation called for men able to bear arms, but women like twenty-eight-year-old Mary Wells and children like ten-year-old Wynie Hempstead, both from Williamsburg, took the chance and joined Dunmore. Their resistance was not about Dunmore's character; it was about pushing an outcome.

Then came military action. At the Battle of Great Bridge in December 1775, hundreds of Black men, organized into Dunmore's "Ethiopian Regiment," took up arms and fought the patriots. They were defeated, and Nancy likely saw the captured soldiers paraded through Williamsburg, destined to be sold to the Caribbean. But they had stood and fought. They had created their own Lexington and Concord.

Through 1776, Nancy was bombarded with contradictions. As the type was set for Jefferson's Declaration of Independence, the most crucial piece of intelligence would have spread through the enslaved community's networks: Dunmore had sailed from Virginia, taking hundreds of Black men, women, and children with him. The patriots had been wrong about Dunmore's intentions, about their claim that the families of people who joined the British side would be abandoned.

Dunmore had made them free.

The governor's promise, however cynical and conditional, had been kept. There now existed a path to resistance that was fraught and imperfect, but it was real. For Nancy, weighing her options in a world of lies, that fact made all the difference.

The Somerset Rule

Nancy watched the war take its toll on Williamsburg. The patriot cause seemed ascendant, especially after news of the French alliance arrived in early 1778. For the people enslaved by patriots, hoping for some opportunity to gain their freedom, this was a dark time. A rebel victory, now made more likely, would close the door on the hopes sparked by Dunmore, cementing the creation of a republic built on the bondage of Black people. And Nancy now had an additional reason for concern, one that perhaps changed everything: the birth of a daughter in 1777. What future could she envision for her child in a world where the primary path to freedom was about to be cut off forever?

Then, in 1779, her world shifted. The British army began a new campaign in the South, with frequent raids along the coast. In May, a British force had landed and spent two weeks capturing and burning patriot supplies and property, without being opposed. More important, Nancy would have heard through her enslaved community's networks how their people had flocked to the British and not been turned away. Simultaneously, the patriot economy in Virginia began to collapse. Inflation skyrocketed. To raise money, the state began confiscating loyalist property — including enslaved people. Nancy watched as men, women, and families she knew were seized and auctioned off alongside furniture and land to the patriot friends of the government. The world was growing more precarious, but also more fluid.

Into this chaos came news that electrified the enslaved community. On June 30, 1779, the commander of all British forces in North America, Sir Henry Clinton, issued a sweeping declaration from his headquarters in Philipsburg, New York.

The Philipsburg Proclamation was not a hasty, conditional offer like Dunmore's. It was official, empire-wide policy. It applied to everyone. After a mild threat to sell any captured Black people found serving the patriots, Clinton made a promise that echoed the *Somerset* decision. He strictly forbade any person from selling or claiming rights over any enslaved person who sought refuge with the British army.

Then he made the offer of liberty unambiguous and universal. "I do promise to every NEGROE Who shall desert the Rebel Standard," Clinton declared, "full Security to follow within these Lines, any Occupation which he shall think proper."

The meaning was unmistakable. This was the Somerset Rule, now backed by the full might of the British army. People are not property. No one can compel them. They would be secure and free to choose their own work. It was not an act of benevolence; it was a military strategy to cripple the patriot war effort. But enslaved people did not care about British motives. They cared about the result.

The reaction was immediate. From Georgia to Massachusetts, enslaved people fled to the British by the thousands. They did not wait for an invitation; they forced the British to adapt and accept them. George Washington blamed the British for creating chaos, but the truth was more straightforward: Enslaved people saw their opening, and they took it.

Nancy watched this unfold from inside the patriot media operation. The pages Dixon printed could not hide the fear. The Virginia government felt so threatened by the British that it chose to move the capital inland, to Richmond. This meant that Nancy and her daughter might be moved, too, along with Dixon's press.

For Nancy, the calculation had now crystallized. The patriots were doubling down, their world contracting in fear. Williamsburg was no longer safe for them, which meant it was becoming a place of opportunity for her. Was that a British fleet in the bay? How close were the lines? The questions were no longer abstract.

Nancy, with her toddler, had to watch and wait for the right moment to make her move. But she didn't need to trust the British. She only had to understand the patriots.

The Enemy's Enemy

By the time the war reached its final phases, the patriots had made one thing clear: Their revolution was never meant for Nancy Dixon. They stated it back in 1775, and they reinforced it with action after action. When faced with the opportunity to match their rhetoric with reality, the patriots failed at every turn. Their vision of liberty was for themselves, built on the foundation of her bondage. Her future in their "new world" would look exactly like her past — excluded, oppressed, and enchained.

Freedom, Nancy recognized, was never going to arrive in Continental buff and blue. It would only arrive in red. Her enemy's enemy would bring it.

That must have been what happened in 1780. We know from Nancy's later testimony that she left Williamsburg with her three-year-old daughter three years before she boarded the ship to Abaco in 1783. That year, the capital moved to Richmond, and John Dixon went with it, but his family — and Nancy — remained behind. The challenge for a historian trying to piece together Nancy's story is that there were no major British raids near Williamsburg for much of 1780, making a journey by an enslaved woman with her toddler through patriot-controlled territory seem almost impossible.

But in January 1781, a new, notorious force arrived in Virginia: a British army led by the traitor in chief of American history, Benedict Arnold. He sailed up the James River, captured Richmond, and for several months brought the war to the heart of the patriot establishment. For so many enslaved people in Virginia, this was the window. This was the opportunity.

For the thousands of enslaved Virginians who fled to his lines, it did not matter that their liberator was Benedict Arnold. It only mattered that he wore a red coat. His raid was a moving zone of British authority, and every step they took broadened the promise of the Philipsburg Proclamation. This was strategic pragmatism in its purest form. It didn't matter what was in Arnold's head; what mattered was what the enslaved people who ran to him had in theirs — a clear-eyed determination to use the British for their own purposes, seizing freedom the moment it came within reach. This was Nancy's war, and a British army led by a traitor was her best, even if most unlikely, ally. To enslaved people like Nancy, Arnold was not a symbol of betrayal but instead a beacon of liberty.

The Summer of Freedom

We can see the war Nancy fought through the eyes of six-year-old Isaac Jefferson, who left the only firsthand account we have from a child who almost gained their freedom. Decades later, an interviewer asked Isaac about his enslaver, Thomas Jefferson, but Isaac also recalled the moment in 1781 when he, his parents Ursula and George, and the rest of Jefferson's enslaved household in Richmond seized their chance and joined the British army. He was carried off by a young British officer, John Graves Simcoe, who was in command of a regiment of white loyalists and who had argued for the value of Black loyalists as people.

Isaac remembered the march away from Richmond, riding in a wagon while the adults walked. He remembered British officers dressing him in a massive red coat. He remembered crossing the James River and ending up in the British camps at Yorktown. Above all, he remembered the kindness. While sickness took many, Isaac recalled that he was fed, with plenty of meat and bread, and allowed to play on the soldiers' drums. "The British," he recalled, "treated them mighty well."

Isaac's story is the story of the thousands who made the same choice as Nancy. This was a mass movement, a resistance facilitated by the British that freed tens of thousands in the greatest act of abolition in America before the Civil War. These people have been called Black loyalists, but their loyalty was not to a king, or even to a constitution; it was to their own liberty. They made a pragmatic alliance with the British because the patriot vision of republicanism, as they saw every day, was explicitly built on their bondage.

This resistance could not have succeeded alone. It required allies, however imperfect. When enslaved families reached the British lines, they were not turned away. They were fed, protected, and transported. As one patriot officer observed with alarm, "2 or 3000 negroes march in their train." This was a massive logistical undertaking. Someone in a red coat had to make a choice, again and again, to say: *Yes, we will take you. Yes, we will protect your daughter. No, we will not turn you away.*

For Nancy, the crucial window opened in the spring and summer of 1781. A British naval victory over the French at the Battle of Cape Henry on March 16, 1781, gave them continued command of the Chesapeake Bay and allowed the landing of two thousand fresh British and loyalist troops in Virginia. This sea power unlocked a summer of freedom, allowing the British to move thousands of Black loyalists out of Virginia by ship, beyond the reach of their former enslavers. Nancy certainly didn't walk to New York City with her three-year-old daughter. She was likely put on a ship by a British officer who, faced with a sea of Black faces, chose to honor the Philipsburg Proclamation and respect her declaration of freedom. The truth, ignored by patriot propaganda, was that most of the enslaved people who reached British lines stayed free.

The British commitment was tested at the highest levels. When Virginia's governor demanded that the British commander, Charles Cornwallis, return the "stolen property," Cornwallis refused. He replied that while no enslaved people had been *taken*, "great numbers have come to us." Any former enslaver was welcome to search the camp, he offered, but there was a catch: They could only reclaim people "if they are willing to go with him."

It was the Somerset Rule, applied on a battlefield. Under the British flag, these people had agency. They could not be compelled.

Isaac and his family were in Yorktown when Cornwallis made that stand. But their luck, and the British commitment, ran out of time. A larger French fleet arrived, defeated the Royal Navy, and sealed the Chesapeake. The British army was trapped. Nothing — and no one — could get out.

The British surrender at Yorktown on October 19, 1781, was a tragedy for the thousands of Black loyalists caught there. The articles of surrender, which it must have pained the young patriot officer John Laurens, a stanch opponent of slavery, to write, stipulated that any "property obviously belonging to the inhabitants of these States ... shall be subject to be reclaimed." In an instant, the people who had been recognized as free were reclassified as property. George Washington turned his army into slave catchers.

As Isaac recalled, Washington's soldiers rounded up "all Mr Jefferson's folks" and sent them back to Richmond. From there, they were loaded onto wagons and returned to a lifetime of bondage at Monticello.

Isaac Jefferson lived for another seventy years. After his ten months of freedom, he spent the rest of his life enslaved. But for a few weeks, but for one naval battle, or the want of a few more ships, this chapter might have been about him.

But it isn't. Isaac's resistance ended at Yorktown. Nancy's was just beginning.

The Public Faith

Nancy and her daughter likely arrived in New York City sometime in 1781, walking off a British ship into a crowded, chaotic, and utterly transformed city. Since the British had expelled the patriots from it in 1776, its population had doubled to twenty-five thousand, making it the headquarters for their entire war effort. Soldiers, sailors, merchants, and white loyalist refugees thronged the strets.

Most important for Nancy, the city was home to the largest free

Black community in North America. Thousands who had escaped slavery under the various proclamations, and none at all, had gathered there. They built a new life in Manhattan, earning money as laborers, laundresses, and skilled tradesmen. They established their own churches and schools. Hundreds of children were born into freedom there between 1781 and 1783. Nancy would have reconnected with people from her old life in this new one; people such as John Jones, who had joined Lord Dunmore back in 1775, and Hannah Jackson, a "fine girl" of twelve, were both there from Williamsburg.

But their freedom was precarious. Life was hard, with overcrowded housing and low wages where there were any to be found. And a palpable uncertainty hung in the air. News arrived in early 1782 that the British government had fallen and a new one wanted peace. Rumors flew that the price of that peace would be the Black loyalists themselves, returned to their vengeful former masters.

Their worst fears were confirmed when the terms of the preliminary peace treaty reached the city. The American negotiators — Benjamin Franklin and John Jay, both enslavers, among them — had insisted on a clause, Article 7, that stipulated that the British must leave without carrying away "any negroes or other property of the American inhabitants."

To Nancy and the thousands like her, the words must have felt like a death sentence. Everything — the refusal of patriot authority, the dangerous escape, the alliance with her enemy's enemy — had run its course. The road back to slavery in Virginia seemed inevitable.

The threat quickly became real. Enslavers and their agents began appearing on the streets of New York to hunt for their "property." George Washington sent his own agent. Then the danger became personal for Nancy. A man named Robert Prentis, whose shop had been just doors away from Dixon's press in Williamsburg, arrived in the city. He was there to trade goods, but also, as he reported back to his patriot business partner, to find and return people to slavery. Prentis knew Nancy. He knew her daughter.

Imagine Nancy's terror, seeing a familiar face from her past now stalking the streets of her refuge, a man who could identify her by name. Rumors spread of free Black people being snatched from their homes, even dragged from their beds as they slept.

But then, in a New York tavern, Prentis ran into a formidable loyalist commander, Beverley Robinson. Robinson, a Virginian-turned-New Yorker whose property had also been confiscated by the patriots, had fought alongside the forces that likely freed Nancy. He laid out the new reality for Prentis: Don't bother looking for the people from home. The British, he insisted, would stand behind the Philipsburg Proclamation. The former slaves who had sought freedom were people, not property, and would not be forced to go anywhere they didn't choose.

Robinson must have been convincing. Prentis soon packed up and left for the Caribbean, his venture a failure.

For Nancy, it was a reprieve. A powerful white ally had, for his reasons, stood up for her freedom. But she and thousands of others still awaited the final judgment, which would come from the new British commander in chief in a direct confrontation with George Washington himself.

The Final Judgment

Nancy's fate, and that of thousands like her, came down to a small room in Orangetown, New York, on May 6, 1783, and one man: Sir Guy Carleton, the new commander in chief of British forces in North America. Born in Ireland, Carleton had been in the army for fifty years, shot at on three continents, and wounded in combat several times. Having overseen the messy details of including Catholic Quebec into the British Empire, he would oversee the messy details of ushering the American colonies out of it. And he would tackle the most thorny issue on that day, in that room, against the most powerful man in America, George Washington.

For Washington, the matter was simple. After all, he wasn't a man given to complexity. When he gave himself the chance to think about it, he regretted owning people. So he didn't think about it. Just look at the peace treaty. The British had to depart without carrying away any "negroes or other property." There you go. Black people are property. They must be returned.

Carleton informed Washington that some six thousand people had already been evacuated to Nova Scotia. Washington was stunned. Six thousand? Yes, and many of them, Carleton continued, were Black.

Regrouping, Washington pressed the point. Again, the letter and spirit of the treaty were clear. Property was to be returned, not evacuated.

Carleton drew a clear line. To return the Black loyalists to their former masters would mean violating the promises of freedom the British had made to Black people. It would reduce them "to the Necessity of violating their Faith to the Negroes who came to the British Lines."

Then came the final judgment, a decision that carried with it the hopes of every Black loyalist praying in New York City. Carleton was unwavering. The British would keep their pledge. The Black loyalists would remain free.

He explained that, if the patriots had a problem with it and his superiors found him in the wrong, then the British government would almost certainly offer compensation for the enslavers' losses. The freed people would not be returned to bondage, but he would order the creation of a detailed register recording the name, age, and former master of every Black person departing. Using that, some valuation could be made.

Washington sputtered. How could one possibly determine the "Value of the Slaves" from a simple register? So much of their worth was based on their unquantifiable "industry and sobriety." Besides, he insisted, they would lie about their origins.

Carleton countered that they had no incentive to lie, with their freedom assured. Because they were free people, they could go wherever they chose, anyway. Better to have a list with errors and omissions than no list. In any event, his decision had been made. It wasn't a matter for Washington to agree with, just one for him to abide by.

In that room, the entire conflict was distilled to its essence, ending a battle that had begun in Westminster Hall in London in 1772. For Washington, as it had been with Stewart, it was a question of property rights. For Carleton, it was about people, and the faith that one group of people, Black men and women, had placed in another, the British government. For Nancy, it was about the ability of a master to abuse his authority over another person. In other words, it was about everything.

The British army may have lost the war for America, but the Black resistance won that final, decisive battle for their independence in Orangetown. The lives of thousands of people — including a thirty-year-old woman from Virginia and her six-year-old daughter — were secured in that moment, for that moment. Their strategic pragmatism, their faith in their enemy's enemy, had been vindicated. Whatever happened next was up to other influences, other circumstances. But for their part in the American Revolution, Black people had pushed their British ally to give them freedom on their terms, and that pledge had held.

To his enormous credit, Carleton never wavered. He never balked. He directed his officers in New York to issue a "certificate of freedom" to every approved Black loyalist, a document proving their freedom, making it illegal for any slave catcher to detain them. Nancy got hers. Carleton gave the patriots the chance to challenge individual determinations in front of a tribunal in the city. But of the thousands of certificates issued, only fourteen were officially challenged. The rest of the Black former slaves, including Nancy Dixon, were now officially free.

The Book of Negroes

Throughout the summer and fall of 1783, transports arrived in New York harbor. They loaded and carried off thousands of loyalists to destinations across the Atlantic world — Nova Scotia, England, and the Caribbean. Among them were three thousand Black loyalists, their names, ages, and circumstances recorded in the large ledger Carleton had ordered to register their information, a book that came to be known as the *Book of Negroes*.

There, on a list for a ship called the *Nautilus* departing on August 21, we find Nancy, her entire resistance distilled into a few words, intended to inform a possible compensation claim:

> Nancy Dixon, 30, sick at present with a girl her daughter, 6 years old. Formerly the property of John Dixon of Williamsburgh, Virginia; left him 3 years ago.

With that entry, her certificate of freedom in hand, Nancy and her daughter boarded the ship and sailed to the Bahamas. There, in an ironic twist of history, she would again cross paths with Lord Dunmore. But that is part of another story. Their future was, indeed, uncertain in that deeply prejudiced world. Still, in the Bahamas, the Black loyalists would build not just communities but a country, founded on the principles of resilience and faith they had forged in their resistance.

Nancy's entry in the *Book of Negroes* was a quiet testament to a clear-eyed goal. In a world of lies, she had maintained a hyper-realism about her options, and when the moment came, she seized it. But her resistance, like that of the thousands who stole themselves from the patriots, required an ally. She and the British did not need to share the same goals or even the same morals. They just needed to suspend their distrust long enough to see a shared enemy and a shared aim. In that strange and pragmatic alliance, Nancy Dixon won her war for independence.

Why We Weren't Told This Story

Why, given its transformative power, is the story of the Black loyalists — the largest emancipation event in America before the Civil War

— a mere footnote in the history of the Revolution? The answer is a foundational principle of resistance: Abusive authority will always work to cover up its abuses.

Every enslaved person who walked away from patriot authority was a living repudiation of the American Revolution's central claim. They were proof that the land of the free was, for them, the land of bondage, and that their enemy's enemy was their only reliable friend. This truth was so damaging to the new nation's founding myth that the denial had to start immediately.

The talking points were established early: The British didn't mean it; they wouldn't honor their promises; those who ran to them would die of disease and neglect. But at a certain point, the patriots and their heirs were no longer talking to Nancy and the tens of thousands of others in her situation; they were talking to us.

Thomas Jefferson led the charge, creating a fiction that would calcify into historical fact for nearly two centuries. He claimed that the British under Cornwallis had "stolen" thirty of his enslaved people and that their neglect led to the deaths of twenty-seven. It was, he wrote, a "useless and barbarous injury." From his own personal and distorted experience, he extrapolated a nationwide tragedy: Thirty thousand enslaved people must have been taken from Virginia alone, and twenty-seven thousand of them must have perished. The Tidewater, he implied, was a mass graveyard, not of British promises, but of Black naïveté.

None of this was true. The records, including Jefferson's own, show that thirty-two people from Jefferson's properties sought freedom with the British. And Isaac Jefferson, who was there, stated plainly that while many died of disease at Yorktown, "non of Mr Jefferson's folks" were among them. In the end, thirteen of the thirty-two were unaccounted for — not twenty-seven — and it is just as likely that they escaped and started new lives as it is that they died. But Jefferson's version — the story of helpless victims and British barbarity — was the one that stuck, because it served the national narrative.

For the next 150 years, mainstream American historians built upon this foundation. The influential "Consensus School" of the post–World War II era, dedicated to crafting a unified, heroic national story, actively diminished the role of Black loyalists. Historians like Daniel J. Boorstin portrayed the Revolution as a conservative affair, a unified patriot front where messy questions of slavery were secondary. Other historians, such as John Alden, described those who resisted as "unhappy and venturesome slaves" and asserted that the majority remained "loyal to their masters and mistresses," becoming "an asset to the Patriot cause." The implication, stated explicitly by others, was that the vast majority of enslaved people were "too uneducated, unsophisticated, or oppressed to take any personal part in the Revolution . . . Few could have been politically aware."

This narrative conveniently ignored the thousands of names in the *Book of Negroes*. It dismissed the clear-eyed pragmatism of people like Nancy Dixon. It took the word of the enslavers as historical fact while treating the actions of the enslaved as footnotes and British statements as empty.

This began to change in the late twentieth century. Historians like Sylvia Frey and Gary Nash started reading the archives "against the grain," challenging the patriot-centric myth. More recently, scholars such as Cassandra Pybus, Maya Jasanoff, and, most recently and powerfully, Christopher Curry have unearthed the incredible Atlantic stories of the Black loyalists after they left America, proving that most of them not only survived but also built new lives and communities, even nations, in places such as the Bahamas. Popular works like Lawrence Hill's novel *The Book of Negroes* (published as *Someone Knows My Name* in the US) have brought this history to new audiences, dramatizing the experiences that academic historians had for so long ignored.

This work of historical recovery remains a form of resistance itself. To tell the full story of the Black loyalists is not merely to add a missing chapter. It is to challenge the very foundation of America's founding myth. It is to show that from the nation's inception, there were competing wars for independence, competing visions of freedom, and that for tens of thousands of people, the true path to liberty meant resisting the men we now call Founding Fathers. Their story proves that history, when honestly told, can be a handbook for the oppressed.

Her Declaration of Independence

Nancy Dixon saw patriot republicanism for what it was: a system that required her enslavement to sustain its vision of virtue. For men like Jefferson, Washington, and Franklin, slavery wasn't a regrettable flaw in their worldview; it was foundational to it. In their republic, Black freedom had no place.

Nancy rejected the patriot cause, but she also knew that British freedom was no guarantee. For every Carleton who defended her liberty, there were loyalists who would have gladly preserved their interests at her expense. The crucial difference was that the British, unlike the patriots, had been forced to live with what Black resistance had made real. From New York to Canada to the Bahamas, loyalist societies were permanently reshaped by the unyielding presence of free Black people. That change had ripples: John Graves Simcoe, the young officer who had carried away Isaac Jefferson, would go on to pass the first anti-slavery law in the British Empire as lieutenant governor of Upper Canada in 1793.

Nancy's story is not a romantic ideal of resistance as symbolic purity or self-sacrifice. It was something harder, more dangerous, and ultimately, more effective. By any measure, her resistance produced what the patriots never offered: a real chance at freedom. Her daughter may well have lived to see the abolition of slavery across the British Empire in 1834. Isaac Jefferson would never see the abolition of slavery in the United States.

Nancy practiced strategic pragmatism. This form of resistance begins with a clear-eyed understanding that no system built on your subjugation will free you out of virtue. Abusive authority must be pressured or bypassed. Strategic pragmatism trusts no one. It moves where power is weak, not where it pretends to be righteous. It makes no claims of loyalty to an ally; it only seeks to make that ally's self-interest serve its purpose. It is a resistance of observation, timing, and negotiation, asking only one question: *What works?*

For Nancy and tens of thousands of others, the answer to their horrific reality was not found in any doctrine. It was in troop movements, shifting policies, and the cracks that opened when empires fought. When the patriots shut the door, the British were forced by self-interest to crack it open. From the *Somerset* case to Carleton's stand, Black resistance compelled an empire to act against its ingrained prejudices.

This mode of resistance is messy, but it gets people free. And in Nancy Dixon's case, it got her daughter free as well — likely long enough to see a future the First Republic was never built to allow.

CHAPTER FOUR

The Haunted Man on Maiden Lane

Resistance Principle #4: Force the fight.

It was nearly dawn on June 8, 1789, on Maiden Lane in downtown Manhattan. The air outside Mrs. Ellsworth's Boarding House was already heavy, the temperature climbing toward seventy degrees before 6:00 A.M. The day promised to be cloudy and stifling. James Madison was already awake, having slept little, if at all.

He was a haunted man, pursued by the ghosts of a revolution that he stood on the verge of betraying.

In New York to participate in the First Federal Congress under the new Constitution, he was trapped, in a very real sense, between his aspirations for the new nation and the demands of the old revolutionaries. Madison wanted his newly proposed national government — much of it his own design, the product of years of study and toil — left untouched. He envisioned a powerful federal system capable of acting with energy on a global stage, with powers to tax and raise armies essential for earning respect in European courts and managing commerce. To curtail its power now, he believed, would be to destroy it before it truly began.

On the desk before him lay his defense against the phantoms of the patriot resistance: a speech and a list of amendments that he hoped would map an escape route. The ghosts of 1775 were in the chamber with him — their language, their fury, their memory of what the Revolution had actually been for. Madison's words were pleading. Evasive. He needed the true believers to "see we pay a proper attention to a subject they have much at heart." If his proposals did "not give that full gratification which is to be wished," they must understand the urgency of other business. He felt "compelled" to seize "the opportunity of proving" his sincerity. He could not "disregard their wishes"; he had to "extinguish" their apprehensions. "We ought not to disregard their inclination," he had written — the language of a man afraid, a man trying to appease spirits he had betrayed, a man looking for the door.

The ghosts haunting Madison weren't just abstract fears; they were the living memories and, in some cases, the actual presence of those who had forged a revolution through a process starkly different from Madison's careful, institutional nation-building. The movement toward independence was a master class in the progression from protest to assertive resistance.

It began with protest in the 1760s — visceral, popular reactions to policies like the Stamp Act, where patriots saw a conspiracy against their liberties. Crucially, this protest coalesced into organized opposition. Groups like the Sons of Liberty, alongside later town meetings and Committees of Correspondence, created a powerful, parallel political infrastructure, operating outside, and often in direct defiance of, sanctioned colonial authority. This organized opposition then escalated into assertive resistance — armed defiance to halt abusive authority. Lexington and Concord weren't isolated skirmishes that began a war for independence; they were the end, the consequence, of a mature resistance movement in which a part of the population, organized and politically mobilized through the process of resistance, met the threat of state violence with their own.

This entire progression — from articulating grievances to building alternative power structures to armed confrontation — created the leaders and shaped the anti-authoritarian thinking of the Revolution. For these individuals, the fight against unchecked authority was not theoretical but rather a lived reality.

The new Constitution, for all its brilliance, lacked the explicit guarantees of individual liberties for which these old revolutionaries had fought. Figures like Patrick Henry and Mercy Otis Warren were thundering against it, seeing the seeds of a new tyranny. Madison's own election to the first Congress against James Monroe (an ally of Henry's) had been secured only after he publicly pledged to support amendments — a Bill of Rights.

So on that stifling June morning, Madison navigated a minefield. His aim was to appease these ghosts while preserving the strength of his federal government, along with saving his own political career. He needed to introduce amendments satisfying the promises he had made in his campaign, yet he was equally determined to prevent them from fundamentally weakening the new national structure or, even worse, opening the door to a second constitutional convention that might unravel his entire plan.

What Madison achieved was a political masterstroke. Cynical, even ruthless, but still masterful. Just as the nationalists had practically forced their constitution through ratification in each of the states, barely holding on to victory, Madison took control of the amendment process in the First Federal Congress, distilling dozens of proposals into a concise set addressing fundamental liberties without crippling federal power. But in doing so, he also established the blueprint for what would become a crucial pattern in American history. The immense, popular, and often radical pressure for a Bill of Rights — a genuine expression of resistance against the perceived overreach of a new authority — was successfully channeled, managed, and ultimately contained within an institutional framework. Madison, ever the institutionalist, co-opted the momentum. He would offer concessions, not surrender, satisfying enough demands to quell the immediate threat, hoping it would go away (or at least quiet down until after the next election), while ensuring that the outcome didn't lead to the more radical decentralization that figures like Henry and Warren envisioned.

The Bill of Rights, a monumental achievement — a major concession of power born of principled resistance — thus also became an early, powerful example of how the American system could absorb and institutionalize even the most potent challenges. The very success of these amendments, enshrined within the Constitution, contributed to the mythologizing of the document itself as a perfect guarantor of liberty. This, in turn, risked obscuring the ongoing need for vigilance and the kind of action in opposition to the institutions of authority that had been so crucial to the Constitution's creation. Here we see an early glimpse of the process of interrupted resistance that will be a central theme of this book.

That June morning, sweating through his pleading speech, Madison faced a problem entirely of his own making. The Constitution he'd helped design lacked the very protections the resistance movement had been formed to secure. And the old revolutionaries — the same people who'd pushed back British authority at Lexington and Concord, who'd stood with Daniel Shays when Massachusetts turned abusive — were forcing him to deliver them.

Force the fight. That's the resistance principle this moment reveals. When abusive authority tries to consolidate power, make them fight for every inch. Force them to respond, to slow down, to pay a price. Extract whatever concessions you can. Understand that partial victories now become foundations for total victories later.

The nationalists at Philadelphia in 1787 had stacked the deck. They were supposed to fix the Articles of Confederation. Instead, they wrote an entirely new constitution, kept it secret, and then rushed it through ratification before opposition could organize.

The Anti-Federalists forced the fight anyway. At each state convention, they pushed. They lost in Pennsylvania, but they learned. They lost in Massachusetts, but they extracted the first promise of amendments. They lost in Virginia, but Madison had to publicly commit to a Bill of Rights to win his own election. They didn't get what they wanted — a second constitutional convention, fundamental restructuring of federal power. But they made the nationalists pay for every victory. They forced concessions that seemed minor at the time but became the constitutional foundation for challenging oppression for the next two centuries.

Plant seeds knowing that someone else will harvest them. The Bill of Rights seemed limited when ratified — it didn't apply to states, didn't free enslaved people, didn't redistribute power. But seventy-eight years later, the Fourteenth Amendment nationalized those rights. Suddenly those "limited" protections became weapons against the very system that produced them. Frederick Douglass understood this when he said in 1852 that "interpreted as it ought to be interpreted, the Constitution is a glorious liberty document" — not because of what the framers intended, but because the Anti-Federalists had forced amendments into it that could be used against the system.

The Bill of Rights emerged not as a gift but as a demand — a product of struggle against established authority. Madison, Hamilton, and their allies fought bitterly against it, not only opposing its inclusion but also attempting to force ratification without debate or modification. Their urgency wasn't born of deep commitment to individual liberties but rather of a desire to foreclose discussion and control the outcome. The Bill of Rights was not a revolutionary act in itself but instead a grudging concession extracted by those who saw in the new Constitution the same violations of rights that had fueled the Revolution in the first place.

This is the resistance history that nationalist mythology has buried. The through line from the New England patriots who organized against the Stamp Act, to the militia at Lexington and Concord who pushed back British troops, to Daniel Shays and the western Massachusetts farmers who used the same resistance patterns against Massachusetts authority, to the Anti-Federalists who forced a Bill of Rights into a constitution designed to consolidate power without one. This is American resistance to be proud of — the continuous tradition of organizing against abusive authority that achieved every major gain for liberty in American history.

And it's been erased by Founders Chic and tales of young patriots building a nation. We've been sold a unified American Revolution, brilliant young minds in the Continental Congress doing something unprecedented, heroes who gave us independence and the Constitution in one glorious burst.

That's not what happened.

This is the story of the resistance movement Madison was never part of — the old revolutionaries who spent decades learning how to push back abusive authority, who kept fighting through every setback, who forced Madison to add protections to his constitution even after he'd won ratification. To understand how they did it, you need to see what that movement actually was, where it came from, how it operated. You need to understand where Madison was while that movement was maturing, because his absence from it explains why he designed a constitution without protecting rights. And you need to see how resistance, properly organized and relentlessly persistent, forced concessions from authority that became the foundation for future freedom.

The story starts not in 1789, but twenty-five years earlier, when a small group of New Englanders decided that Parliament had crossed a line.

The Embattled Farmers

Britain came out of the Seven Years' War victorious and nearly bankrupt. Parliament needed revenue, and the logic was straightforward: Americans should help pay for their own defense. British taxpayers had been carrying the colonial burden for decades.

The Stamp Act wasn't novel — it had been law in England for more than a century. And Parliament knew it was unprecedented in the colonies. They'd consulted colonial agents like Benjamin Franklin, who assured them it would be accepted without problem. Parliament needed to demonstrate, for domestic consumption in Britain, that Americans weren't a special case to be shielded from obligations everyone else accepted.

What they didn't anticipate was how thoroughly colonial Americans had internalized their own self-governance. Not that they had any particular right to it — people in Manchester and Birmingham weren't directly represented in Parliament, either. Virtual representation was how the system worked. But Americans had been making decisions about their own lives for long enough that the imposition of parliamentary authority, however legitimate in theory, *felt* like intrusion.

The men who would later claim to speak for the Revolution were nowhere near it. Young, scattered, oblivious. James Madison was fourteen years old, conjugating Latin verbs at a boarding school a hundred miles from home. Alexander Hamilton was a child in the Caribbean (even he didn't know how old he was). John Jay was a teenage law clerk in New York. The resistance was happening somewhere else, to other people.

Far from any of them, Parliament had decided to make the colonials finally pay their share.

The Stamp Act required colonials to purchase stamped paper for legal documents, newspapers, playing cards, dice — any printed material. The revenue would go to Britain to help pay for troops stationed in North America. To Parliament, this seemed reasonable because it *was* reasonable. The colonials benefited from British protection; they should help pay for it.

To a small group of New Englanders, it was something else entirely: abuse of the consent of the governed. James Otis gave the feeling a phrase: *No taxation without representation.* It didn't matter that the phrase misrepresented how parliamentary authority actually operated. The colonies had no members in Parliament, couldn't vote on the tax, couldn't debate it, couldn't influence it except through agents like Franklin — who had been wrong about how it would be received. In the colonial mind, the tax wasn't negotiated; it was imposed. That made it *feel* illegitimate.

This wasn't what most people thought. The vast majority of colonials grumbled but would have paid. But the small group that saw it as abuse of authority didn't stay small. They organized, and their numbers grew.

In Boston, organized resistance began within a few streets of the South End. A printer, Benjamin Edes, joined a circle of nine associates who met quietly to plan opposition to the Stamp Act. They called themselves the Loyal Nine. They mapped out the local stamp distributors and made sure that each knew what would happen if he accepted the post. On August 14, 1765, they hung an effigy of Andrew

Oliver, the man chosen to enforce the act, from a great elm that Boston soon called the Liberty Tree. That evening a crowd cut down the effigy, carried it through the town, tore down the stamp office that Oliver was building, and burned the figure before his house. Oliver resigned the next day.

The target wasn't some elite British official. Andrew Oliver was Boston-born, from one of the town's old mercantile families, and brother-in-law to Lieutenant Governor Thomas Hutchinson, also a Massachusetts native. He had accepted the post of stamp distributor on Franklin's recommendation, like all the others — local men enlisted to enforce a British tax that was, by any reasonable measure, within Parliament's authority to levy. Every colony had its Oliver. That's what made the resistance so effective: It didn't matter whether the authority was legitimate if you could make it impossible to exercise.

It was violence — targeted, organized, and effective. From the start, the patriots used it as a tool, and they understood how narrow the line was between resistance that would draw followers who saw the response and legitimate, and what would look like simple mob rule. James Otis put it clearly: The patriots needed to remain within "the proper and legal measures to obtain redress." He pointed out that even the commonwealth resistance to Charles I had waited through fifteen years of petition and remonstrance before choosing violence. *The Boston Gazette* articulated the standard: "No mobs, no confusions, no tumults . . . for constitutional methods are best."

The potential for violence in Boston was always barely under the surface. But resistance leaders knew it wasn't time for open conflict yet. "No violence, or you'll hurt the cause," was the watchword. Property destruction, intimidation, making authority impossible to exercise — these were tools the resistance could deploy without losing the allies they needed.

And it worked. No one in Massachusetts would distribute stamps.

The patriots weren't just using local violence, or the threat of it. They were building something more durable. The Loyal Nine linked up with similar groups forming in other colonies — New York,

Connecticut, Rhode Island, Virginia. They merged with another opposition group in Boston: the Sons of Liberty. The name stuck. By early 1766, Sons of Liberty groups existed across the colonies, coordinating through correspondence, sharing tactics, amplifying one another's opposition.

Stamp agents got hounded everywhere. In Virginia, George Mercer arrived in Williamsburg to take up his post and found a crowd waiting. He resigned within hours. In Maryland, Zachariah Hood's house was torn down. In Rhode Island, Augustus Johnston was hanged in effigy and forced to resign under another Liberty Tree, in Newport. Only in Georgia, where royal authority was stronger and the population more dependent on British military presence for protection alongside neighboring Creek and Cherokee territory, did the Stamp Act briefly go into effect. Everywhere else, the strategy that worked in Boston worked again: Make the tax impossible to enforce by making the enforcers' lives impossible.

It was parallel institution-building — operating outside British authority, technically illegal, yet functioning almost in the open because imperial enforcement was thin. In 1765, there were few regular troops anywhere in the colonies, and none stationed in Boston. The Sons of Liberty were not a secret cabal; they met in taverns, published resolutions, and made their opposition public. There was no garrison to stop them.

Parliament repealed the Stamp Act on March 18, 1766. The pattern was set: Perceive authority as abusive, organize resistance — often including targeted violence within accepted cultural bounds — and force concession. The imperial system proved elastic. The patriots had tested its limits and won a measured victory.

Repeal didn't come without conditions, however. To soothe the wounded pride of ministers and merchants who thought Parliament had yielded too much, repeal was coupled with the Declaratory Act — a statement that Parliament's authority over the colonies was "in all cases whatsoever." It was a legal fig leaf, meant to reassure London that nothing fundamental had changed. In America, almost no one cared.

The papers reprinted the text, but the celebrations ignored it. What mattered was the result: Organized resistance had forced Parliament to retreat.

Parliament tried again to raise revenues in 1767 with the Townshend Acts — duties on glass, lead, paint, paper, and tea imported into the colonies. The resistance deployed the same tactics. The Sons of Liberty organized boycotts of British goods. Women formed spinning circles to produce homespun cloth, reducing dependence on British textiles. Merchants signed non-importation agreements. The economic pressure was real — British exports to the colonies dropped significantly.

And Parliament responded. In 1770, they repealed most of the Townshend duties, keeping only the tax on tea as a symbolic assertion of Parliamentary authority. The pattern held: colonial resistance, economic pressure, imperial retreat. This is what representation looked like in practice, even without direct seats in Parliament. Colonial interests were being heard. Authority was adjusting course based on colonial opposition.

The resistance had won. Twice. And both times, they'd won by working within channels that, while not perfectly legal, stayed within bounds the system could absorb. Property destruction, economic pressure, organized opposition — these were tools Parliament could understand and respond to.

Which raised a question the resistance movement wasn't asking yet: If the system keeps working, keeps bending, keeps giving you what you want — what exactly are you resisting? It was a problem that the patriots faced time and again as the process of opposition actually yielded results. Grievances were articulated, protests were mounted, authority responded. And with the disappearance of the grievance came an evaporation of opposition.

Samuel Adams had an answer: You're resisting what *could* happen, what authority *might* do, what troops in the streets *represent* even if they haven't done anything yet. The grievances were real to him, but they were abstract, technical, hard to make other people feel. What he needed was something visible.

On March 5, 1770, a sentry posted at the Custom House on King Street confronted a crowd. A detachment under Captain Thomas Preston came to support him. In the confusion, soldiers fired. Five men died, six were wounded.

Boston at the time had a population of about sixteen thousand people, with two regiments of British army regulars that had been quartered there since 1768 to support customs enforcement. The Townshend Acts had passed Parliament with input from colonial agents. This wasn't abuse of authority in any strict sense, not if you accepted the theory of virtual representation that governed the empire.

The troops guarded official buildings but didn't run the town. Civil authority remained intact. There were no patrols, no passes, no martial law. The soldiers were a symbol, not an occupation. But symbols matter, and Samuel Adams understood that. Eleven days before the shooting, a customs employee fired into a group of radicals, pelting his house with stones. He killed an eleven-year-old boy, Christopher Seider. That death had nothing to do with the troops. But Samuel Adams used Seider's funeral to inflame public anger. The patriot resistance had evolved as Adams formed a keen sense of how to manage messages, drawing on history and culture to create a believable narrative of grievance. He developed an ability to see how situations could be, in his word, "improved" — meaning exploited. He'd watched what happened at St. George's Fields in London two years earlier, when soldiers fired on a crowd. He knew what could be made of a confrontation.

Two weeks later, the soldiers opened fire at the Custom House. Patriot printers and engravers moved fast to control the story. Witness accounts placed blame on the soldiers. Paul Revere's engraving, completed three weeks after the event, showed ordered ranks firing on defenseless civilians — deliberate propaganda designed to reverse the actual confusion of the scene and portray those shot by the soldiers as victims of a massacre. The funerals became processions. Orations were printed and distributed. What had been a street fight became proof of tyranny.

Boston's town meeting demanded that the regiments be removed. The authorities resisted briefly, then folded. On March 10, both regiments withdrew to Castle William in the harbor. They left not because they'd done anything wrong, but because their presence had become untenable once resistance leaders made it the issue. The visible presence of military authority, once exposed as dangerous, couldn't be sustained. Adams had turned a brawl into an object lesson that worked.

John Adams, Samuel's cousin, defended the soldiers at their trial and won acquittals for most of them by shifting responsibility to the crowd — to vague, unnamed agitators who'd provoked the confrontation. The trials proved that British institutions could still function in Boston. Even after men had been shot dead in the street, the system could absorb the violence, channel it through courts, resolve it through law. This was the elasticity of British political culture, the thing that made the empire durable.

Samuel Adams didn't mind. The trials didn't matter to what he was building. What mattered was the story: British authority, when challenged, opened fire, deploying violence to replace argument. The troops had been withdrawn but annual commemorations kept the memory alive, the story going.

Adams had created a template. Provoke a confrontation, control the narrative, make authority visible and threatening, force a response that proves your point. The massacre became a propaganda victory not despite the acquittals but because the whole sequence — shooting, trials, acquittals, annual commemorations — demonstrated that reform within the system wasn't coming.

By July 1771, the opposition had collapsed anyway. All of it. The non-importation associations, the protests, even the boycott on tea — gone. Parliament had repealed most of the Townshend Duties, and the colonists had done what people do when the pressure eases: they went back to their lives.

Adams was not pleased.

Writing as "Candidus" in the *Boston Gazette* on October 14, 1771, he opened by citing the Swiss reformer Zuinglius, who had some thoughts about people who accept oppression: they deserve what they suffer and should perish with their oppressors. Adams agreed. "The truth is, All might be free if they valued freedom, and defended it as they ought."

Then he got to the point, his call for people to rise up in defense of "the liberties of our Country, the freedom of our civil constitution": "It will bring an everlasting mark of infamy on the present generation, enlightened as it is, if we should suffer them to be wrested from us by violence without a struggle; or be cheated out of them by the artifices of false and designing men."

The structure here is not subtle. Don't let them take your rights by violence *without a struggle*—which means, when they bring violence, you fight back. And don't get conned into giving them away. Passive acceptance only "encourages" further attacks and drags "millions yet unborn" into the consequences.

It didn't work. But the argument was on the record: When popular opposition wanes, when the moment needs improving, you improve it.

What came next was indeed quieter but also more dangerous: The patriots started building institutions that didn't need British permission to exist.

The colonial assemblies had been communicating for years through permitted channels, using circular letters to share petitions and coordinate responses to particular acts. This was sanctioned political practice. Richard Henry Lee of Virginia had been pushing for something more systematic since 1768, a way to turn those irregular exchanges into permanent infrastructure.

Then, in June 1772, the HMS *Gaspee*, a British ship under the command of William Dudingston, patrolling the waters off Rhode Island to prevent the smuggling of contraband goods in evasion of taxation, ran aground in shallow water while chasing the merchant vessel *Hannah*. This wasn't an accident. It was a trap. Captain Benjamin Lindsey knew the shallows of Narragansett Bay and led Dudingston's ship exactly where it would run aground. That night, men from Providence — merchants, leading citizens, respectable men who'd been waiting for exactly this kind of opportunity — rowed out to the stranded ship, shot Lieutenant William Dudingston, set him and his crew on the shore, and burned the vessel to the waterline. The attack was organized, deliberate, planned the moment word reached Providence that the *Gaspee* was stuck. Like the massacre in Boston, this was resistance leaders improving an opportunity. They turned it into theater, complete with songs celebrating what they'd done.

The British response was different this time. The attack was ruled an act of high treason. A commission of inquiry convened — colonial Crown officials empowered to send suspects to England for trial. No local juries. The right to trial by a jury of your peers, in your own community, was supposed to be a fundamental British liberty. The threat of being shipped to England for trial violated that, and the colonies understood what it meant.

However, the commission couldn't get anyone to talk. Witnesses claimed ignorance. The attackers were known — Dudingston and his crew had identified most of them — but the community protected them. A five-hundred-pound reward produced no suspects. The commission concluded that persons unknown had destroyed the *Gaspee*.

But the commission's existence, its power to send colonists to England, was what mattered. *The Providence Gazette* called it a court of inquisition. Other colonial papers declared that it made Americans worse off than subjects of any despotic power on earth. The affair showed that the resistance could commit direct, violent acts against royal authority and face no consequences because local institutions wouldn't cooperate. More than that, it showed that when the British tried to work around local institutions, the colonies would unite in opposition. British authority depended on colonial cooperation. When that disappeared, the system had no backup.

News of the commission's power to send suspects to England for trial reached Virginia through the newspapers in January 1773. Richard Henry Lee wrote to Samuel Adams, asking for accurate information — he didn't trust what he was reading. By March, when the House of

Burgesses convened in Williamsburg, the affair was fresh enough that when Virginia's governor moved some counterfeiters from their home county to Williamsburg for trial, the parallel was impossible to miss. Moving suspects away from their communities for trial was exactly what the *Gaspee* commission threatened to do, just on a larger scale.

Patrick Henry, Richard Henry Lee, Thomas Jefferson, Francis Lightfoot Lee, and Dabney Carr met privately at the Raleigh Tavern in Williamsburg on the night of March 11. They drafted a resolution creating a standing committee of correspondence to communicate with other colonial assemblies about threats to their rights. Carr presented it the next day. The House of Burgesses adopted it unanimously. This wasn't the first committee of correspondence — Samuel Adams had created one in Boston the previous November to coordinate among Massachusetts towns, and Virginia had used them before for specific issues — but this was different. This was intercolonial, permanent, and designed to create what Lee called "a large and thorough union of councils."

The resolution went out to the other colonial assemblies. Within months, most had established their own committees. British officials dismissed it — Virginia's governor thought the resolves showed "a little ill humor" but were too insignificant to notice. Lee understood better. He wrote to John Dickinson that the committees were "leading to that union and perfect understanding of each other, on which the political salvation of America so eminently depends."

This was infrastructure: systematic communication networks that could coordinate opposition across distances, share information more quickly and reliably than newspapers, develop unified responses, identify allies. The committees met openly, published their proceedings, functioned almost as if they had official sanction. But they answered to no royal official, operated under no charter granted by the Crown. They were creating a structure of authority that derived entirely from local consent — proving in practice what the patriots had been arguing in theory, that legitimate authority came from the people, not from Parliament's say-so. It was resistance becoming organized at scale, and it was more threatening than any riot because it demonstrated that British authority in America was optional. The colonials could simply route around it.

In 1773, Parliament passed the Tea Act. The legislation was intended to rescue the East India Company from imminent collapse. The Company had massive tea surpluses moldering in London warehouses and couldn't move them. Parliament exempted the Company from import duties on tea brought into England from India and then re-exported to America. The bill substantially lowered the price while keeping the small Townshend duty in place. It also gave the Company authority to choose which colonial merchants would receive the tea as consignees.

This wasn't about raising revenue — no new taxes were imposed. To Lord North's ministry and even friends of the colonies in Parliament, the measure seemed reasonable. Save the Company, undercut smuggled Dutch tea, collect the existing duty, and reassert Parliamentary authority. Simple.

But this was abuse of authority by the definition that matters in this book. Parliament — entrusted with authority to govern in the interests of the people it represented — used that authority to serve private interests instead. The East India Company and its shareholders needed a bailout. Many of those shareholders sat in Parliament. They used their positions, their access to governmental power, to reorganize colonial commerce for their own benefit. Not to raise revenue for the common good. Not to fund defense or administration. To save their investments.

That's the abuse. Authority exercised for the interests of those holding it rather than the people they're supposed to serve. British taxpayers had been carrying the Company's burden for years through the annual four-hundred-thousand-pound payment the Company owed the government. Now Parliament conscripted colonials to bail out the Company by rigging the tea market in its favor, cutting out established merchants and forcing the tea through Company-chosen consignees.

Colonials saw it clearly. The resistance politicians — Adams in Boston, the Sons of Liberty networks across the colonies — had been arguing for years that Parliamentary authority was becoming tyrannical, that there was a hidden force behind it, intent on making the colonies pawns for its own benefit. The Tea Act proved them right, but not in the way they'd been claiming. The problem wasn't taxation without representation. The problem was that Parliament seemed to have stopped representing anyone except narrow interests with access to power.

And the merchant class saw it, too. The Tea Act cut out colonial merchants who'd been operating as middlemen in the legal tea trade and undercut smugglers who'd been importing cheaper Dutch tea. John Hancock in Boston and Benjamin Harrison in Virginia had made a fortune smuggling. Merchants in New York and Philadelphia had built businesses on being the connection between British suppliers and colonial consumers. The Tea Act eliminated both — gave the East India Company direct access to colonial markets through handpicked consignees, bypassing everyone who'd been making money off tea for decades.

Parliament was using its authority to pick winners and losers in colonial commerce. Not for the public good. For the East India Company's shareholders. That's abuse of authority even if the people recognizing it were doing so because it threatened their own pockets.

In ports up and down the coast, radical politicians who'd been building resistance infrastructure for years and merchants whose business interests suddenly aligned with the resistance argument found common cause.

In summer 1773, the Company dispatched tea shipments to Charleston, Philadelphia, New York, and Boston. When ships reached New York and Philadelphia, the Sons of Liberty and local merchants turned them back. In Charleston, the tea was unloaded but left to rot on the docks — the tax unpaid, the tea unsold.

Boston was different. Governor Thomas Hutchinson — whose sons were among the Company's chosen consignees — believed allowing the tea to land was necessary to demonstrate parliamentary sovereignty. He refused to let the ships leave. Boston's town meeting, led by Samuel Adams, refused to let the tea be unloaded.

On the evening of December 16, after a mass meeting at Old South Church failed to resolve the standoff, Adams reportedly said, "This meeting can do nothing more to save the country." That night, a group disguised as Mohawks — including merchants, artisans, and Sons of Liberty members — boarded the three ships and dumped 352 casks of tea worth ten thousand pounds into the harbor.

This was property destruction on a massive scale, organized and deliberate. But it wasn't violence against persons. The patriots were still calibrating. They'd learned from the *Gaspee* that direct violence against British personnel created complications. The Tea Party destroyed thousands of pounds' worth of property but hurt no one. It stayed within boundaries — barely.

But the Tea Act itself represented something that the Stamp Act and Townshend Acts hadn't. Those measures, however much colonials objected to them, were attempts to raise revenue for public purposes. Misguided, maybe. Violations of colonial expectations about self-governance, certainly. But not abusive in the sense that matters. The Tea Act was different. It was authority used to serve those holding power rather than those they were supposed to represent. That's abuse that justifies resistance.

And the colonial response — the destruction of property and direct defiance of a governor determined to enforce compliance — crossed a line the system couldn't absorb the way it had absorbed Stamp Act riots or Boston Massacre trials.

This was the moment when resistance to authority that had been mostly responsive met authority that had actually become abusive. What came next would push both sides past the point where British political culture's elasticity could contain it.

The British ministry initially saw it that way, too. The prime minister, Lord North, understanding that too many members of Parliament were exhausted by the patriot resistance's consistent disturbance of colonial affairs, wanted to keep the matter out of the House of Commons.

When news of the Tea Party reached London, it appalled almost everyone. Even friends of the colonies couldn't condone the destruction of that much private property. George Washington thought the Bostonians had gone too far. Benjamin Franklin was mortified. Radicals in other colonies were outraged at the lawless destruction. The Tea Party had accomplished what successive British ministries had failed to do for a decade: isolate Boston as out of step with the rest of the colonies.

Lord North wanted to contain the resistance. Handle the matter quietly, the way the Boston Massacre had been handled — through courts, through existing channels, let things calm down.

He couldn't. Both the attorney general and solicitor general told him that the Crown had no authority to prosecute individuals or close Boston's port. The Crown had no criminal jurisdiction over the colonies — only Parliament did. Ten thousand pounds' worth of East India Company tea had been destroyed in full view of thousands of witnesses. Real money connected to people with seats in Parliament. Members who'd had enough of Boston disrupting imperial commerce.

North had no choice but to take the matter to the House of Commons. His own political survival required it.

During the early months of 1774, North's ministry brought forward the Coercive Acts: The Boston Port Act closed Boston Harbor to all commerce effective June 1 and moved customs officials to Salem. The Massachusetts Government Act revoked the colony's 1691 charter — eliminated the elected council, gave the royal governor power to appoint all officials, restricted town meetings to once a year without gubernatorial permission. The Administration of Justice Act allowed royal officials accused of capital crimes to be tried in Britain rather than Massachusetts. The Quartering Act authorized billeting troops in unused buildings.

These were punitive measures, designed to make an example of Massachusetts. The revocation of the charter was an intentional display of parliamentary supremacy, a lesson for all the colonies.

And they were abusive. Collective punishment for the actions of a few dozen men. Revocation of chartered self-governance that had existed for eighty years. Removal of accused officials from local justice. Not measures to raise revenue or regulate commerce for the common good. Measures to punish a population for resisting. To satisfy MPs who wanted Boston broken. To demonstrate power. To make people afraid of what would happen if they kept fighting back.

The Tea Act had crossed a line, using Parliamentary authority to bail out private interests. And now the Coercive Acts crossed another one. Parliament wasn't trying to govern Massachusetts anymore. It was trying to punish it into submission.

The Coercive Acts proved the patriots right.

Abusing Authority

News of the Coercive Acts reached the colonies in spring 1774. The Boston Port Act closed the harbor effective June 1. The 1691 charter, the elected council, local authority to appoint officials, town meetings without gubernatorial permission: eliminated.

Parliament's measures backfired spectacularly.

Word of the Acts spread through the correspondence networks the resistance had spent years building, and the response came fast. Virginia called for a continental congress. Then every other colony joined in. Virginia mattered most here — steadiest colony in the empire, loyal, cautious, the one that made other colonies nervous about getting too radical. When Virginia's House of Burgesses called for a day of fasting to protest Boston's closed port, the royal governor dissolved it.

Its members met anyway. Walked down the street to the Raleigh Tavern, banned British imports, demanded a congress. George Washington was there. His position: "The cause of Boston now is and ever will be the cause of America." That sentence worked. If Virginia was in, everyone was in.

In Massachusetts, things moved faster because Major General Thomas Gage arrived in May as both military commander and royal governor, sent to enforce Parliament's will. Gage had commanded the forces that occupied Boston since 1768. He'd seen what happened after the massacre — how the resistance turned five dead into proof of tyranny, how the propaganda machine converted a street brawl into an atrocity. But he'd been on leave in England when the tea went into the harbor, still there when the Boston Port Bill sent transatlantic relations into a tailspin. Distance apparently clarified things. Gage assured the king that Americans "will be Lyons, whilst we are Lambs but if we take the resolute part they will undoubtedly prove very meek." Four regiments would handle it.

He moved the capital from Boston to Salem. Started appointing councilors under the new system. Restricted town meetings. The Coercive Acts weren't empty threats — Gage would make sure of it, backed by almost four thousand British soldiers. He'd forgotten what he once knew, or convinced himself that firmness would succeed where prudence had. Either way, he was about to relearn the lesson.

The colonials were happy to teach him. They refused to cooperate. Counties across Massachusetts organized conventions and rejected the new government. Closed courts rather than operate under a revoked charter. Formed committees of safety with authority to call out militia. Built a parallel government and dared Gage to stop them.

When Gage tried to confiscate gunpowder stored in Charlestown in early September, thousands of militiamen showed up. He looked at the situation and canceled the next seizure. That was the test. Could the resistance mobilize armed men fast enough to make British military action too risky to attempt? Turned out, yes.

Six days later, Suffolk County representatives met. Joseph Warren drafted what became the Suffolk Resolves: Nineteen points declaring the Coercive Acts unconstitutional and urging colonials to ignore them completely. Economic boycott of Britain. Form militias; learn the art of war. Establish alarm systems for British attack. Create a provincial congress to govern Massachusetts outside any British authority.

Paul Revere rode it to Philadelphia, where the First Continental Congress was meeting. On September 17, as its first official act, Congress unanimously endorsed it.

The resistance went from coordinating protest through correspondence committees to coordinating defiance through an actual congress. Not protest within permitted channels anymore — organized opposition building authority structures wholly outside British control. Congress adopted the Continental Association: non-importation, non-exportation, committees of inspection in every town to enforce the policy. These committees became functioning government, under the authority of the Continental Congress.

Concord, Massachusetts, twenty miles from Boston, had ignored most of the colonial disputes for years. While Boston raged about British policies through the 1760s and early 1770s, Concordians fought about roads and schools and whether their minister was acceptable. Local squabbles. Real problems. Let Boston make noise about parliamentary authority. Concord had actual issues to resolve.

Then the Massachusetts Government Act restricted town meetings.

Town meetings weren't political theory. They were how Concordians ran their lives. How they settled disputes about roads, managed schools, hired ministers, made community decisions about daily existence. Basic self-governance. When Gage said they needed his permission to meet, the abuse became immediate and personal. Not abstract. Not something happening in Boston to other people. Something affecting whether Concord could function as a town.

The comfortable sorts started paying attention. The middling farmers who'd avoided choosing sides, who'd thought the whole dispute was overblown radical nonsense, started listening to patriot arguments. Loyalist talking points — just pay the tax, submit to parliamentary authority, things will calm down — carried less weight when patriots could point at suspended town meetings and British troops in Boston enforcing a revoked charter.

Concord organized. Formed a militia company — minutemen who could be ready at a moment's notice. Stockpiled weapons and ammunition. Created a committee of safety with authority to mobilize. Built the resistance infrastructure that could take on armed conflict if Gage decided to push.

Other towns across Massachusetts did the same. Across all the colonies, actually. British administrative control was unraveling. Tax revenue got diverted from royal officials to resistance committees. Local committees assumed government functions. Militias drilled every week.

Gage sat in Boston and wrote increasingly desperate letters back to London. Need thousands more troops. Need a naval blockade. Can't enforce the acts without massive reinforcements. The entire colony was in organized rebellion, and he couldn't stop it.

The resistance had been building infrastructure for a decade. In response, the system bent, adjusted, made concessions. Parliament repealed the Stamp Act. Repealed most of the Townshend Acts. The elasticity had worked to contain the pushback.

The Coercive Acts broke that pattern. These were punitive measures designed to make an example, to break resistance through overwhelming force.

Instead, they strengthened the patriot position. Demonstrated what authority exercised abusively looked like. Not raising revenue for public purposes. Not regulating commerce. Punishing a population for resisting. Using governmental power to serve those holding it rather than those they were supposed to represent. That's the abuse that justifies resistance by the terms that matter in this book.

And the acts expanded the resistance beyond Boston radicals and port-city merchants. Brought in the comfortable, the cautious, the people who just wanted to run their towns and be left alone. The Coercive Acts did what a decade of patriot organizing couldn't do on its own: made the threat feel real and immediate to people who'd been successfully ignoring it.

In April, Gage got new orders. Take decisive action. Seize the military supplies colonials were stockpiling. Arrest radical leaders if possible. Demonstrate that British authority still existed in Massachusetts in some meaningful form.

He chose Concord as the place to set an example. Weapons and ammunition were known to be stockpiled there. It was far enough from Boston to send the desired message of authority's reach, yet close to available troops.

What Gage didn't fully grasp: Alarm systems were already in place. The militias were organized and had been drilling for months. The committees of safety had authority to mobilize armed men. The colonials had spent those months preparing for exactly this scenario — British troops marching out of Boston to seize their weapons and eliminate their ability to resist with force.

On the night of April 18, 1775, British troops marched out of Boston toward Concord. Gage intended for his mission to be secret. It wasn't. Riders spread the alarm across the countryside. Revere, William Dawes, Samuel Prescott — moving through the network of committees, using the alarm systems the Suffolk Resolves had formalized. Every town along the route got word: British troops are marching, heading for Concord to seize weapons. By dawn on April 19, when the troops reached Lexington, armed colonials were waiting on the common.

The resistance had built the capacity to fight. Parliament had given them the reason. Now they'd find out if their preparations would actually work when British regulars were standing in front of them.

About seventy militiamen were assembled on the Lexington common under Captain John Parker. Armed colonials, organized under local authority, refused to disperse when ordered. Someone fired — accounts differ as to whom. The British line fired a volley. Eight militiamen died. Ten were wounded.

This was the moment. Not property destruction or intimidation; this was actual combat, the body count that makes most resistance movements fracture or retreat into channels where they can be managed.

The Lexington militia scattered. The British troops marched on to Concord, six miles farther. They'd won the confrontation. Demonstrated superior force. Shown that colonial militia would break when faced with British regulars.

At Concord, the calculation changed.

The troops entered the town center around eight in the morning. Started searching for weapons and supplies. The resistance had moved most of it already, but the British found some cannon balls, destroyed gun carriages, dumped flour. Set a fire that spread to the Town House.

Companies of militia had been gathering outside of town. Hundreds of armed men from Concord and surrounding towns watched smoke rise from the town center. They didn't know what was burning. Thought maybe the British were torching the entire town. Colonel James Barrett made the decision: Advance on the British position.

At the North Bridge, about four hundred militiamen confronted three companies of British regulars — maybe one hundred troops. The British fired. Two militiamen fell. The militia fired back. British soldiers fell — dead, wounded, breaking formation. The regulars retreated back toward the town center. Colonial militia had engaged British troops in direct combat and driven them back.

That was new. That changed everything about what the resistance was capable of.

The British commander made the decision to retreat to Boston. By noon, seven hundred troops were marching back down the road they'd come up that morning. And all along the twenty miles back to Boston, militia companies were waiting.

This was the resistance infrastructure functioning as designed. The alarm systems had brought out militia from every town in the region. Not mobs. Not spontaneous violence. Organized companies under officers, acting under authority of committees of safety, executing tactics they'd been practicing. They positioned themselves behind stone walls, trees, buildings. Let the British column pass. Fired. Fell back. Repositioned. Fired again.

The British troops couldn't respond effectively. Couldn't see where fire was coming from. Couldn't force battle on their terms. Had to just keep moving, taking casualties the entire way. By the time they reached Lexington, they were almost out of ammunition and close to breaking completely. A relief brigade of a thousand troops, guided by a Harvard student, met them there — Gage had sent reinforcements when he realized how badly things were going. The combined force continued the retreat to Charlestown, under fire the entire way.

By the time they reached safety, the British had suffered 73 killed, 174 wounded, 26 missing. The patriots suffered 49 killed, 39 wounded, 5 missing.

Those numbers mattered. Real casualties, sustained in combat, forcing British troops into retreat. This wasn't the Stamp Act riots where property got destroyed and everyone went home. This wasn't the Boston Massacre where soldiers fired into a crowd and got tried for it afterward. This was organized military action by colonial militia against British regulars, resulting in British defeat.

The resistance had pushed back abusive authority. Literally, physically, all the way back to Boston. Gage's troops were besieged in their own headquarters within days. Militia from across New England — thousands of armed men — converged on Boston and held British forces contained. The Massachusetts Provincial Congress coordinated the military action. Committees of safety supplied it. The parallel government the resistance had built over ten years was functioning as actual government, directing operations.

This was what the resistance had been building toward since 1765. The infrastructure to organize at scale. The experience to coordinate across distances. The willingness to accept violence and its consequences. The parallel institutions to exercise authority independently of British control. All of it working exactly as needed when tested by actual combat. The resistance succeeded in doing what resistance movements are built to do: stop authority from being exercised abusively by making it impossible to exercise at all.

But success created its own problem. What happens when you've actually pushed back the authority? When you're holding British troops under siege and operating your own government? When you've demonstrated that you can fight and win but now you have to figure out what comes next?

That's where the resistance started losing control of what it built.

The Nationalists Take Over

After April 19, militia from across New England converged on Boston. Thousands of armed men. Organized by committees of safety. Coordinating through the Massachusetts Provincial Congress. They besieged British troops in their own headquarters. Gage and his reinforcements — Generals Howe, Clinton, and Burgoyne had arrived in late May — couldn't break out. The resistance had pushed back abusive authority and was holding it contained.

Loyalists were trapped inside the city. The siege physically separated Massachusetts into two camps. Inside Boston: British troops and colonials who'd refused to join the resistance. Outside: the resistance forces, operating their own government, directing military operations, exercising authority without reference to British control.

On June 17, 1775, the resistance fought what turned out to be the bloodiest battle of the entire war.

The British planned to take Dorchester Heights for artillery control. The resistance intelligence network caught their intentions and patriot forces moved first, fortifying Breed's Hill on the Charlestown peninsula overnight. The British woke up to find colonial militia dug in behind fortifications overlooking Boston.

General Howe ordered a frontal assault, and he led twenty-five hundred regulars up the hill. About three thousand militia waited behind their hastily built walls. The resistance held fire until the British were close — "don't fire until you see the whites of their eyes" actually happened — and repulsed the first assault. Repulsed the second. Ran out of ammunition during the third and had to retreat.

The British took the position at a cost of 1,150 men killed or wounded — about 40 percent of those engaged. One out of every eight British officers who would be killed in the entire war died at the Battle of Bunker Hill. The resistance lost about 440, including Joseph Warren, thirty-four years old. He had drafted the Suffolk Resolves and was killed in hand-to-hand combat during the final assault.

Black soldiers fought at Bunker Hill. Peter Salem, enslaved in

Framingham before joining the militia, was credited with shooting British Major John Pitcairn. Salem Poor fought with such distinction that fourteen officers signed a petition praising his conduct. Cuff Whittemore, Barzillai Lew, Titus Coburn, Alexander Ames, Seymour Burr — all were Black men in the resistance ranks who fought alongside white militia. Not as auxiliaries. As soldiers.

Indigenous men from Wampanoag, Nipmuc, and Stockbridge communities stood in the same lines.

The resistance militias were local forces drawn from whomever their towns depended on. That's the part modern historians and storytellers get backward when they're desperate to find some founding diversity story. Nothing in colonial America was integrated by design or principle. The inclusion of Black men, Indigenous men, other men of color in New England resistance ranks was begrudging at best, a function of local necessity, not enlightened ideology. But they were there. Free men and some enslaved men who'd earned or bargained for freedom. Fighting because these were their communities and they were defending their homes.

The resistance force that fought Bunker Hill was the most inclusive American military force of the eighteenth century. Not because of ideology. Because resistance was local.

George Washington ended that when he arrived.

Congress had adopted the New England forces as the "Continental Army" on June 14 and elected Washington commander in chief. When he reached Cambridge on July 3, 1775, he found an army that included hundreds of Black soldiers. Within weeks, he and his officers debated whether to continue that practice. On November 12, orders were issued barring further enlistments of "Negroes, boys unable to bear arms, or old men unfit for duty."

Free Black men already serving could stay until their enlistments expired, but there would be no new Black soldiers. Enslaved men were banned entirely, even those who'd fought at Bunker Hill.

Washington, and the Virginia enslaver establishment of which he was a part, required enslaved people to be classified as property, not persons. This was Southern ideology imposed immediately on a New England resistance force. The Continental Army would reflect Southern priorities: Black men — free or enslaved — excluded from bearing arms in defense of liberty.

Lord Dunmore's proclamation that December changed Washington's calculation. Dunmore promised freedom to enslaved men who joined the British. In response to this new security concern, on December 30 Washington authorized reenlistment of free Black men already serving. Congress confirmed the changed policy mid-January 1776. But it didn't reopen enlistment broadly, and it didn't change anything for enslaved men.

The transition from militia to Continental control valued uniformity and political reassurance to Southern states over the improvised, local, mixed composition of resistance forces.

This wasn't the New England resistance under new leadership. This was Continental authority replacing local resistance, immediately signaling whose interests mattered.

The resistance movement that dominates American Revolution storytelling — midnight rides, tea parties, Sons of Liberty, shots heard 'round the world — all happened in New England. All of that was over by spring 1776. Everyone — the British ministry, the rest of the patriot movement — recognized the shift at the time.

By the time resistance movements reach that final point — violence justified by higher law, accepting that people will die — hearts and minds have already changed. What came next was war. Conventional military conflict with logistics, finance, diplomacy. The progression from grievance to organized opposition to armed pushback was complete.

Coalition politics among competing colonial establishment interests now dominated the action, managing a conflict the original resistance leaders hadn't wanted. Striving toward independence few of them had considered, much less desired.

The resistance succeeded in pushing back abusive authority. In succeeding, it got absorbed into something that would betray what it had been fighting for.

The New England resistance was over by spring 1776. Not because it failed, but because it won, and then discovered that winning meant being taken over by people who had very different ideas about whose rights mattered and what all that fighting had been for.

The Articles

The New England resistance never aimed for independence. That wasn't the goal. The resistance knew what it was against — abusive authoritian, punitive measures, Parliament using power to serve narrow interests rather than the people it represented. It knew what it was for — the rights they'd defined through years of opposition, the self-governance they'd been exercising through parallel institutions, the ability to push back when authority became abusive. Independence wasn't part of that equation. It wasn't even on the list until the coalition managing the war decided that it needed to be.

John Adams said this plainly later, when he was old and cranky and tired of people getting the story wrong. The Revolution happened in hearts and minds before the war started. The resistance was that revolution — the transformation in how colonials understood their relationship to authority, their willingness to organize opposition, their capacity to fight when necessary. When shots were fired at Lexington, that phase ended. What came after was something else entirely, and Adams resented what it had become.

Thomas Jefferson agreed, for once. He wrote in 1815 that he hadn't considered independence inevitable or even desirable until 1776. The resistance had been pushing back specific abuses, trying to force course correction within the imperial system. That's what all the petitions and declarations and committees of correspondence were doing — articulating grievances, demanding redress, building the case that parliamentary authority had become abusive and needed to be contained. Independence emerged from different dynamics after that — how the British government responded to armed conflict with more force instead of negotiation, how the coalition managing the war decided that independence was the only way to frame what they were fighting for, what became politically necessary once engaged in a conventional war and in need of support from a powerful ally, France.

The war that followed the resistance wasn't the resistance continuing under different management. It was conventional military conflict between armies, managed by a coalition of colonial establishments with competing interests and profoundly different visions of what authority should look like once British power was gone. That coalition declared independence in July 1776, eight months after Washington took command, a full year after the resistance phase effectively ended when he arrived in Cambridge and started issuing orders about who could and couldn't fight.

Managing that war exposed problems: The Continental Congress had no power to tax, no way to compel states to contribute money or troops. It could request contributions. It could beg, which it did constantly. States could and did ignore those requests whenever it suited them to do so, which was most of the time.

The money situation was catastrophic from the start. Congress couldn't pay soldiers, couldn't supply the army, couldn't meet the most basic obligations of a government trying to fight a war. So it printed Continental currency to cover the gap — more than four hundred million dollars' worth by 1780 — which triggered exactly the massive inflation you'd expect when you print money with nothing backing it. By 1781, saying something was "not worth a Continental" meant that it had no value at all.

The young men managing these impossible institutions during the war years learned specific lessons from the chaos. James Madison entered the Continental Congress in March 1780 at twenty-nine years old, five years into the war, long after the resistance phase had ended. His formative political experience wasn't organizing against abusive authority; it was trying to get sovereign states to contribute their requisitions so Congress could function at the most basic level. He watched states ignore Congress's requests. He wrote countless letters trying to convince state politicians to honor obligations they'd agreed to. He drafted proposal after proposal to give Congress more authority to act without depending on state cooperation. Every single day reinforced the same message: Scattered power among jealous, sovereign states made everything harder than it needed to be. Madison spent the war years becoming convinced that centralized authority with real enforcement power was the obvious solution.

Alexander Hamilton's education was even more direct and more bitter. As Washington's aide-de-camp from 1777 through 1781, he managed correspondence between military and civilian authority, coordinated logistics, handled the endless practical problems of keeping an army in the field when the government supposedly supporting that army couldn't or wouldn't provide basic necessities. He watched the Continental Army nearly collapse multiple times because Congress couldn't supply it. He saw soldiers go unpaid for months, go hungry, go without adequate clothing or equipment in winter, and he understood that all these struggles traced back to the same structural problem: Congress had no power to compel compliance from the states.

In June 1783, about four hundred armed Pennsylvania Continental soldiers surrounded the State House in Philadelphia where Congress was meeting. They were owed years of back pay. They'd been furloughed, which meant Congress was done with their service, and they'd correctly figured out that meant they'd never be paid. Their show of force scared off enough delegates that Congress couldn't achieve a quorum to conduct business. Congress fled Philadelphia for Princeton, which was humiliating but also perfectly summarized the problem: A government that couldn't protect itself from hundreds angry veterans couldn't do much of anything.

Hamilton absorbed the lesson completely. A government incapable of paying its soldiers, incapable of protecting itself, incapable of compelling states to meet basic obligations — that wasn't a government worth having. It was worse than worthless. It was dangerous. Authority that couldn't enforce compliance wasn't real authority at all.

The war ended in 1783. British troops left. The coalition that had agreed on independence immediately fractured over what to do with it, and the fracture revealed two completely different understandings of what the pursuit of independence had been for.

For most patriots — especially the New England resistance leaders who remained active — the Articles of Confederation were working exactly as intended, doing exactly what patriots had spent a decade learning was necessary: keeping authority weak enough that it couldn't become abusive, dispersed enough that it had to remain responsive, limited enough that it couldn't threaten the rights they'd fought to protect.

For the young men who'd spent the war years trying to make continental institutions work, the articles were an obvious disaster. Too weak, too decentralized, too unable to act when action was needed. But here's what they missed, or what they'd never learned because they hadn't been part of the resistance: The articles were "weak" only if you thought federal authority needed to be strong. Most patriots didn't think that. Strength in central authority was the problem they'd been resisting. The whole point was to avoid creating exactly the kind of powerful centralized government that the nationalists wanted to build.

Two completely different understandings of what independence meant had emerged from two completely different experiences. The old resistance leaders had spent decades learning how authority becomes abusive — what it looks like when power gets concentrated, when it stops being responsive to the people it's supposed to serve, when it starts serving those holding it instead. They'd learned to recognize those patterns, to organize against them, to build structures that prevented them from forming. And they'd created the Articles of Confederation to embody those lessons: minimal federal power, maximum state sovereignty, authority kept dispersed and weak enough that it couldn't threaten rights.

The young nationalists had spent the war years learning how to make authority function efficiently. They'd watched the confederation struggle to manage a war, to coordinate states, to enforce decisions, to act with any kind of dispatch or effectiveness. They'd learned that scattered authority created chaos, that state sovereignty made everything harder, that government without real power to compel compliance couldn't accomplish basic tasks. And they'd become absolutely convinced that concentrated power, properly structured, was the solution to every problem they'd encountered.

By 1783, the divide was set. The old revolutionaries understood how authority becomes abusive and how to guard against it. The young nationalists understood how to make authority strong enough to function. Those two understandings were about to collide.

Whether you think the Articles of Confederation "failed" reveals more about where you stand on the question of nationalism than about any objective analysis of the historical moment. The articles did exactly what they were designed to do. They just weren't designed to do what the nationalists wanted.

The collision arrived in western Massachusetts in 1786, when farmers reached for the resistance playbook the nationalists had never learned.

The Playbook Returns

Daniel Shays was born in 1747. He was twenty-eight when Massachusetts farmers first took up arms in 1775, answering the Lexington alarm that turned protest into open war. Within weeks he was on the heights above Boston, fighting at Bunker Hill. He enlisted again when the Continental Army formed, served through nearly the whole war, rose to captain, and saw hard action at Ticonderoga and Saratoga. When it was over, he went home to Pelham — back to the stony ground his family had worked — trying to start a new life in the republic he had helped win.

He wasn't alone. The western Massachusetts farmers facing ruin in the mid-1780s weren't agitators or victims of circumstance. They were the embattled farmers — the same men who had answered the alarms in 1775, who had stood behind the works on Breed's Hill, manned the siege lines at Roxbury, and built the networks that had broken British authority. They had done the work, fired the shots, and carried the cost of independence.

Now their own government was coming for them.

The Massachusetts government — controlled by commercial interests in Boston and the eastern counties — had imposed crushing taxes to pay off the state's war debt. The taxes had to be paid in hard currency. Gold or silver. Which farmers didn't have and couldn't get. When farmers couldn't pay, courts foreclosed. Farms they'd spent their lives building were being seized and sold at auction to satisfy debts the farmers had no way to pay. The men who'd fought for independence were losing everything.

This was property seizure on a scale that had never happened under British rule. While the British had imposed taxes without representation, Massachusetts was seizing the only means farmers had to pay the taxes it imposed. What exactly had independence been for?

The Westerners were underrepresented in the legislature, overburdened by taxes designed by creditors who controlled the assembly. They'd spent a decade in the 1760s and 1770s learning to recognize abusive authority. Parliament imposing taxes without consent. British officials restructuring colonial economies to benefit imperial interests. Courts enforcing rules that served power rather than protecting rights. They'd built a resistance movement to push back that abuse. They'd articulated grievances, exhausted permitted channels, organized opposition, and finally met British force with force when authority wouldn't bend.

This was the same thing. Different authority, same abuse. The location had just shifted from London to Beacon Hill.

So they reached for the playbook. The one they'd written, and that had worked.

First, articulate the grievance. The taxes were unjust — too high, payable only in currency farmers couldn't obtain, enforced through foreclosures that destroyed livelihoods. Western farmers were underrepresented in the legislature that passed these taxes. The court system had become a mechanism for transferring property from farmers to commercial interests. This was taxation without adequate representation. This was abuse of the consent of the governed.

Second, petition for redress. Through 1785 and into 1786, town meetings across western Massachusetts sent petitions to the state legislature. Lower the taxes. Issue paper currency so debts could be paid in something farmers could obtain. Reform the court system. Stop the foreclosures. Provide relief for men who'd fought for independence and now faced ruin.

The legislature — dominated by Eastern creditors — refused to be responsive. Rejected their petitions. Denied their requests.

Third, organize. County conventions assembled to articulate positions, coordinate response, present unified demands. This was the committee of correspondence model, adapted to their circumstances. Build the infrastructure. Make sure everyone understands the grievances, agrees on the demands, coordinates action.

Fourth, organized opposition. In August 1786, farmers began preventing courts from sitting. At Northampton, about fifteen hundred men surrounded the courthouse, physically blocking entry. The judges couldn't hold session. Foreclosure proceedings stopped. The machinery of oppression became impossible to operate.

At Worcester, hundreds of men prevented the court from sitting. At Concord — where they'd fired on British troops eleven years earlier — they did it again. Surrounded the courthouse. Made authority impossible to exercise. The judges went home.

This was the resistance playbook, deployed with precision. No property destroyed. No one attacked. Just the systematic prevention of an abusive system from operating. Make authority unworkable, force it to respond, extract concessions.

The farmers were doing exactly what the patriots had done to stamp distributors, to customs officials, to British authority when it tried to enforce illegitimate power. They were some of the same individuals, and certainly the same communities and culture.

The difference was the response.

In September 1786, about six hundred farmers marched on the Supreme Judicial Court in Springfield. The militia had been called out to protect it — but many militiamen refused to serve. They recognized what they were seeing. This was resistance to abusive authority. They wouldn't serve against their own.

Governor James Bowdoin, a wealthy merchant close to the commercial interests benefiting from the tax system, saw anarchy. Mob rule. The breakdown of order. A threat to legitimate government that had to be crushed.

He called on the Confederation Congress for military help. Congress had no authority under the articles to provide it. So Bowdoin turned to neighboring states. But the force wasn't sufficient, and parts of it weren't reliable. Too many recognized the farmers' resistance as legitimate.

In January 1787, Boston merchants raised six thousand pounds — private money — to fund a military force. They put General Benjamin Lincoln in command of a private army of forty-four hundred men, paid for by the same commercial interests whose debt collection the farmers were resisting, and sent it west to break the resistance by force.

The farmers knew escalation was coming. On January 25, 1787, about fifteen hundred farmers assembled outside the federal arsenal at Springfield. They needed weapons. If a private army was marching West to crush them, they'd need arms to defend themselves.

General Shepard commanded the arsenal's defense with twelve hundred militia and artillery. The farmers approached in a column. Shepard sent a messenger warning them to stop. The farmers kept coming. He ordered warning shots fired over their heads. They kept coming.

Shepard ordered his artillery to fire directly into them.

Four farmers died. Twenty were wounded. The rest scattered.

This was government violence — or private violence deployed by government — against men who'd won independence. Not property destruction like the farmers had been doing. Not even the targeted violence the 1770s patriots had used against officials. This was grapeshot fired from artillery into a crowd of farmers trying to arm themselves against a privately funded army sent to break their resistance to abusive authority.

The farmers had done everything the patriots had done. Articulated grievances. Petitioned for redress through proper channels. Organized when petitions were rejected. Used the same tactics — preventing courts from sitting, making authority unworkable — that had successfully pushed back British power. They'd been disciplined, organized, restrained in their use of force.

The response was artillery fire. Then a monthlong military campaign.

Lincoln's private army marched through western Massachusetts in late January and February 1787. They scattered farmer assemblies wherever they found them. Pursued leaders. Arrested hundreds. Shays fled to Vermont. By late February, the resistance was broken. Not by argument or concession or negotiation. By military force. Fourteen resisters were sentenced to death, though most were eventually pardoned.

In this, John Adams saw the creation of something that would shape American political culture for the next two centuries: a containment mechanism that would make resistance to abusive authority — even when that authority was demonstrably abusive — seem illegitimate by definition.

The farmers had worked within the system. They'd petitioned the legislature. They'd used permitted channels. The system rejected them. To Adams, that should be the end of it. Once "we" the people have established our own government, once the institutions are "ours," resistance to those institutions threatens everything the revolution achieved. The farmers weren't defending rights against abusive authority. They were threatening legitimate government.

This was borrowed straight from Britain. The Glorious Revolution of 1688 had answered all fundamental questions about authority and rights. Parliament was supreme. Rights were protected through representation. Therefore, any resistance outside institutional channels was unnecessary and illegitimate. Adams was inserting 1776 into the same framework on American soil. The founding answered the questions.

The institutions protect rights. Any challenge to those institutions, even when they're operating abusively, delegitimizes itself by threatening stability.

Mercy Otis Warren went even further in the same direction. She'd been part of the patriot resistance — her plays and pamphlets had articulated resistance principles through the 1770s. But she refused to connect Shays to that tradition. A "rebellion" could never be justified against a government of "the people's own making," she wrote.

Except the patriots hadn't fought a tyrannical monarch. They'd fought parliamentary abuse of authority. Warren knew this — she'd written about it. But now she was rewriting the resistance she'd helped build. "The ignorance of this incendiary and turbulent set of people might lead them to a justification of their own measures, from a recurrence to transactions in some degree similar in the early opposition to British government," she wrote. "They knew that a successful opposition had been made to the authority of Britain . . . but they were too ignorant to distinguish between an opposition to regal despotism, and a resistance to a government recently established by themselves."

This was the containment mechanism being built in real time. The farmers weren't ignorant. They understood exactly what they were doing — using the resistance playbook against authority that was abusing its power. But Warren needed them to be wrong. Because if they were right — if the same tactics that worked against British authority were legitimate against Massachusetts authority — then the revolution never ended. Resistance remained permanently available against any abusive authority, including "ours." That threatened the entire institutional settlement.

So the resistance had to be reimagined. The patriots of the 1770s were heroes. The farmers of 1786 using the exact same tactics were dangerous radicals. The difference wasn't the tactics or the abuse or the legitimacy of the grievances. The difference was that "we" were in power now. And resistance to "our" institutions was rebellion, not a defense of rights.

Both Warren's son Henry and her nephew Harrison Gray Otis went west to serve in Lincoln's private army putting down Shays.

But there was a different sense among the people. In 1787, they elected a new assembly to reflect the mood. James Warren — Mercy's husband, who'd been part of the old resistance — returned to office and was elected speaker. He hadn't supported Shays's aims or methods, but he sympathized with their situation. He thought they were right about the grievances — the previous legislature hadn't properly addressed them, and it had unfairly taxed them. More important, he believed the authority used to put them down was oppressive and unnecessary.

The Massachusetts government had suspended habeas corpus to suppress the resistance. It had denied resisters trial by jury in their vicinage — trial by their actual peers from their own communities — an ancient constitutional right that had been central to patriot resistance in the 1770s. Warren saw this clearly: The authority used against the farmers was the kind of abuse the patriots had fought against. In taking their side, in recognizing their resistance as consistent with the patriot movement, he suffered political consequences from nationalist opponents who needed Shays to be wrong.

The nationalist faction saw something else in all of this: opportunity. They'd been waiting for a crisis that could justify consolidating federal power. Here it was. Massachusetts couldn't suppress domestic resistance without buying a private army. The Confederation Congress had no military force, no power to intervene, no capacity to prevent this from spreading to other states. The nation was vulnerable to exactly the kind of resistance that had built it.

That analysis missed everything important. The farmers weren't chaos. They were resistance — organized, disciplined, following a proven playbook against authority that was objectively abusive. The fact that Massachusetts couldn't suppress them through militia meant that the militia recognized the resistance as legitimate. Half wouldn't serve because they understood: This is what resistance to authority when it becomes abusive looks like; this is the tradition we built together.

But the nationalists didn't see resistance. They saw disorder that required stronger central authority to suppress. And they saw how to use it to achieve their ends.

In September 1786, while farmers were surrounding courthouses, delegates from five states had met in Annapolis to discuss commercial issues under the Articles of Confederation. Madison and Hamilton were there. They accomplished nothing on commerce. But they issued a call for a broader convention to meet in Philadelphia in May 1787 to consider revisions to the articles.

Shays's resistance had given that call urgency. States agreed to send delegates. The nationalist faction had their moment. They were going to Philadelphia with a plan — not to revise the articles but to replace them entirely. And they were going to use the specter of Shays to justify consolidating exactly the kind of centralized power the articles were designed to prevent.

The old revolutionaries made a catastrophic miscalculation. Most didn't go to Philadelphia. Patrick Henry famously "smelt a rat" and refused to attend. But others stayed away for different reasons. They thought the young nationalists would play by the implied rules. There would be proposals for amendments to the articles. Debates. Opportunities to head off anything dangerous. Time to organize opposition if necessary.

They were wrong. The nationalists weren't going to follow norms. They were going to seize control of the entire process, work in secret, and ram through a complete replacement of the articles before opposition could form.

Through lack of participation, the old revolutionaries made a tremendous blunder they would seriously regret.

Forcing the Fight

Patrick Henry was fifty-two years old. He'd been thirty-eight when he delivered his "Give me liberty, or give me death!" speech in Virginia in March 1775, the month prior to Lexington and Concord. He'd been part of the patriot movement since his 1765 speech against the Stamp Act. He'd spent more than two decades learning how authority becomes abusive, what rights need protecting, how power consolidates if you don't stop it. He hadn't gone to Philadelphia — he'd smelled the rat. Now he was going to make the young nationalists explain every piece of what they'd done.

At the Virginia Ratifying Convention in 1788, Henry cut to the structural heart of it. The Constitution's authority derived from "We, the people" — not from the states as sovereign entities. That shift, he argued, was "a revolution as radical as that which separated us from Britain." The document didn't just reorganize government; it consolidated power in ways that endangered "our rights and privileges" and hollowed out state sovereignty. Everything turned on "that poor little thing — the expression, We, the people."

Henry kept forcing the convention back to first principles. When had the Revolution become about commerce and geopolitics, "How your trade may be increased" and "How you are to become a great and powerful people"? — Those weren't the questions that drove men to answer the Lexington Alarm. The question that mattered, the only one that had ever mattered, was "How your liberties can be secured; for liberty ought to be the direct end of your Government . . . Liberty the greatest of all earthly blessings — give us that precious jewel, and you may take everything else."

Henry heard Madison and the other nationalists reaching for words the patriots had never used. They wanted something "great" and "splendid" — "a great and mighty empire; we must have an army, and a navy, and a number of things." That language had no roots in the resistance that led to independence. "When the American spirit was in its youth," Henry reminded them, "the language of America was different: Liberty, Sir, was then the primary object." Where did the nationalists' aspirations, the ideas, the goals come from? They didn't come from the American Revolution.

The spirit of the nationalists, the new continental spirit, "the American spirit, assisted by the ropes and chains of consolidation, is about to convert this country to a powerful and mighty empire," which was "incompatible with the genius of republicanism," at the heart of what the resisters to British oppression had hoped to achieve.

At fifty-two, Henry positioned himself as a man out of time — deliberately. He'd entered the resistance before most of the nationalists were old enough to hold a musket. Their history began with independence; his began with the Stamp Act. "I am fearful I have lived long enough to become an old fashioned fellow," he told the convention. "Perhaps an invincible attachment to the dearest rights of man, may, in these refined enlightened days, be deemed old fashioned; If so, I am contented to be so." And to those who called him suspicious for saying that rights and privileges were in danger by the Constitution: "Suspicion is a virtue, as long as its object is the preservation of the public good."

Where others found compromise, Henry found only danger. The Constitution's admirers pointed to its balance; Henry saw "deformities" — including "an awful squinting . . . toward monarchy." A president who could be reelected indefinitely. A Senate that could dominate through a minority of states. The checks and balances the nationalists celebrated looked to Henry like the machinery of consolidation dressed in republican language. And there would be no recourse for the people to defend their rights if they were abused or to punish officeholders for violating their trust. With a federal government with a standing army and control of the militia, "Will your Macebearer be a match for a disciplined regiment?"

Henry rejected the nationalist premise entirely. Where was this crisis they kept invoking? Where were the followers of Daniel Shays, ready to topple American freedom at the slightest provocation? There was no evidence, anywhere. Virginia had no uprisings. Europe posed no imminent threat. The danger was "imaginary" — manufactured to justify haste. The real danger, Henry argued, came from rushing an untested government into existence on the strength of fears that couldn't survive examination.

Edmund Randolph, Virginia's thirty-four-year-old governor, was another of the young nationalists. Although he had joined with the opposition at the Philadelphia convention, and refused to sign the Constitution, he'd been persuaded to join Madison in supporting it in Richmond. He answered Henry the next day by staking his own revolutionary credentials, but actually reinforced the point. "I am a child of the revolution," he declared, but it was a different revolution from Henry's. Randolph had come of age inside continental institutions: Washington's staff at Cambridge, the Virginia convention of 1776. The resistance that preceded those institutions had formed Henry; the institutions themselves had formed Randolph. That difference shaped everything that followed. "I feel the highest gratitude and attachment to my country — her felicity is the most fervent prayer of my heart," Randolph said.

The generational fault line ran through every exchange. Randolph insisted that the nationalists were "true republicans, and by no means less attached to liberty, than those who oppose." But attachment wasn't the issue. The issue was formation. The young nationalists had been produced by the Revolution's institutions — the Continental Congress, the army, the wartime committees. They consumed its rhetoric without having built it. Adams, Henry, Richard Henry Lee, Warren — they'd spent decades constructing the arguments before anyone fired a shot. The language sounded the same. It didn't mean the same thing.

Many of the old revolutionaries turned to one another in this moment, seeing how Washington and Franklin — not real revolutionaries, either, both embedded early and for the duration in the continental vision — had shaped this outcome. They found each other across state lines. Richard Henry Lee wrote to John Lamb — a New York Son of Liberty from the Stamp Act days — in June 1788, bewildered by what they were watching unfold: "'Tis really astonishing that the same people, who have just emerged from a long and cruel war in defence of liberty, should agree to fix an elective despotism upon themselves and posterity!"

Both Randolph and Madison bristled and retreated under Henry's attacks. They both attempted to diminish their aspirations. Randolph did not long for America to be "a grand, splendid, and magnificent people . . . We want Government, Sir" that would provide stability and security. Madison added that "national splendor and glory are not our objects," but to be "respectable abroad" was not inconsistent with being secure and happy at home.

And they continued their insistence on an immediate threat, even though they could only really point to Daniel Shays. Their argument was oddly circuitous. Why did every state but Rhode Island send delegates to the Constitutional Convention if there was no danger? They invoked the perils of commercial weakness without a strong central government and added that many states had only themselves to blame, because they ignored both their own constitutions and their obligations under the articles. Much heat with little fire.

Madison gave a history lesson: Confederations didn't work in the long term. They were dismembered. Only a centralized government could protect the country from attack. And then he got into the confusion of federalism. The proposed government was both federal and consolidated. It was unprecedented in its innovative blend of being formed by the people but operating on the power the people lent to the government, which they could always recall.

But for all of this talk about the power of the people, and the uniqueness of a federal republic that drew power from the people, the nationalists still fought against including specific protections for the people. Individual rights could be sufficiently protected at the state level. Or they were unnecessary for the limited power that the consolidated government would have. But those whose sympathies lay with the concerns of the old patriots asked: Even with the power coming from the people, was there still not a need to protect the people from the power accrued by that government?

One after another, it was the young framers — Madison, Randolph, John Marshall, and Francis Corbin — who stood up to dismiss the arguments of experience and history. America was special. The United States was unique. None of the issues that applied to other republics could ever apply to the one they created, which was unique in world history.

Henry went back on the attack and took apart what Madison and Corbin argued. There was debate over an amendment, the first one over an amendment, to limit the power of the federal government to tax only when a state failed to provide its share. President of the Convention Edmund Pendleton and others said that would only be in extreme circumstances, otherwise duties would cover the costs of the government. But it would sometimes have to borrow money — again, back to the nation on the world stage — and lenders would not have confidence in lending money to a country that had no means of imposing taxes to pay back loans. So the power of taxation was "essential to the very existence of the Union."

The Federalists saw comprehensive federal power to tax, and to compel, as a core element of their idea of an effective national government. But the old revolutionaries didn't see it that way. Taxation, as they had first argued decades earlier, and continued to argue, was about rights, not national efficiency. Since the people were only represented in the House, and the House's representation was so small, where would the consent to tax actually rest? How could representatives of so many people actually understand what their constituents could bear? What was all that talk about "taxation without representation" if it wasn't reflected in this Constitution?

Henry continued to insist that fears being addressed by the Federalists were hypothetical at best, while dangers posed by the Constitution against individual rights were real and present. What countries would send armies to settle debts? Henry pulled in Jefferson, who noted that France was more interested in trade agreements with the United States than it was with debt collection. And he threw down that Jefferson, too, only supported the Constitution with amendments — particularly, a bill of rights attached to it.

The nationalists tried to argue that bills or declarations of rights were useless. They did nothing to stop abuses. The people in the states without them were as free as those in states with them.

Henry had outmaneuvered them. Virginia's Declaration of Rights wasn't an abstraction to Virginians — it was a point of pride and a practical guarantee. Adding one to the federal Constitution was "a favorite thing" among them. Henry drove the point: "A bill of rights may be summed up in a few words. What do they tell us? — That our rights are reserved. — Why not say so? Is it because it will consume too much paper? . . . My mind will not be quieted till I see something substantial come forth in the shape of a Bill of Rights."

Madison's arguments didn't move Henry. The Constitution required "the surrender of our great rights," and for what? A promise that Congress would fix it later? "It is our duty to rest our rights on a certain foundation," Henry countered, "and not to trust to future contingencies." Even trial by jury — a bedrock, fundamental right — wasn't adequately secured. In 1776, Americans had refused to depend on Parliament to protect their rights. Now they were being asked to depend on a Congress with fewer constraints. Henry made the parallel explicit over several days of debate. "I trust that I shall see Congressional oppressions crushed in embryo," he pressed, because, "[a]s this Government stands, I despise and abhor it." But still, there remained the ultimate point of resistance should the nationalists persist: "Old as I am, it is probable that I may yet have the appellation of rebel."

On June 24, George Wythe moved to ratify. The motion came loaded. A preamble declared that all powers granted to the federal government were a gift of the people — who could take them back if they were ever perverted into oppression. Liberty of conscience, liberty of the press, the right of trial by jury — essential rights that no one holding authority under the Constitution could touch. Any imperfections? Fix them through the amending process afterward, not before. Ratify first, then recommend amendments.

But here was the kicker: Virginia's ratification would "cease to be obligatory" if those amendments never came.

Madison joined Randolph in the counterattack. The opposition had no unified intellectual framework — every opponent was of a different opinion. Speed and secrecy had bought the nationalists a resistance caught flat-footed. Madison pivoted to deflection. A bill of rights was unnecessary, because the government had only the power given to it by the people. A bill of rights might even be dangerous, because "an enumeration which is not complete, is not safe." What if they missed one? Better, apparently, to guarantee nothing at all.

But never in his life had Madison been challenged so forcibly — and so publicly. He usually avoided confrontations, yet here he was at the center of a powerful one. And what was worse, he knew he was on the losing end of it. He started to bend. Could he at least make it look like a win? Or at least not such a bad beating? Henry had him, and everyone in that chamber knew it. So, he would agree that amendments were an inherent feature of the Constitution. Sure, there were imperfections. But how could anyone know what actually needed fixing until the thing went into effect and revealed its problems? He'd support amendments, as long as they weren't "unsafe." But not before ratification. His position, for all the tactical give, remained all or nothing.

So, all of the arguments came down to this set of differences: What were the Constitution's defects, and should they be resolved before or after ratification? Even that was a major shift in the nationalist position from the days right after the ratifying convention when the Constitution's advocates believed that the government they envisioned was the best that could be derived by any group of men ever and that any change would weaken its genius. That was no longer ground they could stand on, thanks to the opposition.

Henry ended where he'd begun, with the Revolution as touchstone. If the opposition lost the vote, he would accept it. But he wouldn't stop working to "retrieve the loss of liberty, and remove the defects" through constitutional means. He hoped that "the spirit which predominated in the revolution" was "not yet lost," that it could still be summoned to make whatever government emerged "compatible with the safety, liberty and happiness of the people."

Randolph closed by reframing the question. Eight states had ratified. Virginia's choice wasn't really about the Constitution's merits anymore — it was "Union or no Union."

That ended the debate.

The critical vote came on Henry's motion to require a declaration of rights before ratification. It failed, 80–88. Eight votes. Henry demanded the names be recorded. Then the main question: ratification with recommended amendments. It passed, 89–79. George Mason asked for those names to be recorded, too.

There was no celebration.

The mood in the chamber was somber.

Madison won ratification and lost control of what ratification meant. He told Hamilton that many of the recommended amendments were "highly objectionable" but "impossible to prevent." To Washington, he admitted that the amendments "could not be parried," not in Richmond, anyway. The fight would continue in a different venue. The recommendations weren't binding. Congress could ignore them entirely. Madison was already calculating how to do exactly that.

But the Anti-Federalists also knew that. The battle was yet to come.

With the Constitution now ratified, the opposition could organize more broadly across the states to work for amendments. That would be their last chance. Madison knew this, and feared it. He wrote to Jefferson that, yes, the opposition agreed to abide by the vote and be peaceful, but that didn't mean that they wouldn't resist.

The old revolutionaries had lost ratification. But they'd extracted something crucial: a public commitment to amendments. And they'd made clear that any representative who didn't fight for those amendments wouldn't survive politically.

James Madison was running for the First Federal Congress. His district was Virginia's Fifth. His opponent was James Monroe — backed by Patrick Henry, who'd redrawn the district to make Madison's victory harder.

Madison needed to win. But he couldn't win without convincing Virginia voters that he would deliver amendments.

In January 1789, he wrote a letter to a Baptist minister that got published widely: He would support a Bill of Rights.

That's what forced him to his desk on Maiden Lane that June morning in Manhattan.

The Forced Founder

Madison couldn't sleep that June night because he knew what was coming. Patrick Henry. Henry was coming for him. Henry controlled Virginia. As Washington put it, "He has only to say let this be Law — and it is Law."

The Virginia legislature had just chosen two opponents to the Constitution as its first senators: Richard Henry Lee and William Grayson. They handily defeated Madison's bid for a Senate seat. Henry had explicitly opposed Madison's aspirations because he was "not to be trusted with amendments" since he had said in the ratifying convention "that not a letter of the Constitution cou'd be spared."

Madison had to fight for a seat in the House to become a member of Congress, against another opponent to the Constitution: James Monroe. And Monroe was positioned to beat him.

So what did Madison do? He supported amendments, of course.

He wanted it known to voters that he would support amendments that would "serve the double purpose of satisfying the minds of well-meaning opponents, and of providing additional guards in favour of liberty." After more than a year of fighting them, he embraced them on the campaign trail to get elected.

Henry had made sure that Madison couldn't escape to a safer district. The election law required one year's residency in the district. Madison's home congressional district included Orange County, where he lived, and seven other counties. He left the Confederation Congress in New York in late 1788, spent Christmas at Mount Vernon, then headed into a five-week campaign against Monroe — or rather against his own past, to make sure he wasn't shut out of the very government he'd created.

Much of it was spent in ice, rain, snow, even hail.

He encountered "multiple falsehoods" against him in Culpeper — or were they inconvenient truths Madison had to re-create in himself?

Madison had opposed amendments before ratification because he feared they would cause dissension among the states and help those who wanted to dissolve the Union. But now he embraced amendments. Was all for them.

And he would take the lead. No second convention, as New York had called for and others supported. Amending the Constitution should be done in the First Federal Congress. Article V said amendments could be introduced either at a convention or by Congress. But Congress could act faster than a convention because it would meet sooner, as early as March. A convention could never be put together so quickly. And Congress, because it was already acting as the government, would be the safer option. It wouldn't gut the very structure it was part of. A convention would be dangerous. Anything could happen because anyone — like Henry — might be elected to it. That would "turn every thing into confusion and uncertainty."

He kept writing letters to supporters for them to publish or otherwise circulate, sharing these fresh convictions of his. He would always oppose an amendment on the direct taxation power, though — any other plan would lead to wars between the states. So the power to directly tax was absolutely essential, sacrosanct. It had to stay as written.

He won election to the House, but not without committing not only to supporting amendments but also to leading the effort. On February 2, 1789, a snowy frigid Election Day, of the district's 5,189 voters, 972 came out for Monroe and 1,308 for Madison. The rest stayed home — more than 60 percent. But they all would hold him accountable to his pledges, which had been unambiguous.

In the Virginia ratifying convention, he'd said that "a solemn declaration of our essential rights" would be "unnecessary and dangerous." There he'd supported amendments if they would calm discontent, but not to secure the people's rights. He didn't change his mind. He remained opposed to securing individual liberties, but he was open to doing so as a matter of political expediency.

When Congress got going, members of the House — the Federalists, who now in power wanted to use it — thought the government had more pressing issues. Create a revenue system and federal judiciary, set up executive departments and determine the president's power over them. Everything took time with representatives who were inefficient. "We are in a wilderness without a single footstep to guide us" in starting a national government from scratch. So thinking about amendments was not a priority for the Federalists.

But Madison still had to face his constituents. He had made promises. And the opposition remained strong enough in the states that the other option for amending the Constitution — a convention called by the states — was a threat. That needed to be headed off even if his colleagues couldn't see the need.

In May, he moved for consideration of amendments, but that was put off until June 8. Even then some wanted it delayed further, to March 1790, after the government was fully organized.

But Madison needed to show his constituents something — or Henry would eat him alive. They needed to at least introduce the subject "so our constituents may see we pay a proper attention to a subject they have very much at heart" and "to quiet that anxiety which prevails in the public mind." All they needed to do was take up the subject for a day, just one day, and then they could put it off to address more urgent needs. That might be enough to calm down the opposition.

He could not fulfill his duty to himself — the duty to get reelected — and to his constituents by letting the subject "pass over in silence." Couldn't they just talk about the amendments he proposed?

John Page, another representative from Virginia, one of Jefferson's closest friends, who'd been in Virginia through everything — the conventions, the militia during the war, the House of Delegates — knew the opposition because he was part of it and could speak directly, maybe even threateningly, to Madison: If Congress didn't act on amendments, the opposition "will clamor for a new convention."

Page essentially embodied Henry's intentions and will, standing right there in the House of Representatives.

Madison operated quickly — he wasn't about to recommend anything that would change the government or its powers. Just those amendments about "the security of rights" to which no one had really objected and that would likely get the votes in Congress and ratification of the states. So if Federalists in Congress achieved that, they could head off the opposition and keep control of the process and the substance. "We have in this way something to gain and, if we proceed with caution, nothing to lose."

The opposition was centered on a bill of rights, so Madison could ignore possible amendments addressing other concerns, such as limiting the power to tax. If they focused on the most abstract of the amendments, the Bill of Rights — the parchment barriers — they could solve all kinds of political problems: "satisfy the public mind that their liberties will be perpetual . . . without endangering any part of the constitution."

That was the strategy.

Madison then proposed nine amendments. A declaration that all power is vested in and derived from the people. Change the representation size formula for the House of Representatives. Add a prohibition on increasing compensation for representatives until after the next election. Freedom of conscience, speech, press, petition, assembly, and right to bear arms. But he wanted to beef up this language for the folks back home. Instead of the "ought" in so many of the state declarations: "The people shall not be deprived or abridged of their right to speak, to write, or to publish their sentiments." And "the freedom of the press, as one of the great bulwarks of liberty, shall be inviolable."

Then he went further. One amendment was original to Madison — to explicitly apply the rights of conscience, press, and trial by jury to the states. This was going very far and invading exactly the territory that the Constitution's opponents feared. Now Madison was setting the federal government up as the protector of rights of the people . . . even against the states. That was consolidation and centralization of authority, and exactly what the opposition feared.

Madison even wrote that the rights of the people were in "more danger of those powers being abused by the state governments than by the government of the United States."

But then he was done. He did what he thought he needed to do to buy himself some time.

Madison's proposal was sent to a select committee in July.

A month after the French stormed the Bastille, the House took up debate on the report from the committee. Opposition members saw through Madison's strategy and called the report "whip-syllabub ... formed only to please the palate," not the "solid and substantial amendments which the people expect." In fact, it was really just a diversion, "like a tub thrown out to a whale" by sailors to divert the whale from attacking their ship.

Which is precisely what it was.

The House — dominated by Federalists who were now not helping Madison's personal politics — entirely erased his first proposal. It also rejected any idea of actually changing anything in the Constitution itself. Roger Sherman and others insisted that the Constitution remain unchanged because that's what had been ratified and it, in its original form, was "sacred." So any amendments should just be tacked on the end. Madison had to accept that to get the two-thirds necessary for approval.

The House agreed on August 24 and sent amendments to the Senate. Its debates were closed. Richard Henry Lee and William Grayson introduced all of Virginia's amendments. All were rejected by the Senate. It revised and approved twelve amendments on September 14.

They grouped all of the conscience amendments into one amendment that began "Congress shall make no law ..." They eliminated Madison's limitation on state authority and expansion of national authority. They eliminated the separation of powers amendments, the exemption from military service, a vicinage requirement for criminal trials. They changed the language of the reservation of rights amendment to make it clear that the people retained powers and rights that were not delegated anywhere.

The House agreed. A conference committee made only two changes. Then the proposed amendments were sent on.

President Washington, without comment, sent them to the states on October 2.

Richard Henry Lee was furious. He saw that the opposition had made a major mistake in its tactics by giving in to a post-ratification amendment process. They didn't foresee that the process would be dominated by the nationalists, and so dictated by them. They had been under a "delusion" that the states' recommendations would be taken seriously, when they could be disregarded as a matter of Madison's personal politics. Unlimited power of taxation and standing armies had actually made it into the Constitution. Grayson admitted that they had lost the game by agreeing to play it.

Madison wasn't happy, either. But he was mad because of what the Senate had done to his latest hobbyhorse: expanding national power by making sure the amendments applied to the states, too. That was now the most important amendment of all to him.

But Madison had never wanted amendments to protect personal liberties. And he never fought for them as such. His project, in mid-August 1789, on "the nauseous project of amendments" was to "kill the opposition every where" — which meant Henry. Theodore Sedgwick said that Madison was "constantly haunted by the ghost of Patrick Henry." Robert Morris of Pennsylvania said that Madison, in his fight with Monroe, "got so Cursedly frightened in Virginia" that he "dreamed of amendments ever since."

Others observed that the opposition in Virginia had so spooked Madison that he was imagining threats to the Constitution that weren't there and treating them with placebos. And that was the Bill of Rights to Madison — a placebo to treat a nonexistent ailment.

And they had a point. Only Virginia was pushing for the second convention. New York joined, but no other state acted. So if Madison had not acted in the House, the opposition might have died away. The Federalists could have achieved their goal.

But the opposition in Virginia struck. And they stuck. The weakness, in fact, wasn't the Constitution in practical terms. It was Madison's fragile ego, and the specter across all of Virginia of Patrick Henry.

A resistance lesson here is that victory does not have to be on perfect terms. It just has to be enough, in the right way.

But another resistance lesson is that resistance has to be sustained or it will lose support. This is the weakness of temporary oppositions of convenience. When the threat seems to diminish, so does the opposition to it, since opposition, and then resistance, requires persistence and sustainability. The opposition groups in other states faded away after the election of the first Congress.

But the way things played out worked for Madison, politically. He almost immediately became "the patron of amendments." And no one talked about the direct taxes.

And for Mercy Warren, "the amendments and amelioration of the constitution united all parties in the vigorous support of it."

By November 1789, Madison could tell Washington that "the late opponents are entirely at rest."

But the resistance had achieved its goal: the protection of liberties. The last battle of the American Revolution had been fought and won, mainly by those who had started the Revolution in the first place.

Madison had won everything. His Constitution was law. His vision of centralized power had prevailed. And yet the old revolutionaries still haunted him, because they represented something that can't be killed by winning an election or ratifying a constitution: the continuous tradition of American resistance to abusive authority. The refusal to accept that any system — no matter how well designed, no matter how republican its form — deserves trust without explicit protections for the rights it claims to serve.

That tradition haunts America still. Buried under celebratory mythology designed to keep it in its grave, hidden beneath Founders Chic and nationalist narratives that credit Madison with rights he fought against. The containment mechanism works overtime to keep those ghosts quiet — to convince you that the system already protects everything that needs protecting, that the founders generously bestowed your freedoms, that resistance outside approved channels is unnecessary because enlightened leaders built everything you need.

But the ghosts are always there. On call. Waiting.

Henry Wadsworth Longfellow got it on the eve of the Civil War when he wrote about Paul Revere's ride. A legend, sure. Longfellow knew it wasn't exactly history. But there's truth in legends — sometimes the truest kind. What else was he doing but summoning that patriot resistance that had stood up to abusive British authority in 1775, connecting it to his own era's resistance to the abusive authority of the Slave Power in 1860?

A cry of defiance, and not of fear,
A voice in the darkness, a knock at the door,
And a word that shall echo forevermore!
For, borne on the night-wind of the Past,
Through all our history, to the last,
In the hour of darkness and peril and need,
The people will waken and listen to hear
The hurrying hoof-beats of that steed,
And the midnight message of Paul Revere.

Madison was haunted that morning by the knowledge that the resistance he'd tried to outmaneuver, the old revolutionaries he'd tried to sideline, the continuous tradition of organized opposition to abusive authority — none of it could be permanently defeated. It could be buried, contained, interrupted by mythology and institutional worship. But it remained. Waiting to be called on again.

The ghosts that forced Madison to deliver amendments he never wanted are still available to every American generation that faces abusive authority and has to decide whether to submit or resist.

Force the fight. Never stop. Not through days. Not through generations. Authority will always try to consolidate, to contain, to convince you that the fight is over and you've already won everything you need. The ghosts know better. They've always known better.

Madison knew they were there. That's why his speech read like pleading from a cornered man. He'd won the constitutional battle, but the resistance hadn't accepted defeat. It never does. And in the hour of darkness and peril and need, those ghosts show up again.

They always do.

CHAPTER FIVE

The Fugitive President

Resistance Principle #5: A lifetime of persistence.

PHILADELPHIA, MAY 21, 1796

The late-afternoon sun slanted across the cobblestones of High Street, casting long, uneven shadows between the bustling shop fronts and elegant brick town houses that lined Philadelphia's main street. The air, thick with the scent of horse manure, woodsmoke, and the distant tang of the Delaware River, hummed with the ceaseless activity of a growing port and a young nation's capital.

Inside the president's house, Black hands were busy preparing dinner, following the meticulous directions laid down for them by the First Lady, Martha Washington. She was explicit about what she wanted them to do and how they must do it. She was no less a disciplinarian with affairs inside the house than her husband, the president, George Washington, was outside it. She shared his reputation as an exacting, unforgiving master, where every detail of household management, including every aspect of the lives of the enslaved people, was subject to their rigorous control.

Among those enslaved people was Ona Judge, around twenty-three years old, "the perfect mistress of her needle." Born in 1774 to an enslaved seamstress and a white tailor who came to Mount Vernon from England as an indentured servant, she was only ten years old when she was assigned to address Martha's every personal need, every day of her life. Called Oney by the Washingtons, Ona helped Martha bathe. She helped Martha dress. She made sure Martha's clothes were clean and mended them when they frayed. Tired or awake, sick or healthy, Ona was indispensable to Martha's life.

But on that spring evening in Philadelphia, as the household prepared for its customary rituals of refinement and propriety, Ona had something else on her mind. Her timing needed to be impeccable. The Washingtons would only be distracted by their meals and their company for a little bit. Martha might call for her at any time. Ona's foresight in planning, the trust she placed in others, the trusted network of resistance accomplices that she had created — all were about to be put to the ultimate test. As the Washingtons sat down to their table, Ona quietly and deliberately stepped into the shadows and the uncertain twilight of freedom. Carefully considered, yet fraught with danger, Ona's leap into the dusk was a calculated risk against the overwhelming power of the First Republic and its chief representatives, George and Martha Washington.

She carried little with her, perhaps only a small bundle of personal belongings, necessities she could manage discreetly that would be of use. In a testament to the deliberation and secrecy required for such a determined act, Ona had already sent belongings ahead to her trusted network. What she mainly carried with her was a fierce determination, born from a lifetime of observation, understanding, and frustration. And fueled, perhaps, by the stories of those who had gone before her, enslaved people from Mount Vernon who had also become free only by running from the greatest of all the patriots.

A person "stealing" their own freedom was resistance in the earliest days of the First Republic. America's independence movement and the young nation's founding documents and laws institutionalized the clearest form of abusive authority, that which used the mechanisms of government, and the authority derived from the governed, to deny not only liberty but also life.

What then were Ona's options? In those early days, so much was on one individual, relying on groups of other individuals. The opposition was not yet organized, the grounds of its contest only beginning to emerge, because the nature of the abusive authority, powered by every arm of this new American state, was novel. The opposition's scope and composition needed to be tested for its strengths and its weaknesses. For Ona, the grounds of protest were painfully clear; the onus would be on her to muster for herself the most fundamental resources for any personal resistance: the persistence to keep going, almost single-mindedly, in pursuit of a resistance goal and the resilience to rebound from the blows that would inevitably strike her down as she pursued her ultimate objective.

Gilded Cages

To those on the outside, Ona's position, of one so clearly favored by Martha, might have appeared privileged — she was well clothed, fed, and even allowed her own time, attending theatrical performances and circuses in the city — but that was a façade or, at best, a double-edged sword. Ona's skills did make her especially valued to Martha. But in reality, her elevated status within slavery was a gilded cage, its relative comforts serving only to mask her fundamental lack of autonomy. Its bars were constructed by deceit, reinforced by the continuous threat of arbitrary and absolute power.

As a "dower slave," she did not legally belong to Martha. Instead, like most of the enslaved people in Washington's quarters and fields, she was the property of the Custis estate, a legacy of Martha's first husband, Daniel Parke Custis. Like a farming tool or a plantation field, Ona was only to be used by Martha until it was time to pass her to one of Martha's four grandchildren. And that's precisely what Martha planned to do with Ona after her granddaughter Elizabeth Parke Custis married an English lawyer in Philadelphia in March 1796. Why give new dishes or a carriage as a wedding gift when you can give a talented young enslaved woman?

And therein was the problem. Ona knew Martha. She knew her temper, her whims, her conceits. The enslaved people in and around the household could manage life around her demands, her caprices. Enslaved life was intolerable, but in the First Republic, one's only option was to negotiate the difficult terrain.

But Eliza was another matter. Ona knew her, too. A regular presence in the Washington household, Ona had a front-row seat for

Eliza's tantrums. Even Gilbert Stuart, perhaps the foremost American portraitist of the time, noticed her "willful personality," capturing her for posterity in a stance that Ona would have recognized: arms crossed, privileged, aware of a world that existed to serve her inclinations. In that brutal world, where enslaved people had to manage so much evil, a future with Eliza was an especially unbearable prospect. Years later, Ona confirmed that she "was determined never to be her slave," even though she lived in a republic that did not recognize her as a person.

Ona's personal vow of self-determination would have to overcome forces greater than the gilded cage that was her position in the Washington household or even the impersonal slave economy that had been in place for more than 150 years. The entire state structure of the newly founded country in which she lived was based on the ultimate abuse of authority — the exclusion and oppression of others as a political tool. Far from turning "the world upside down," the patriots created a republic that went far beyond the exclusions and oppressions of the British colonial world. Federal law tied slavery to the mathematics of political power and "democracy" through the three-fifths clause. The Constitution's reference to enslaved people as "persons" brought little comfort given that it explicitly made them less than whole. The First Federal Congress barred the door of exclusion even more tightly with the passage of the Naturalization Act in 1790, which declared that only "free white persons" could become citizens of the United States. Attorney General Edmund Randolph stated the obvious when he recorded the sincere belief of the patriots that enslaved people, "not being constituent members of our society . . . could never pretend to benefit from" any claim that all men were created equal. The Fugitive Slave Act of 1793 drove that point home — in a direct riposte to Carleton's defeat of Washington in that room at Orangetown ten years before — when it empowered slave catchers anywhere in the country to recover free Black people, with the support of the federal court system, and made it a criminal act to stand in the way of their return to slavery.

So the moment that Ona stepped into the Philadelphia night,

stealing herself from the Washingtons, she knew that she was turning herself and everyone who helped her into criminals. Every act to assist her, to harbor her, to conceal her, even by failing to report her, was a conscious act of resistance to civil government. And yet there existed a nascent network of support, well aware of the risks and ready to provide information, safe passage, and secure spaces for Ona.

If anything closed the door on the promise of the patriots' war for independence, even in Northern states, it was that such a network was necessary to help Ona, and so many like her, escape from the new country the founders had created, an entire nation that functioned as a cage for hundreds of thousands of enslaved people.

Closing Doors, Opening Windows

Ona's awareness of the possibilities of a broader Atlantic world was sharpened and reinforced by the unique environment of Philadelphia. Right outside her windows was an alternative reality, a counterfactual existence represented by free Black people who revealed every day that liberty was not an unreachable dream. Leaders of the free Black community, such as Richard Allen and Absalom Jones — both of whom had once been enslaved — were prominent figures in the bustling temporary national capital. Black residents of Philadelphia built thriving parallel institutions in churches, mutual aid societies, and civic associations that openly challenged, even mocked, America's founding hypocrisy. The Free African Society, for example, founded in 1787, provided a foundation of financial and social support to the city's Black population, while the establishment of independent Black churches like Bethel African Methodist Episcopal Church, created in 1794, and the St. Thomas African Episcopal Church became the institutional centers of their community. Like Black loyalists in New York City during the war, their very presence, their organized efforts, and their public advocacy served as a constant, living testament to the possibility of Black freedom and self-determination.

Pennsylvania itself stood apart, shaped by Quaker morality and Revolutionary-era principles, culminating in An Act for the Gradual Abolition of Slavery, passed near the end of the war, in 1780. The first of its kind in the Western Hemisphere, the law gave any enslaved adult brought into Pennsylvania and residing there for six continuous months automatic eligibility for freedom.

Washington, however, saw this virtuous piece of legislation as a threat — a problem to be circumvented, even dismissed, as a restriction that did not need to apply to him. His reaction was perversely inspired by the example of Edmund Jennings Randolph — the first attorney general, appointed by Washington — who used the state's abolitionist law to strategically free his own enslaved people, relocating them to Philadelphia expressly for that purpose. As Randolph later wrote, slavery was "riveted in Virginia by disabilities of emancipation." For him, one of those disabilities was the fact that, in a world in which people were property, Black people freed in Virginia would belong to those whom an enslaver owed money, like a carriage or horses. Freedpeople could not, then, be truly free, so long as the enslaver was in debt. But Randolph had earlier expressed to James Madison that, in Pennsylvania, he could grant the enslaved people whom he owned their freedom and, under the law, they would not have to worry about any entanglements. If he just moved to Pennsylvania as a member of Washington's new cabinet and became a citizen of the state, he was sure that the law would make his enslaved people free and place them safely and legally beyond the reach of his many creditors.

So on April 5, 1791, Randolph visited Martha Washington at her Philadelphia home to tell her something extraordinary in that exclusionary world: "Three of his Negroes had given him notice that they should tomorrow take advantage of a law of this State, and claim their freedom," and the Washingtons ought to think about that as a possibility for their own enslaved people. Note what he said. Not that his enslaved people had taken their freedom and informed him after the fact. Not that they had told him of their intent, and he was taking steps to stop them. But, in an exchange of politeness that Jane Austen would have appreciated, they asserted that they were going to "claim their freedom" the next day. They just wanted him to know. It was a moment powerful in its quietude.

But Randolph fundamentally misread the Washingtons' character, and not for the first time. The president and his wife would never, ever relinquish control over their human property. Instead, Washington devised a covert, systematic counter-resistance — an illegal conspiracy to deny enslaved people their freedom under Pennsylvania law by rotating them out of Pennsylvania before they had remained in the state for six months straight. The result was a secretive scheme designed to reset the residency clock. Washington's explicit instructions to his personal secretary, Tobias Lear, underscored the duplicitous nature of his strategy: The rotations had to occur "under pretext that may deceive both them and the Public." Why? Because the Washingtons were breaking the law, and they knew it. In 1788, the Pennsylvania legislature had acted against that particular abuse, explicitly making it illegal.

Perhaps the older enslaved men and women in the household whispered to Ona that, despite all evidence to the contrary, she had a choice. It would take courage, persistence, and resilience, but one could resist the most powerful man in America and win. They knew people who had done it.

Ona was a child when the HMS *Savage* anchored off the Potomac in April 1781. She would have been around seven years old — too young to remember the details, but not too young to grow up with their weight. At least seventeen people from Mount Vernon escaped to that British warship, taking advantage of the chaos near the war's end and risking everything for freedom under the protection of the British, only to end up a few months later facing the same fate as Isaac and the other free Black people who had once belonged to Thomas Jefferson. Washington, predictably, was furious. He wrote to his estate steward, his cousin Lund Washington, demanding explanations and expressing a kind of possessive outrage that makes sense only if those escapes had struck a nerve, challenging his absolute authority and control. For a man who had always tried to portray himself as calm and in control but actually demonstrated a hot temper throughout his life, the departures stung, perhaps for what they revealed about the fragility of his dominion.

At Mount Vernon, the event could not have quietly disappeared. Enslaved families would have talked about it for years afterward — the moment someone made it out, even briefly. The names of those who boarded the *Savage* would have been remembered, whispered as symbols of daring. For those whom Washington captured at Yorktown, their return to slavery was a bitter lesson about what American victory meant for enslaved people. But they had been free, even for a few months, by running away from Washington, not relying on him. That incident likely lived on in Ona's world not as a historical event but as a warning and an inspiration, a story of risk and consequence, of what it meant to reach for freedom and then be dragged back, but also a testament to the enduring desire for it.

As she grew older, other stories would have entered Ona's world — sharper, clearer, and less distant — such as that of Thomas, who ran away from Mount Vernon during the war, too, to Philadelphia, staying free even longer before he was tracked and recaptured, and Washington paid a bounty to the slave catcher who returned him. Ona might have been old enough to absorb not just the story but also the lesson Washington meant it to teach: He would find those who ran, and his reach was long. But it also proved something else — that people were still running, still willing to gamble everything on the chance that somewhere there might be a place where their personhood would be recognized, where the chains of bondage could be broken.

And then, crucially, there were the names whispered with something closer to reverence, of the people who didn't come back, the people who had made it to freedom and remained there. Deborah Squash. Daniel Payne. Harry Washington. All three had once lived and labored at Mount Vernon, all three had taken their freedom during the Revolution, and all three had made it out when the British evacuated New York City in 1783. Carleton was talking about them, among thousands of others, when he pledged protection of their freedom to Washington on that day in Orangetown . . . and Washington knew it. Deborah met and married an enslaved man in New York City, and Daniel ended up in Nova Scotia, building a new life in a colder, but freer, land. The older Harry, who claimed to have joined Dunmore in 1776, joined the Royal Artillery as a pioneer, then eventually sailed to Sierra Leone to help found a new Black settlement in Africa, a testament to self-determination on a grand scale. They would not have been distant figures in a Mount Vernon world built around oppression. They would have been part of the shared memory that circulated in enslaved quarters as a parallel history, one not recorded in Washington's ledgers but spoken aloud when safe — repeated and remembered — a counternarrative of successful resistance.

Under Washington's illegal rotation plan, Ona was about to be sent back to Virginia and then handed over to the hated and feared Eliza. But, perhaps inspired by the stories of those who had resisted Washington and won their freedom, she saw that she had a choice. She could refuse: if she dared to seize the moment, allies would help her in the fight, and she had the persistence and resilience to fight against the onslaught she knew would come. In Philadelphia, there were not just friends but resistance allies, fighters in the battle against the abusive authority of enslavers backed by the full force of the First Republic.

So on that May night, she seized her moment in a leap of faith that her clandestine network would be there to catch her.

And they did. They made sure she made it aboard the sloop *Nancy*, safely bound for Northern ports, first to New York and, finally, to Portsmouth, New Hampshire.

A Relentless Pursuit

Washington's reaction to Ona's escape was not one of introspection. He was not given to reflection. The less he thought about things, especially slavery, the better. Instead, his perspective — as a general, a politician, an investor, a plantation manager — was that of a master whose authority was almost always in a state of being challenged.

His pursuit of Ona was not really about the loss of labor; it was a response to an act of defiance that threatened his sense of absolute control. We might fill an entire book with Washington's uniform reactions to such moments throughout his life. But Ona had a broader context in which to operate. She was not George's property. Ona belonged to Martha. She was part of her late husband's estate, and Martha placed the responsibility for "losing" Ona, and the responsibility of getting her back, on George. Wasn't he the president, after all? Plus, if Washington did not recover Ona, he would be on the hook for reimbursing the Custis estate for her value, and he wasn't inclined to do that. Adding to the pressure on George, Martha was personally bothered by the loss of so personal an attendant. Who would wake her up? Who would care for her clothes? And no one else in their household was so good with a needle and thread. The combination of George's rigid authoritarianism, his financial liability, and Martha's agitation fueled a campaign to reclaim Ona that would last the rest of Washington's life.

Constitutionally incapable of understanding how a piece of property could harbor such an intense desire for freedom, Washington acted. First, he put the world on notice through ads in the newspapers that Ona had escaped and, given that enslavers lived perpetually in a surveillance culture, sent notice to his many connections, family, and friends to keep an eye out for her. George and Martha then constructed a narrative that made her departure make sense to them, given their moral blindness to the inherent violence of Ona's condition. She had been treated with exceptional kindness, "brought up and treated more like a child than a Servant." Ona was "simple and offensive." There was no way she ever would have wanted to run, so she must have been "seduced and enticed away by a Frenchman." Ona was nothing more than a gullible victim rather than a rational actor making a calculated bid for liberty. This convenient fiction, which Washington returned to again and again in his correspondence, allowed him to frame himself, as all enslavers did, as a benevolent patriarch betrayed by ingratitude and outsider influence rather than as the perpetrator of an oppressive system that an enslaved person had purposefully and knowingly rejected.

In Portsmouth, Ona did not hide; she constructed a new life. The growing free Black community embraced her upon arrival, providing the shelter and connections she needed. She found work as a domestic servant and met Jack Staines, a free Black sailor, whom she wanted to marry. But just a few months later, Elizabeth Langdon, the daughter of John Langdon, a US senator from New Hampshire, and a friend of Eliza's sister, Nelly, recognized Ona on the street. When he heard the news, Washington acted swiftly.

And he was not going to limit himself to the resources available to a private person. Some might have seen Washington's use of his official powers to resolve a private matter an unethical abuse of his public office, but he certainly would have thought the larger abuse would be to allow Ona to flaunt his authority. After all, the First Republic had been designed to protect the interests of landowning and slaveholding elites. So he reached out to the secretary of the treasury, Oliver Wolcott, who then directed Washington to Joseph Whipple, the collector of customs in Portsmouth.

Whipple, the brother of a signer of the Declaration of Independence who had also been an officer under Washington in the Continental Army, would surely obey instructions, wouldn't he? He told Whipple that Ona was probably inclined to return, given how well he and Martha had treated her and other rumors he had heard about her. So Whipple should first try to persuade her to return. If not, Whipple should just grab her and put her on a ship to Virginia.

But Washington had a history of assuming facts not in evidence. He assumed that Whipple was on his side, but that does not seem to have been the case. Whipple knew that his position required him to be responsive to Washington, but the request violated the very Fugitive Slave Act that Washington had signed into law in 1793, which required that captured Black people who were assumed to be formerly enslaved must first be taken before a judge to ensure the legality of the ownership claims being asserted. The president, Whipple wrote to Wolcott, should just act within what the law provides. But just as with the 1788 Pennsylvania law banning the rotation of enslaved people out of the state, Washington didn't feel the restriction applied to him.

Moreover, the people of Portsmouth, whose opposition to slavery was growing by the week, might have something to say about Whipple abetting such an abuse of authority. Whipple noted that any move against Ona "will be governed by the popular opinion of the moment."

On top of all that, the example of Prince Whipple loomed over the situation. Prince had just passed away in Portsmouth, maybe in his home on a corner of property owned by Joseph's brother William. Prince Whipple had been enslaved by William, had gone to war with him, and had been promised his freedom in exchange for his dedicated service. Prince fulfilled his part of the bargain, but, as was often the case with white slaveholders, William didn't keep his word. Even Prince's petitioning of the New Hampshire assembly did no good. William finally did get around to freeing Prince in 1784, not long after a court in the state next door, Massachusetts, effectively ended slavery there. So it's quite possible that Joseph thought that Ona should be allowed to remain free.

At first, Whipple reported to Wolcott that he tried to act on Washington's representation that Ona had been enticed away, that she had never really wanted to leave the Washingtons. He learned that she was about to get married, so he stopped the issuance of her marriage certificate. Then he lied to Ona, telling her that he wanted to talk to her about a job with his family. But then, he told his boss, the secretary of the treasury, something happened. Whipple discovered that Washington was wrong. Ona hadn't been "decoyed away" but in fact had fled her bondage compelled "by a thirst for compleet freedom" that she was told she'd find in the North.

Then Ona made a pivot that not only showed persistence, resilience, and flexibility but also was an assertion of her personhood. She offered to negotiate, and property cannot negotiate, can it? Ona said she would return to Mount Vernon if the Washingtons agreed that she was free and released her from her service to their family upon their deaths. But — and here was the key point — "she should rather suffer death than return to Slavery." Whipple was thrilled. Freedom in exchange for service? That was a terrific outcome. Circumstances, though, scuttled the deal. The ship on which Ona might have returned was delayed, and, in the meantime, Ona simply changed her mind. She decided that staying free where she was, in Portsmouth, was a much better outcome.

Washington's response to her offer was a little bizarre. He wrote directly to Whipple, telling him that he never would have agreed to any deal giving Ona her freedom. He then returned to a theme common for him whenever the subject of slavery arose in a potentially public setting, saying that he might be in favor of gradual manumission, or even abolition, if it were "practicable at this moment." Maybe. Perhaps. He'd been saying the same thing, or something similar, for thirty years, without change, without evolution. As an abstract point, he was against the idea of slavery and would be for ending it should any practical way, meaning a way of dealing with the inevitable problem of free Black people, be found to do it. It was a common refrain among enslavers of his time and place. But he, and they, could not — would not — see a way to manage that problem.

In any case, Ona's situation, in the Washingtons' minds, had nothing to do with the larger question of if, how, and when slavery might be ended. She'd been unfaithful to them and shouldn't be rewarded for bad behavior. She somehow owed George and Martha for being such a good master and mistress to her. And, crucially, acknowledging her freedom would set a bad example for the enslaved population. George then went on to spend an entire paragraph belaboring what he thought was the more important point, trying to convince Whipple that he had been right all along about Ona's motivation for leaving. Whipple shouldn't accept Ona's version. She was lying. She had been talked into it by a Frenchman, and he had proof. And his word was worth so much more than Ona's.

In the end, the Washingtons' position remained firm. Ona could return to slavery with them. Martha would forgive her. And, George added cryptically, "all the rest of her family" would receive the same treatment from Washington, suggesting that there was an alternative, a veiled threat.

Whipple could not push the issue. Anti-slavery sentiment was running high in Portsmouth. Any overt move to take Ona might tip that protest sentiment into organized opposition, even active, violent resistance. It might excite "a riot or a mob." The only way to resolve the issue, he pointedly informed Washington, was to end slavery. Gradually, sure, but keeping things as they were would only guarantee wave after wave of future Ona Judges.

Resistance won that moment. Ona's persistence gave her a reprieve. Her resilience gave her a husband, as she shifted to get married in Greenland, New Hampshire, as a way to sidestep Whipple's interference with her marriage certificate. And then she had a little girl, Eliza, born in freedom.

Over the next year, the Washingtons, transitioning back to life at Mount Vernon, found another resistance moment to fixate on: Their celebrated chef, Hercules, had followed Ona's example and left. They spent the next year as they had the previous one with Ona, enlisting people to find him, developing plans for his return, complaining about the effect on their lives. Martha wrote that she was "sadly plaiged" by the loss of her cook and having to act as her own housekeeper. Failing on every count, as he had with Ona, Washington admitted by year's end that he'd have to give up the effort and, regrettably, purchase another human being to ensure that he and Martha had nice dinners.

But the Washingtons still would not forget about Ona and just let her live her new life. They would test her resilience yet again.

In the late summer of 1799, as the warm days on the Potomac became stifling, Washington's health was failing, and he had a lot on his mind. Only a few weeks before, he had finalized his will. Despite what many historians say, Washington's active views on slavery did not evolve throughout his life. He was never going to give his enslaved people their freedom and chose not to in the end. While there are those who, for some reason, insist that Washington was some sort of aspiring anti-slavery advocate, he did the least he possibly could in his will for the people he owned. As the yellow sun baked his crops, Washington looked across his fields and quarters at the hundreds of people whom he claimed responsibility for, knowing that he would abuse his authority in his final act. He would set one enslaved person free. One. William Lee, who had accompanied him through the Revolutionary War as his personal valet. That's it. The problem that he saw as being the foremost hurdle to even a discussion of abolition, or gradual manumission — with the practical implications of granting Black people their freedom — would never be his problem. Nor would it be Martha's. His enslaved people would be free only upon her death. Martha was sixty-eight years old. She might live another decade or more. It didn't matter. Neither of them would be around to see what happened. He wouldn't give it another thought, nor would he mention it.

What would he mention? Ona Judge. He would spend some of his last moments on earth not trying to free people, but trying to return one to slavery.

In August, he dispatched Martha's nephew, Burwell Bassett, with instructions to take Ona and forcibly return her to Mount Vernon. And there was now an added value to Washington: He learned that Ona had a child, maybe more than one. Perhaps owning them, too, would cover the cost of all of his trouble.

According to Ona, Bassett tracked her down "and used all the persuasion he could" to get her to return on her own. She "utterly refused." So Bassett planned to take the next step, local sentiments and threats of mob violence be damned. He would take her — and her infant daughter — by force. Staying the night in the house of Senator Langdon, Bassett was perhaps too free with Langdon's Madeira, and as a result, too free with his plans. He revealed everything to Langdon. The senator might have been a friend of Washington's in Federalist politics, but he was not, it turns out, an accomplice when it came to abusive authority. And maybe, even quite possibly, he was trying to make up for his daughter's betrayal of Ona. It was she who had alerted the Washingtons to Ona's being in Portsmouth in the first place. That very night,

Langdon told Ona to get away from Portsmouth. His warning to her was itself a criminal act. She quickly hired a carriage, collected her baby girl, and got away, out of Bassett's reach. He returned to Virginia, his kidnapping mission a failure.

Bassett wouldn't have long to endure Washington's reaction. The president died in December, ending the attempts to recover Ona. However, as far as Ona knew, the threat remained. Martha would live another three years. More to the point, the power of the state ensured that the Custis estate would endure beyond Martha's life. The abusive federal authority that ensured her status as a fugitive, and as property, would strengthen. She would remain in a state of resistance for the rest of her life.

Ona's experience is the marker of all effective resistance against abusive authority, and she embodied the twin pillars of effective resistance: persistence and resilience. She withstood the efforts of Washington, which were backed by the authority and resources of the First Republic, and she had to remain vigilant for the rest of her life. Ona achieved her resistance goal: freedom.

From Property to Protagonist

Almost everything that we know about Ona comes from two sources: Washington's correspondence and her oral history. For generations, historians and storytellers sidestepped the first source and ignored the second one as they created a dominant narrative of an exceptional First Republic with Washington at its core. History and biography were deployed as muscular tools of nationalism, celebrating the central cadre of patriot leaders as both representative and normative of the American experience, and therefore of American identity, while excluding all others. In this biased and often fictionalized narrative, slavery was nothing more than a regrettable but necessary sideshow, irrelevant to the themes of liberty and equality that the patriots themselves attempted to establish as central to the record of their accomplishments. And so slavery was largely ignored, especially since it continued to be an essential feature of the First Republic through the 1800s.

And the sources left behind by free Black people themselves were deemed irrelevant and smeared as untrustworthy, unreliable. Falling into a genre that we today call slave narratives, they were dismissed as fictive products of anti-American abolitionist propaganda.

In the end, a nationalist propaganda emerged and coalesced during the nineteenth century, one that manufactured broad acceptance of American exceptionalism mythology. This narrative dominates to this day, requiring an act of interpretive resistance to push against its ongoing abusive authority.

To do that, we must continue to recover the experiences of people like Ona, rescuing their narratives from exclusion and then from distortion. It requires prying their stories from the perspective of historians such as Ulrich Bonnell Phillips, a committed white supremacist and Yale University professor who trained a generation of scholars in methods and assumptions that systemically erased the Black experience. His 1918 book, *American Negro Slavery*, actively promoted racial bias by privileging the sources of the enslavers as the only sources through which to understand the experience of enslaved people. Phillips's work provided a usable past for segregationists, one in which resistance like Ona's was unimaginable because Black people were presumed incapable of it, lacking the intellectual or moral capacity for defiance. The result was a long shadow over the field.

The refusal to recognize Ona's experience served a deliberate function: It naturalized the authority of the enslaver and rendered opposition to that authority unthinkable. If enslaved people had no political consciousness, then there was nothing to resist. If they accepted their condition, then any history that told otherwise could be dismissed as fiction or even unpatriotic. For decades, that framework has dominated textbooks and classrooms across America. It has reinforced the racial hierarchies that outlived slavery, and it trained generations of scholars to ask the wrong questions, draw biased conclusions, or avoid facts and primary sources entirely. Even those who did not share Phillips's open racism often inherited his basic assumptions about what counted as agency, whose voices mattered, and where history was thought to reside.

Recovering Ona's resistance, then, has always required more than archival work. It has required the rejection of the frameworks that made resistance illegible. It has meant challenging the authority not only of slaveholders but also of the historians who took — and continue to take — their word alone for the way things were under slavery. That recovery work — led in later decades by scholars like Herbert Aptheker, who meticulously documented slave revolts, John Blassingame, whose detailed studies of slave communities revealed daily acts of defiance, Eugene Genovese (despite his own compromises), who explored the complex relationship between master and slave, and more decisively by Black feminist historians like Deborah Gray White, Stephanie Camp, and Saidiya Hartman, who centered the experiences and agency of enslaved women — went beyond scholarly intervention to be resistance in its own right. It demanded that historians not only write about resistance but also practice it — by refusing to accept the sources of power on their terms, by reading against the grain, and by insisting that those who were meant to be erased from the historical record had inserted themselves into it through their defiance. The task now is to follow that example and continue pulling back the layers of interpretation that still obscure more than they reveal — especially in the most revered corners of American memory, including the lives of the founders.

The mid-twentieth century witnessed a much-needed correction through scholars such as Kenneth Stampp and Stanley Elkins, who highlighted slavery's violence and psychological trauma. Yet even their portrayals often depicted enslaved people as victims whose capacity for meaningful resistance had been broken by systemic abuse. Theirs was a reductive view that inadvertently denied enslaved people the dignity of their selves, portraying them as damaged rather than actively resistant. The true historiographical revolution began with historians like Blassingame, whose groundbreaking book *The Slave*

Community (1972), alongside Herbert Gutman's detailed explorations of enslaved family life and Genovese's analyses of slave resistance in works like *Roll, Jordan, Roll* (1974), re-centered the narratives around enslaved people's own experiences, voices, and cultural expressions. Their scholarship illuminated the complex, multifaceted resistance of enslaved communities, revealing not passive submission but continuous, active defiance through daily acts like work slowdowns, sabotage, theft, self-education, and ultimately escape.

Yet despite these historiographical shifts, George Washington's personal history has been insulated from any real scrutiny. The early fictionalization of Washington, first for elite circles by John Marshall, then turbocharged into the public consciousness by Mason Locke Weems with his cherry tree fable, created an impenetrable national fairy tale — Washington the virtuous patriot, the flawless statesman, the embodiment of American ideals, a figure beyond reproach. Washington's ownership of enslaved people, including Ona, was minimized or rationalized as incidental rather than fundamental to understanding his character and power, a necessary evil of his time rather than a defining moral choice. Historians such as Douglas Southall Freeman, despite his rigor, never questioned the moral failings at Washington's core, perpetuating a nationalist narrative that rendered enslaved people invisible, the very fact of their beings irrelevant to the grand narrative of the First Republic's founding.

But no cultural force has been more potent in promoting the nationalist aims of the patriot mythology than the farce of the late-twentieth-century publishing and media production juggernaut known as Founders Chic — the popular culture-driven revival of the small cohort of arch-patriots such as Washington, spearheaded by writers such as Joseph J. Ellis and Ron Chernow. Their bestselling works, read predominantly by a white male audience, reinforced, and even resurrected and retrenched, comfortable myths about American exceptionalism, presenting the founders as complex but ultimately heroic figures. Ellis's *His Excellency: George Washington* (2004) and Chernow's *Washington: A Life* (2010) framed Washington's life as a synecdoche for all of the American founding, as the "great contradiction" of a man who fought for liberty while holding others in bondage, forcing Washington into "moral contortions." That interpretation, which continues to dominate popular history, is an act of evasion, twisting words like *nuance* and *complexity* into a moral quagmire that only Washington himself would have appreciated. They acknowledge the brutality of slavery, briefly, occasionally, despite its centrality to Washington's life, only to soften its every impact and their verdict on the enslaver. Storytellers such as Ellis and Chernow and their circle have invented a moral struggle in the mind of Washington, and almost every other founding enslaver, where the evidence points only to a consistent pattern of behavior: that of a master who used any means necessary — legal, illegal, and extralegal — to protect his property and his power. There was no evolution; there was only the relentless pursuit and enforcement of his authority.

It took historian Erica Armstrong Dunbar's powerful book *Never Caught: The Washingtons' Relentless Pursuit of Their Runaway Slave, Ona Judge* (2017) to bring Ona's life from the shadows into the spotlight. Her signal achievement, as an act of resistance history, was to rescue Ona's story from the dismissive paragraphs of Ellis and Chernow, restoring her experience, and telling Ona's story on her own terms. Dunbar painstakingly reconstructed Ona's world, relying on her words and on deep research into her contexts. Building on the work of Annette Gordon-Reed and Philip D. Morgan to center the humanity of enslaved people in an inhuman world, Dunbar brilliantly recovered Ona as a truly complex person faced with almost unimaginable challenges.

More recently, Alexis Coe's *You Never Forget Your First: A Biography of George Washington* (2020) represents a new generation of unflinching, direct historians. They are not afraid to represent honest history by challenging the "Thigh Men" who see it as their role to protect Washington and his compatriots, lavishing praise and excuses for them within a hypermasculine, heroic framing. Coe's refreshingly irreverent yet rigorously researched biography positions Judge's story not as peripheral but pivotal, a vital corrective necessary for understanding Washington — and by extension, the First Republic — in his full complexity and darkness.

It is no coincidence that Coe's most powerful interventions come from her position outside the academy, liberated from the institutional pressures and professional expectations that constrain many scholars into equivocation or complicity with nationalist mythmaking. Free from these limitations, Coe has demonstrated how honest history itself can function as a profound act of resistance, one urgently needed in an era when powerful institutions continue to prefer reassuring myths over unsettling truths and when the past is often weaponized to serve present political agendas.

Seizing the Narrative: The Final Resistance

Ona Judge's escape from the Washingtons marked the beginning of a lifetime of resistance against the abusive authority of both a set of controlling masters and an entire system. Her lifelong defiance required persistence and resilience to sustain her through decades of poverty, loss, precarity, and fear as she bobbed and weaved in a nation almost literally designed to re-enslave her. Settling in New Hampshire, she lived a life forever shadowed by the threat of recapture, yet remained defiantly free long after the deaths of both George and Martha.

However, Ona's ultimate act of resistance might not have been her physical escape from the reach of the Washingtons and the application of inhumane First Republic laws but rather her reclamation of her narrative. In her seventies, penniless and widowed, she recognized that memory itself is a battlefield — a contested space in which history and identity are shaped, and where the stories of the powerful often overshadow the truths of the oppressed. She was not out of danger, not beyond the reach of the Custis heirs. Yet she seized the opportunity to take her place in a corrected, and corrective, historical record, through two oral histories.

The first interview was conducted at her home in Greenland, New Hampshire, a few miles from Portsmouth, in 1845. A Baptist minister, Thomas Archibald, wrote down Ona's recollection of her escape, taking the reader back to that moment in Philadelphia in 1796. The account was published in *The Granite Freeman* and picked up a few months later by William Lloyd Garrison's *The Liberator*, the most well-known and far-reaching abolitionist newspaper in America.

In the wake of the annexation of Texas and the emergence of manifest destiny, forces designed to expand slavery across the continent, an anti-slavery activist in New Hampshire, the Reverend Benjamin Chase, sensed a chance to undermine both the heroes of the First Republic and reverence for its Constitution when he conducted his own interview with Ona. In it, she again recounted her background and the moment of her escape, but she went beyond the details of her own story to take on the myth of the Washingtons' devoted Christian faith. Were they as pious as the nationalist storytelling would have Americans, in a nation driven by God, believe? No, recalled Ona, "the stories told of Washington's piety and prayers . . . have no foundation." Sundays were for "card-playing and wine-drinking." She had already said, and would have been in a position to know, that "Mrs. Washington used to read prayers but I don't call that praying." And, Chase noted, Ona remained yet enslaved, only shielded from return to bondage by her age and infirmity, by her diminished value, not by law or justice. Ona's lived experience was an indictment of Washington, his uncomplicated values, and the Constitution he championed.

So Chase asked, in a question for the ages, "So good a man as Washington is enough to sanctify war and slavery; but where is the evidence of his goodness?" If the Constitution is a moral document, and Washington a moral man, then Langdon, who had enabled Ona to remain free by frustrating Bassett's grab, and all those who would overthrow the Constitution's abusive authority, were morally guilty of violating what they stood for.

Garrison published Chase's interview in *The Liberator* as a letter to the editor in January 1847.

But from both of these narratives comes no more powerful statement of resistance than this: Asked if she was sorry that she had left the Washingtons, given how difficult, in the eyes of a white person, her life had become, she responded, likely with ease and clarity, "No, I am free, and have, I trust, been made a child of God by the means." Her persistence was rewarded. Her resilience was redeemed.

Ona's life spanned an era in which slavery, rather than diminishing, became more deeply entrenched, more institutionalized, and legally protected as it spread broadly across the continent. That wasn't despite the war for independence that Washington had fought and the country he had established, but because of it. Ona knew that better than almost anyone. Freedom came from running away from the authority Washington had established and strengthened, from resisting it, not embracing it. And so her story — publicly recounted and widely circulated by abolitionists — became a weapon in the broader resistance movement, fueling growing organized opposition against slavery, providing a powerful human face to the abstract arguments for freedom. Ona's experience served as a powerful reminder that slavery was neither a benign institution nor an inevitable one; it was an abusive authority, deliberately upheld, not yet fiercely contested, and the nation's revered founders were responsible for it.

Ona's resistance was, ultimately, her successful reclamation of the power to define her own life and to articulate the profound moral victory of asserting one's humanity against systemic oppression. She persisted in the knowledge that she should have the last word on determining the course of her life. Like Giles Corey, and James Somerset, and Nancy Dixon, she refused to be sacrificed to a lie that her life, that her reality, could be determined or twisted by an abusive authority. And she drew on deep reservoirs of resilience that are essential to any effective resister, especially against the most powerful authorities: How do you recover from the blows that will fall, and fall hard?

Ona's narrative — built on nothing more or less than the truth — provides an enduring model of resistance that illuminates a pathway for others, demonstrating that even the most marginalized person, against the most powerful of opponents, can seize control of their own stories — but only if they persist in their commitment, only if they are resilient. Ona transcended anyone's claim to her as property, no matter how powerful they seemed to be or historians have said they were, leaving a legacy that continues to challenge the nation's foundational myths and stir its collective conscience.

CHAPTER SIX

The Right to Refuse

Resistance History Principle #6: Ideas matter.

CONCORD, JULY 1846

Henry David Thoreau woke before the sun fully claimed the sky, the early light peeking through the rough-hewn boards of his cabin, illuminating the dust specks floating in the pine-scented air. Outside, the woods around Walden Pond were quiet but stirring: A wood thrush began its song while the water's surface was glassy in its stillness, only to be ruffled, momentarily, by the lightest murmur of a passing breeze.

Across Walden Pond lay a reminder of his modern world: the new Fitchburg Railroad cut a straight line through the forest. The twenty-nine-year-old teacher, writer, and thinker could hear the distant echo of its whistle — an intrusion that "penetrates my woods . . . reminding me that the earth is wider than my field."

But on that morning, the intrusion felt heavier. The United States had, just two months earlier, started a war to expand slavery, to abuse further the consent of the governed in the active exploitation of people in bondage. It stabbed at Thoreau's conscience, at his morals, at every sense he had about what was right and just in the world, invading the peace of the pond. But that was a peace that millions of people held in chains could never enjoy.

That afternoon, noticing that a pair of worn shoes needed the attention of the cobbler, he began the mile-and-a-half walk into town. Along the way, he met Sam Staples, the constable of Concord. Thoreau liked him. Staples was "quick, clear, downright, and on the whole a good fellow." But he was also Concord's tax collector, and the state wanted its due from Thoreau. So Staples arrested the young teacher and took him to the town's jail, right off the green, locking him behind thick stone walls and iron grates.

It turns out that being jailed for resistance against abusive authority was something of a family tradition.

CONCORD, JUNE 1775

Josiah Jones had not been sentenced; he had not even been tried. There was no charge the law could name against him — only the accusation that he would not stand with the patriots. That was enough. The order from the provincial congress was blunt: He was to be "confined in the jail at Concord until further order." No date for release. No hearing to plead his case. Just the certainty that, until he bent to their will, he would remain behind its wooden bars.

The *Polly*, an eighty-eight-ton sloop, had been chartered in Boston to carry thirty-one-year-old Josiah Jones to Nova Scotia for hay and oats to supply the forces trapped in Boston under patriot siege. For Josiah, this wasn't about loyalty to a king. He never mentioned the word. It was an act of principle. And principle was the currency of the Jones family. The patriot "mob" in his hometown of Weston had already learned that the Joneses were formidable. They had driven them from their home for refusing to bend the knee to a new set of masters, but they hadn't broken them. Now, with his parents taking refuge in a city under siege, Josiah was doing what his conscience — and his duty to his family — demanded.

He didn't know that the captain of the *Polly*, Ephraim Perkins, intended to betray him. Perkins had put out from Kennebunkport, Maine, weeks before with cargo for Plymouth. On the return, a Royal Navy ship detained his vessel, and British officials in Boston persuaded him, for a hefty fee, to carry shipments for the army. Perkins agreed — and then immediately set a course not for Nova Scotia, but back to Kennebunkport, where the Arundel Committee of Correspondence was waiting.

The seizure was quick. Jones, some fellow passengers, a few weapons, and a sealed packet of letters entrusted to Jones were all taken. His protests meant nothing. The committee did not weigh whether he intended harm or whether hauling fodder counted as aiding the British cause. His actual intentions were irrelevant. What mattered was his refusal to accept that their liberty gave them the right to take away his. The patriots spoke of freedom, but what they were building on the ground in towns across New England was a system that tolerated no dissent. You either joined their cause or you were an enemy of it. If you weren't with them, you were dangerously against them — and dangerous men belonged in jail.

They marched him to Watertown to face the provincial congress. Josiah's own admission of guilt — that he opposed taking up arms against Britain — was taken as proof of his hostility to "the liberties of America." On June 10, Congress ordered him confined in the jail at Concord "until further order." No trial. No sentence. Just punishment for refusing to submit.

He would stay there for more than three months — until his sister Mary decided that the patriots' authority wouldn't decide Josiah's fate. She smuggled him the knives he used to saw through the jail's wooden bars. Then, in an act of sublime defiance, she stole the local sheriff's horse and spirited Josiah out of Concord, a ghost riding away from the reach of men who claimed to be fighting for freedom.

So when Thoreau was locked in that Concord jail in 1846, he was living out a family legacy. The man who had been imprisoned there seventy years before for defying the patriots, Josiah Jones, was his great-uncle. And the woman who broke him out — the audacious, principled Mary Jones — was Thoreau's grandmother. She wasn't a distant ancestor. Mary was the woman in whose house Henry was born, who helped raise him until he was thirteen. And in an act that would ripple through American history, it was Mary who first introduced her young grandson to the shores of Walden Pond.

The product of Thoreau's night in jail, an experience that focused his thoughts and feelings about what was happening in America, was the subject of a lecture he gave in Concord on "The Rights and Duties of the Individual in relation to Government." A few years later, they were revised and published as *Resistance to Civil Government*. After his death, an editor renamed it simply *Civil Disobedience*. It remains the first — and still the most precise — articulation of the American idea of resistance. And it became the ideological foundation, and even a practical playbook, for resistance movements around the globe.

Often confused with an argument for nonviolent protest, *Civil Disobedience* is far from that. It is, on the one hand, an angry and cynical work, born of years of experience and frustration with the American state that the First Republic had evolved into by the 1840s. On the other hand, it is deeply hopeful in its insistence that change through resistance is possible, if an opposition has the courage and the realism necessary to stop wasting time on tactics that won't work, such as tepid reform or mistaken reliance on traditional politics, and focus on what might work — outright refusal to accept abusive authority.

For those who know Thoreau primarily through *Walden*, you might think that the author of the earthy, vital *Civil Disobedience* comes across as a person different from the detached philosopher steeped in transcendental thought. The dissonance is all the more striking when you learn that the two works, which define Thoreau's legacy, were written at the same time. The extraordinary simplicity of his experiment in living deliberately at Walden Pond was interwoven with the complexity of his wrestling match with the injustice embedded in America's government. But on a closer reading, you can hear the same voice in both, aware of and reflective about the world around, and at the same time insisting that to live deliberately is also to refuse complicity with the world's harms — to refuse a life of quiet desperation.

But Thoreau's resistance has an ancestry, a lineage. In those jails in Concord — Josiah in 1775, Thoreau in 1846; separated by seventy years yet joined in experience — we can trace the ideological origins of American resistance. The continuity is plain: both men confronting abusive authority, both refusing to submit to demands they did not accept.

In those jails in Concord, the American tradition of resistance was born.

Inheritance

He remembered the moment. March 4, 1838. Twenty-year-old Thoreau, home on a Sunday afternoon, newly out of Harvard and looking for work in Concord, bounded down the stairs into the parlor and took in the room. He noted in his journal:

> Here at my elbow sit five notable, or at least noteworthy, representations of this nineteenth century — of the gender feminine. One a sedate — indefatigable knitter, not spinster, of the old school — who had the supreme felicity to be born in days that tried men's souls — who can, and not unfrequently does, say with Nestor, another of the old school — "But you are younger than I. For time was when I conversed with greater men than you. For not at any time have I seen such men, nor shall see them, as Perithous and Dryas, the shepherd of the people."

The "indefatigable knitter" was his mother, Cynthia, born in 1787, "in days that tried men's souls." Those lines fit the tone of her house and her history. When she said "greater men," she might have been measuring her son against lives she knew.

They might well have been her own — and his own — family.

In the 1770s, the New England resistance pushed patriot politics toward coercion, especially in towns like Weston, the Joneses' home. After the Tea Act, patriot committees had created a culture of coercion and surveillance, as mobs demanded public declarations, punished dissent, and branded neighbors "enemies to liberty." The committees were not debating societies; they enforced conformity through public pressure, loyalty oaths, boycotts, and intimidation. In Weston, that pressure was personal. Mary's father, Elisha, publicly opposed the committees; neighboring towns took notice. The Golden Ball Tavern, run by her cousin Isaac, was attacked when neighbors whispered — quietly but accurately — that he sold tea. The result was not a debate of the issues of the day. It was intimidation that reordered daily life. Loyalists like the Joneses did not see the patriots as guardians of liberty; they saw their neighbors claiming a new power and enforcing it.

What drove the Joneses and many other loyalists away was not "loyalty to tyranny," as patriot propaganda had it, but a refusal to surrender conscience to a movement that had hardened into orthodoxy, that demanded total submission. By the mid-1770s, dissent in Weston was punished, not argued. For Mary Jones and her family, the question was no longer Parliament or tea; it was whether committees had the right to dictate belief, business, and even what her husband, the Reverend Asa Dunbar, said from the pulpit — what her cousin Isaac could place on his tavern's tables. The choice was stark: submit to the new order or stand apart and accept the cost. In Thoreau's reckoning, that is what they did: They resisted one more abusive authority.

The events of April 19, 1775, pulled the Jones family in a different direction from most of their neighbors. In Cambridge, twenty-one-year-old Stephen Jones — only a few weeks from graduating — was standing by the Harvard gates when a British brigade sent to rescue the troops under fire at Concord reached town. In those morning hours, Stephen chose to guide the column down that "Battle Road" from Cambridge to Lexington. When they arrived, under fire from patriot reinforcements behind every wall and tree, the commander sent Stephen galloping back to Boston with critical dispatches for General Gage. On arriving back in the city, Stephen, with his brothers, joined the first military company of loyalists to support the British troops. He would never see Harvard again.

Josiah's turn came six weeks later. He had been living in New Hampshire but joined his family in Boston after the Lexington Alarm. While there, he also joined the loyalist company and helped their father supply the growing number of troops and families in the besieged city. On May 30, with food and fodder running dangerously low, he accepted the mission to fetch hay and oats from Nova Scotia. The ship's master betrayed him, sailing instead into that harbor in Maine, delivering Josiah to the patriot committee, which led to his being thrown into the Concord jail, branded "a notorious enemy to his Country." No indictment, no sentence — just confinement for refusing the patriots' authority. He had done nothing wrong. He had not taken up arms against anyone. But he did refuse to join the patriots. That was enough.

But for his sister Mary, it was too much. Every day she rode the eight miles from Weston to carry him meals — and knives. And still Josiah remained in jail. An exchange proposed by Gage failed. Petitions were ignored. July's heat gave way to September's chill; the saw marks deepened in the wooden bars to Josiah's cell. On the night of September 27, the opening was finally large enough. Josiah slipped out to Weston; Mary took the sheriff's horse and then got her brother clear. He would never return to Massachusetts.

Simeon, another brother, was then jailed by the patriots under suspicion of helping Josiah escape — no one thought of Mary — and for his own lack of enthusiasm for the rebels' cause. He was eventually released but went straight to the British army, also never to return to Massachusetts.

In 1795, when Cynthia was eight, she met those men. After years of struggle, having been chased by patriots from Weston to Keene, New Hampshire, Mary's husband, the Reverend Asa Dunbar, died, leaving it to her to raise their four children alone. Mary turned their home into a tavern and a shop, but her health began to fail. Fearing it was a last chance to see the family, separated from her by the war, she turned her teenage son, Charles, over to friends, then gathered her three daughters and set off on a perilous journey.

They first took passage on a sloop that weathered a harrowing storm to enter Frenchman's Bay, to see Mary's brother in Gouldsboro, Maine. After a few days in the shadow of Cadillac Mountain, they crossed the Bay of Fundy. There Mary came face-to-face with Stephen, Simeon, and Josiah, none of whom she had seen since 1775. And yet there was also one missing, with a palpable absence — her favorite, youngest brother Charles, after whom she had named her son. He had left Harvard during the war to join the British army like his brothers had. But Charles was killed in battle outside Williamsburg and buried in Virginia's soil.

The moment. Those men and that woman. Were they the "greater men" collective that Thoreau put into his mother's mouth? A catalog of losses, choices, and refusals that did not fit the patriot story and yet defined the American Revolution.

The Joneses were not outliers. They represented a current of colonial life that nationalist fictions have obscured. More recently, historians have recovered the experience of the 10 to 15 percent of the population that opposed the patriots, revealing how loyalists like them are too often miscast as self-interested or fearful. Yet what the Joneses stood for — constitutional order, moderation, and the rule of law — was perhaps not as necessary or as harmful to the mythology of the revolution as what they stood against: an exclusionary, coercive authority that claimed to speak for everyone. That opposition has been so neglected in the historical record that it seems unthinkable — surely, the myth tells us, no one in their right mind could have been against the patriots. The Joneses remind us that principled opposition, against their personal interests, was not only possible, it was common. But the myth of the Revolution refuses to see it. The Jones family's story exposes how much has been forgotten — and how much has been deliberately erased — in the creation of America's founding legend.

Cutting through that legend, Thoreau called their moment the "Revolution of '75," not for battles or flags but for the legacy of quiet defiance it left in his family. There were no parades for them, no statues, no places in the popular tale. What they carried was an inheritance of conscience — saying no when obedience meant surrendering integrity. Cynthia's stories, and the lives that made them, preserved that heritage: Do not yield belief to power; do not let authority make a test of loyalty out of your conscience. Thoreau made that his creed. It was not the Revolution of the textbooks but instead a revolution in principle — a family tradition of resistance to abusive authority he claimed as his own.

"For not at any time have I seen such men, nor shall see them," Thoreau put in his mother's mouth, directed at him. It was Cynthia speaking, but she was pointing to her mother, her uncles, even her cousins. Mary had lived through a revolution that, for her family, meant holding the high ground of conscience. Two of her brothers were seized and locked away for their beliefs. Four of them fought the patriot cause in British ranks. Charles gave his life. Thoreau's grandmother had stood with them through it all, never yielding to an authority she judged unjust. That was the family tradition Thoreau was born into in her house on Virginia Road — liberty of conscience not as a slogan but as a duty worth the cost. In Thoreau's hands, the principles imparted by the only grandparent he knew became a philosophy: Ideas matter; morality matters; and the obligation to resist stands above any power that demands you betray either.

Conjuring the Spirit of '76

By 1846, the Revolution that bound Thoreau's night in a Concord jail to Josiah Jones's months-long earlier imprisonment had already been cast in terms of nationalist myths. Thoreau's legacy of liberty of conscience — the Jones family's refusal to bow to the patriots' coercive demands — lay buried under the narrative that had come to dominate the country. That rewriting began early, woven into the very process of creating the American nation.

The earliest histories of the Revolution were not written to memorialize its realities but rather to lock in a narrow story of a single, linear path from monarchical tyranny to the world's first republic governed by the rule of law. David Ramsay set the template: The Revolution produced the patriot movement; the patriot movement produced the War for Independence; the War for Independence produced the Constitution. One clean arc, driven by the same actors from start to finish. In that version, the Revolution existed only to justify its endpoint — the Constitution — and everything else was stripped away. White loyalists, Black loyalists, Indigenous nations, even many of the old revolutionaries themselves — all vanished from the story.

Their presence would have complicated the origin myth, and complication was, as it still is, the enemy of nationalism.

By 1826, that mechanical narrative had hardened into political culture. Independence was marked each July 4, but emptied of its original purpose; the Constitution was treated as the inevitable and unquestionable fulfillment of the Revolution. The heroes — Washington, Jefferson, and the rest — were celebrated as the cause itself, immune from scrutiny. It was the age of nation-building, and the Revolution had been retrofitted to serve it.

That baffled many who had lived through it. Mercy Otis Warren, in her history, was among the first to reject the notion that there had been one coherent path. Benjamin Rush warned against mistaking the war for the Revolution — "The American war is over but this is far from being the case with the American Revolution" — insisting that the real work of reshaping the political and moral order had only just begun.

Adams and Jefferson shared the view, but with even less optimism. Jefferson told Adams that no one could ever truly write the history of the Revolution because "the life and soul of history" had been sealed behind closed doors, unrecorded and unrecoverable. Adams went further: "I consider the true Victory of the American revolution & of the establishment of our present Constitution as lost forever. And nothing but misrepresentations or partial accounts of it, ever will be recovered." For Adams, the Revolution was never the war itself but instead "a radical change in the principles, opinions, sentiments, and affections of the people," a transformation in political character that had already taken place before 1775.

But Adams also saw how swiftly that transformation had been claimed and rebranded by the "men of '87" for purposes far removed from the original resistance. And he didn't have to look far to find it — only to his son, John Quincy Adams.

The younger Adams, born in 1767, initially embodied the very nationalist narrative his father distrusted when he entered public life. He was part of a generation that came of age with the new government and saw the Revolution, the war, and the Constitution as a single, triumphant, and divinely ordained story. In that regard, John Quincy Adams was more the political heir to James Madison and Alexander Hamilton, the nationalists, than he was to his father's generation of patriots.

The nationalist fervor was on full display in the old chamber of the US House of Representatives on July 4, 1821, when the younger Adams, as secretary of state, celebrated the Declaration of Independence and the Revolution that produced it. Short on facts and long on rhetoric, John Quincy Adams traced a narrative path to nationhood familiar to most Americans today — and breathtaking for its blindness to historical truth. From the first settlers in Plymouth, "conquest and servitude had no part. The slough of brutal force was entirely cast off: all was voluntary; all was unbiased consent; all was the agreement of soul with soul." And then Adams leaned into the emergence of the exceptional American nation. Jefferson's document declared, "The people of North America were no longer the fragment of a distant empire, imploring justice and mercy from an inexorable master in another hemisphere . . . They were a nation, asserting as of right, and maintaining by war, its own existence." What the patriots did was not only unique in world history, asserted Adams, but "it can never be repeated. It stands, and must for ever stand, alone, a beacon on the summit of the mountain, to which all the inhabitants of the earth may turn their eyes for a genial and saving light till time shall be lost in eternity, and this globe itself dissolve, nor leave a wreck behind."

And there was an unbroken narrative, too, that strung the Revolution to the war to the Constitution in one unchallenged, unitary progression of America's national greatness.

All of that would have been news to his father, who had fought through the battles that his son glossed over. At nearly the same time that his son was thinking about the glorious emergence of the American nation, John Adams explained that it wasn't any such thing. He wrote to Hezekiah Niles, a Baltimore publisher interested in what had actually happened almost fifty years earlier, that "the Revolution was effected before the War commenced." It was "in the Minds and Hearts of the People." That, to Adams, was "the real American Revolution." But it operated differently in each of the thirteen colonies, given that Americans were *not* one people. They were "all distinct, unconnected and independent of each other," to such an extent that historians would have to examine what had happened in each colony even to begin to understand what the revolution really was, how it really came about.

Not one nation. Not one people. Perhaps one Revolution, but in at least thirteen parts. And there was no connection between it and the war, and no direct link from either to the Constitution.

But by the middle of the nineteenth century, it was, indeed, too late to recover the elder Adams's revolution. The younger Adams's version had taken hold. The nationalist myth had done its work — fusing Revolution, war, and Constitution into a single, state-serving narrative, endlessly celebrated yet never questioned. It was not history to be learned from but rather memory to be managed. And in that managed memory, the Revolution's principles — the refusal of abusive authority, the defense of liberty of conscience — lay buried beneath the demands of loyalty to a nation-state that claimed their legacy while betraying their meaning.

By the time Thoreau came of age, Concord itself had been remade into a shrine to the nationalist version of the Revolution. Its past was no longer a web of divided loyalties, competing visions, and dangerous acts of conscience — it had become a stage set for myth. Ralph Waldo Emerson, more than any other figure, supplied the script. In 1836, for the dedication of the town's battle monument, he wrote the "Concord Hymn" — verses that would fix the opening shots of the war in the national imagination:

By the rude bridge that arched the flood,
Their flag to April's breeze unfurled,
Here once the embattled farmers stood,
And fired the shot heard round the world

It was a masterstroke of mythmaking — compressing a tangled, local skirmish into a moment of universal destiny, the birthplace of liberty itself. Emerson's toast at a later commemoration was even more explicit, likening the spot where Captain Isaac Davis fell to the burning bush — "where God spake for his people." In those few words, Concord was sanctified, its history bound to divine will, its meaning fixed as the starting point of an unbroken march toward American greatness.

This was the same Emerson who, in his 1837 "American Scholar" address, declared, "Our day of dependence, our long apprenticeship to the learning of other lands, draws to a close." He cast the United States not as a contested republic but as an emerging civilization with a singular destiny — a distinctly nationalist vision wrapped in the language of intellectual liberation. In Concord, that vision meant elevating one thread of the town's past — the patriot resistance of 1775 — while erasing others, including the loyalist families whose stories paralleled Thoreau's lineage. Emerson's own grandmother, Phebe Bliss, had been close friends with the daughters of the Royall family, the wealthiest loyalists in New England. Her brother Daniel Bliss was Concord's most prominent loyalist, who memorably pointed out in defending an enslaved man, John Jack, who had gained his freedom, the patriots' hypocrisy: "Tho' he lived in a land of liberty, He lived a slave."

Like the Joneses, the Revolution tore apart the Bliss family. Two brothers joined the patriots, two joined the British army. One was a prisoner of war; Daniel found refuge in Canada. Their Concord property was confiscated and sold. Yet in Emerson's hands, the Concord of memory belonged to his other grandfather, the Reverend William Emerson, a Continental Army chaplain who died returning from service at Fort Ticonderoga in 1776. It was that legacy — not the divided one — that he chose to enshrine.

This selective remembering was not Emerson's alone; it was the work of a generation. In 1841, Nathaniel Hawthorne's *Grandfather's Chair* offered young readers a pantheon of patriot heroes — Adams, Hancock, Warren, Otis, Quincy — each portrayed as Heaven-sent for "the one objective of establishing the freedom and independence of America." It was history as a sermon, a story with no room for dissenters or alternative outcomes. And in the hands of professional mythmakers like nineteenth-century historian George Bancroft, the Revolution was folded seamlessly into the rise of the American nation, its principles rendered indistinguishable from the state's expansionist ambitions.

Together Emerson and Hawthorne were shaping the emotional and moral register of the Revolution's memory, turning local events and familiar figures into sacred symbols of national birth — a project that George Bancroft would elevate into the sanctioned history of the republic, binding poetry and sermon to the machinery of state.

Bancroft was more than the most influential historian of his age — he remains the most influential historian of ours. He was the chief architect of the national origin story that still governs American self-understanding. Shaped by the German romantic nationalism he absorbed as a student in Göttingen, he brought to American history the same tools European nation-builders used to bind fractured states into a common identity: a unifying narrative, the language of divine destiny, and the erasure of dissenting pasts.

In Bancroft's hands, the Revolution was no longer one contested moment among many but a single, seamless, and inevitable chain of events — from colonization, to the Revolution, to the War for Independence, and finally to the Constitution — each step portrayed as the work of one people, with one will, guided by one God. This was not history as it had been lived; it was history as it needed to be remembered to serve the nationalist project. That memory could not tolerate ambiguity. Anything that blurred the line of inevitability — white loyalists, Black loyalists, the old revolutionaries who resisted the Constitution, even the fractures within the patriot cause itself — had to be removed or subordinated.

Bancroft didn't merely fuse patriot memory with divine purpose — he sanctified the very structures of authority the Revolution's most principled resisters had fought against. Slavery, in his telling, could be regretted, but only for its corrupting effect on white society; its place in the national story could still be justified as part of God's design — an evil destined to vanish in the fullness of America's manifest destiny. This was providentialism married to exceptionalism, producing a narrative in which the United States was not simply one nation among others but also the chosen beacon of liberty to the world — foreordained, infallible, and, above all, indivisible.

By casting the Revolution as the prelude to the nation's birth — rather than a struggle over conscience and rights — Bancroft ensured that the memory of resistance could be used to legitimize the state, not to challenge it. His version of the past did more than dominate the history books of his century; it still frames how Americans are taught to think about their founding, shutting down the possibility of true American resistance by defining the Revolution as a finished, flawless achievement rather than an unfinished, contested inheritance.

By the summer of 1846, the nationalist version of the Revolution was so complete that it was almost impossible to imagine it any other way. Emerson had sanctified Concord as holy ground, Hawthorne had turned patriotism into children's scripture, and Bancroft had written God into the nation's birthright. The Revolution was no longer the messy, uncertain "Revolution of '75" that Henry's family had lived, fought, and paid for — it was the "Spirit of '76," a single, unbroken arc from Lexington to Philadelphia, from war to Constitution, from independence to destiny. In that telling, the "men of '87" were not the younger generation who had hijacked the resistance and built their own authority into the bones of the Constitution but rather the inevitable heirs of liberty itself. And by the middle of the nineteenth century, that story had hardened into something far more dangerous: a mythology so total that it not only excused the state's abuses but also made changing them almost unthinkable. "In point of fact," a Massachusetts publisher wrote, "there is now no probability that the whole record of the revolution will ever be played. In America, we have heard but one version of the tale."

But by then, even John Quincy Adams had come to recognize that he had been wrong. After serving as a US senator, secretary of state, and the nation's sixth president, Adams was elected to the House of Representatives and entered Congress to fight against the enslavers' republic. He had come to see the Constitution as an instrument that had betrayed the Revolution's promise. In his House speeches against the gag rule, Adams insisted that the republic had become merely a cabal of states bound by a pro-slavery charter. But there was a Union that mattered more in the greater fellowship of people who had once risked everything for liberty: "The Constitution is a covenant with death, and an agreement with hell," abolitionists thundered, in a message that Adams carried forward. He conducted a three-week floor fight against Texas annexation in 1838 that powerfully cast the Constitution as corrupted rather than sacrosanct. He ultimately returned to his father's belief that the revolutionary principles of 1775 trumped the political choices of 1787. He concluded that "the indissoluble link of union between the people of the several states of this confederated nation, is after all, not in the right, but in the heart." Not in the Constitution, but in the deduction to the founding principles that should have guided it.

Sitting in the Concord jail for refusing to pay his poll tax, Thoreau saw it that way, too. He knew the difference between the fight his grandmother's family had waged against the patriots' coercion in 1775 and the government born in 1787 — a difference the nationalist myth was designed to erase. The real Revolution, the one that had lived in his family's conscience, was about resisting abusive authority wherever it appeared. The Constitution, and the political culture it created, had instead built that authority into law and wrapped it in legend. That was the danger of the "Spirit of '76": It was not merely a misremembered history but also a usable past — deployed to bind the present to the authority of the state and to sanctify obedience as a civic virtue. In *Civil Disobedience*, Thoreau would tear at that foundation, stripping away the patriotic pieties to expose the central fact his family had always known — that liberty of conscience demands resistance, and that any government requiring you to betray it forfeits its claim to your loyalty.

The Right to Refuse

After being released from jail, Thoreau went back to Walden Pond and began to think about the relationship of the individual to government, and the question of obedience. To what extent was a person's conscience entirely one's own, representing a majority of one? How much of the self did an individual have to give up to a government to be protected by its structures? Did one have to surrender one's conscience to government's priorities and deliver to it the resources it demanded, regardless of the purposes to which those resources were put? What if that government acted only in the interests of a few, or of a faction, in ways that violated the obligations that it owed to the people, especially in a government of, by, and for those people?

"Must the citizen ever for a moment, or in the least degree, resign his conscience to the legislator?" he wondered. "Why has every man a conscience, then?"

Those were the questions Thoreau carried back to his cabin, as he thought about what it meant to live deliberately. Drawing on his experience, his family's history, and his philosophy, he arrived at a pointed conclusion: "The only obligation which I have a right to assume is to do at any time what I think right."

Then, in early January 1848, word arrived at Hillside, the Concord home of the reforming educator and abolitionist Bronson Alcott, that Thoreau was going to speak at the Concord Lyceum on Sunday the 23rd on "The Relation of the Individual to the State." Alcott was enthusiastic about the question. He, too, had protested the state by not paying his taxes. He had refused its authority by providing his home as a stop on the emerging clandestine network that would come to be called the Underground Railroad, spiriting away enslaved people to Canada and freedom.

What was in his mind and those of his neighbors when they walked through the doors of the Unitarian church on that cold New England evening to hear the familiar voice of their eclectic friend? Whether they had heard about the speech given in Congress by a young representative from Illinois, Abraham Lincoln, condemning President Polk's justification for starting the war with Mexico, or read Frederick Douglass's January 21 editorial in *The North Star* demanding attention to that war, or even seen Ona Judge's published recollections of Washington only a year earlier — that is the wider context in which Thoreau rose to speak.

Thoreau met the moment, delivering the lecture that would eventually become *Civil Disobedience*.

"I heartily accept the motto 'That government is best which governs least,'" he began, repeating an old adage. But then he pivoted. "That government is best which governs not at all." Government was an expedient, a means to an end, "but most governments are usually, and all governments are sometimes, inexpedient." His implication was clear: Citizens should be governed by their conscience, not by an external, often inexpedient, force. The only end of government should be the good of the governed, not of the few who were elected to lead it.

But what happened when those elected few started to use the tools of government for their own ends? Thoreau pressed the precedent of the "revolution of '75," which had begun as a resistance against an abusive authority, raising questions of conscience on all sides in America. "All men recognize the right of revolution; that is, the right to refuse allegiance to, and to resist, the government, when its tyranny or its inefficiency are great and unendurable."

Just look at what the patriots did, he argued, and for a cause that amounted to an annoyance. Taxation without representation is, all other things being equal, an annoyance, not an existential threat, and yet the patriots of old were willing to go to war over it, to destroy their relationship with their government, their neighbors, and their families over it. They thought that was sufficient grounds for a resistance to become a rebellion, as the revolution of 1775 became the rebellion of Washington and Franklin.

But the "men of '87," in Thoreau's terms, turned the promise of that revolution into something else, something sinister. As more and more writers and speakers, from Douglass to John Quincy Adams, were exclaiming, following on the criticisms of the "Old Revolutionaries" in the debates over the ratification of the Constitution, the document that emerged out of the Philadelphia convention had run roughshod over the resistance principles that had driven the Revolution. In its operation, as Ona Judge's experience revealed, the enslavers at the top could further abuse the authority they gained from the people to advance their interests.

And they continued to abuse it, with increasing severity and barbarity against the chained part of the population. Thoreau charged that now they had expanded that abuse to deploy, for the first time, the most coercive arms of the state — its army and its revenue — to serve their narrow agenda, one that every day made laughable the claims of the revolution of '75 and its supposed accomplishments.

At what point was resistance legitimate? If it could be deployed over the annoyances of taxation in 1775, what about the abuses of the government against all the vast majority of Americans' broader interests in 1848?

Thoreau drove the point home to his audience seated in the pew boxes before him by comparing the grievances directly. While most of his contemporaries believed the conditions for revolution did not exist in their time, they certainly thought "such was the case . . . in the Revolution of '75." But he dismissed the tax on foreign commodities that sparked that conflict, noting that if he were living through it, "it is most probable that I should not make an ado about it, for I can do without them." Frankly, he argued, the point at which the patriots drew their line was, at most, an inconvenience, and the friction caused by their resistance as productive of bad things as of good. "At any rate," he leveled, "it is a great evil to make a stir about it."

And yet, look at the moment in which he and his audience were living. Their government, captured by the interests that constructed it, was supposed to be the mode through which "the people have chosen to execute their will." Instead it was now "equally liable to be abused and perverted before the people can act through it." The war in Mexico was all the proof one needed. It was "the work of comparatively a few individuals using the standing government as their tool; for, in the outset, the people would not have consented to this measure." Compare that with the mere "friction" that was the basis of the American Revolution. Think deeply about that, he urged, "when a sixth of the population of a nation which has undertaken to be the refuge of liberty are slaves, and a whole country is unjustly overrun and conquered by a foreign army [the United States Army invasion of Mexico], and subjected to military law."

But Thoreau was only warming to his message. That was just the structure of American government. What of the practice in its sixty years of operation? Where was the path for change and correction, especially when it came to injustice? "Its very Constitution is the evil," he stated. So "as for adopting the ways which the State has provided for remedying the evil, I know not of such ways."

American democratic culture had developed troublesome traits in the emergence of rituals that conditioned deference toward its founding institutions. The accepted forms of protest and petition favored incremental reform. "They take too much time, and a man's life will be gone," he said. Life was meant to be lived, not wasted away, with the hope that the world would someday become a better place.

And yet the state had provided no effective way to bring about change. Even voting, by both the electorate and its elected representatives, was a hollow act. "All voting is a sort of gaming, like checkers or backgammon, with a slight moral tinge to it, a playing with right and wrong," he wrote. Instead, "a wise man will not leave the right to the mercy of chance, nor wish it to prevail through the power of the majority."

All of it seemed empty, especially in the face of real change when it was required. People were in chains. Dying. Being robbed. Only to serve the economic interests of a narrow few, and directly in opposition to the supposed principles of the country.

Yet what did people do when they felt a law or governmental action was wrong? Vote against it. Maybe even protest against it. And then go home. Have dinner. Read the newspaper. Go to bed. Feel like they had done their part in a democracy. And wake up the next morning with the same horror having been perpetuated for yet another day because they were unwilling to go any further than that. "They hesitate, and they regret, and sometimes they petition," he charged from the church's pulpit, "but they do nothing in earnest and with effect."

People's compliance, Thoreau argued, made them agents of the state's crimes, for "Law never made men a whit more just; and, by means of their respect for it, even the well-disposed are daily made the agents of injustice."

What was the limit? Thoreau drew a hard, bright line between the "revolution of '75," which he understood as a living principle of conscience against abusive authority, and the compromised state built by the "men of '87." The first was an act of moral necessity; the second was a political arrangement designed to manage dissent and protect its own structural injustices.

The Constitution, in his reading, was not the fulfillment of the revolution but rather its containment. Its framework enshrined slavery and conquest while creating channels of "reform" that were designed to fail. When the state's very machinery is organized for injustice, then the precedent of '75 becomes a present duty. In such a moment, he declared, it is "not too soon for honest men to rebel and revolutionize."

But American democratic culture, he argued, had emerged and developed to insulate the Constitution. The comfortable American voter was anesthetized by it into a kind of political inertia that deadened their principles, content allowing injustices to be committed by their government so long as the performance of democracy made them feel as if their voice was somehow heard in the process.

He reserved special scorn for the thousands who claimed to oppose slavery and the war but who "in effect do nothing to put an end to them; who, esteeming themselves children of Washington and Franklin, sit down with their hands in their pockets, and say that they know not what to do, and do nothing." These were the people who would "wait, well disposed, for others to remedy the evil, that they may no longer have it to regret. At most, they give only a cheap vote, and a feeble countenance and God-speed, to the right, as it goes by them."

Reform, moreover, was actually big business, he charged. "We love better to talk about it; that we say is our mission. Reform keeps many scores of newspapers in its service, but not one man."

And America's lawyers and politicians were agents of inertia, enemies of change. Look at Daniel Webster, he told the Lyceum crowd. Their aging US senator from Massachusetts reveled in talking about policies that suggested change, joining the vast majority of reformers who offered little but "cheap professions."

What such men preached was not wisdom, but prudence. To Thoreau, Webster was no leader but merely a follower of those men of '87. He pointed to Webster's own words defending the Constitution's sanctioning of slavery: He could not think of anything that would "disturb the arrangement as originally made, by which the various states came into the Union," even if that was an evil bargain.

Most Americans had come to accept that in their political culture, the men of '87 were to be defended at all costs. But the absurdity of such a position was made plain when you considered that, as Webster admitted, this meant the framers needed to be deferred to even when it came to slavery, "because it was a part of the original compact — let it stand."

Despite all of Webster's supposed ability, Thoreau noted, neither he nor his reformer compatriots could bring themselves to consider the central moral issue of the Constitution separate from the mere political architecture that scaffolded it. Knowing "of no purer sources of truth," they simply went to the Bible and the Constitution and stopped there, "with reverence and humility."

But for those who could see where truth "comes trickling into this lake or that pool," Thoreau argued, the journey past those documents was a moral necessity.

The primary moral duty, then, he stressed to his audience, is not to persuade the majority or to patiently work for reform from within but to immediately withdraw from the machinery of injustice. To cast a ballot or pay a tax to a government that wages unjust wars and protects slavery is to become an agent of that very injustice. But "any man more right than his neighbors," he said, echoing the experience of his family in Weston, "constitutes a majority of one."

Yet people remained in chains, soldiers were being sent to die, another country was being taken over and destroyed. Was that what the revolution of '75 was all about? No. But it might well have been what the men of '87 had in mind. And it was why the government they created not only allowed it but also enabled it.

So according to Thoreau, what are the options? Resistance, pure and simple, drawing on the lessons of the old revolutionaries. "Action from principle — the perception and the performance of right — changes things and relations; it is essentially revolutionary," he argued.

Leave behind empty reform and take steps outside the comfortable, permitted channels that only anesthetize the governed. It's not enough to know that one is right against injustice and then go to sleep, comfortable in that knowledge. That knowledge must be paired with action.

And the first step in that principled action must be the refusal of abusive authority, especially in a democracy that takes its authority from the consent of the governed. At the very least, do not be complicit in the perpetuation of the wrong.

Thoreau said on that Sunday evening, "It is not a man's duty, as a matter of course, to devote himself to the eradication of any, even the most enormous, wrong . . . but it is his duty, at least, to wash his hands of it, and, if he gives it no thought longer, not to give it practically his support." This is the entry point of all resistance. Not the dramatic act, not the confrontation with armed authority, not the clandestine network or the raid. Just this: Stop making it easier for abusive authority to function. Stop providing the resources, the legitimacy, the silent acquiescence that lets the machine run smoothly.

And then take the next step, whatever form that takes, but let it be effective. "If the injustice is part of the necessary friction of the machine of government, let it go," he said, "but if it is of such a nature that it requires you to be the agent of injustice to another, then, I say, break the law. Let your life be a counter-friction to stop the machine."

But suppose blood should flow? It was already flowing. "Is there not a sort of blood shed when the conscience is wounded?" he asked his audience.

Thoreau, of course, wanted to be a good, quiet, patient citizen. He yearned to live in a country where the government took the work of correcting gross injustice out of his hands.

If one looks at the Constitution from a point of ignorance, he instructed the assembled crowd, the Constitution "with all its faults, is very good; the law and the courts are very respectable; even this State and this American government are, in many respects, very admirable and rare things."

But his neighbors before him were educated, informed, and perceptive. He pressed them on what the Constitution and the American government looked like from a knowledgeable, more aware point of view. Might they then not be "worth looking at or thinking of at all"?

Thoreau allowed that the revolution of '75 got much right and acknowledged that Americans loved to associate themselves with it and its heroes. But, Thoreau charged, most Americans did not understand that the men of '87 robbed the nation of much of what that revolution achieved and constructed instead a government that perpetuated and strengthened injustice, in a perverse way, in their name.

And that led to a political culture — traditions and practices and performances, from voting to permitted forms of opposition — that insulated it from the change that was required to move it back to its revolutionary principles.

Far from John Quincy Adams's 1821 celebration of America as carrying the beacon of freedom to other nations, the reality was, in Thoreau's eyes, an enslavers' republic that expanded oppression at the point of a bayonet.

His analysis that night was conditioned by Thoreau's understanding of his own family's experience. He could appreciate the symbolism of Washington and Franklin, which he invoked, while knowing the stories of Ona Judge and of the loyalists.

"There will never be a really free and enlightened State," Thoreau argued, "until the State comes to recognize the individual as a higher and independent power, from which all its own power and authority are derived, and treats him accordingly."

He yearned to live deliberately, which is what he wrote about in *Walden*. But he couldn't do so if his government was using his taxes to take life from or deny freedom to others.

Reformers, incrementalists, were, to Thoreau, just another arm of the abusive state.

That was his message. Not nonviolence. Not peaceful protest. But principled action.

Those are the ideas that Bronson Alcott and their neighbors took with them into the dark, cold Concord night. That's what became *Civil Disobedience*, the resistance playbook born of American history and American experience.

Reflecting on the forces that had put him in jail, Thoreau pressed home the fact that reform was not possible given America's compromised founding institutions and the political culture that had emerged to protect them. The First Republic, born in hypocrisy and fortified by the framers of the Constitution — those he derisively called the men of '87 — had only deepened its foundations of inequality as it grew. Expansion had carried those dynamics westward, binding the nation's future to slavery and conquest. The political machinery had hardened to make the most urgent change not just improbable but structurally impossible.

Refusal, for Thoreau, was not the end of resistance — it was the beginning. To withdraw consent was to clear the ground, to strip authority of its legitimacy, to force it to reveal the coercion beneath its laws. What came after depended on the scale of the wrong and the depth of the state's entrenchment. If slavery, war, and the Constitution itself stood in the way, then strong measures might be not only justified but also required.

Closing — The Inheritance of Action

Two jail terms, seventy years apart. Josiah Jones in 1775, locked up in Concord for refusing to bow to the patriot committees; Henry Thoreau in 1846, locked up in the same town for refusing to fund a war of conquest and a state that protected slavery. Different causes, different regimes, but the same act: standing on conscience in the face of authority that demanded surrender.

For both men, the point was not protest for its own sake. It was the refusal to legitimize an authority that had already broken faith with the governed. For Jones, that authority was the patriot movement in its coercive, purging phase — no longer defending liberty, but enforcing orthodoxy. For Thoreau, it was the American state born of the men of '87, built to protect its own power and unwilling to change when justice demanded it. Neither man mistook obedience for order, or legality for morality.

The resistance principle they embodied was not just practical — it was moral. It begins with the belief that ideas and values matter, that they might matter more than anything else. Conscience is not a private ornament; it is a public obligation. When power demands that you violate your own conscience, your first duty is to refuse — and refusal is only the beginning. Resistance, in this view, is not limited to what is permissible but expands to what is necessary. That clarity of principle — rooted in the lived experience of the Revolution's resistance phase and sharpened against the hard edges of the republic's betrayals — gave Thoreau's thought its enduring force.

Civil Disobedience promotes the essence of American resistance, in practice and in principle: born from the rise of the republic in response to its particular challenges but universal enough to be embraced across the world and into our own century. Thoreau did not offer a single tactic or doctrine but rather a way of thinking: Resistance must be anchored in moral truth and pursued by whatever means that truth demands. The clarity of this principle has been claimed by movements from Gandhi's campaigns in India to anti-colonial struggles in Africa, from Eastern Bloc dissidents to Martin Luther King, Jr. *Civil Disobedience* does not prescribe nonviolence. Rather, it demands that every act of resistance be honest about its purpose and willing to bear its cost. This is the legacy that Thoreau's grandmother established when she helped her brother escape from unjust incarceration in Concord: refusal to yield to a power that has forfeited its legitimacy.

The republic that Thoreau challenged has changed its shape, but not its nature. It still wraps itself in the rhetoric of liberty while concentrating power, still demands loyalty to its myths while punishing those who question them, and still mistakes its survival for the survival of what's right in a world that still relies on the consent of the governed. All around us, the same pattern repeats — states invoking history, tradition, or security to justify abuses, and citizens left to decide whether to comply, to protest within approved boundaries, or to resist outside of the tolerated pathways.

Thoreau's conclusion that the last option is the only one that can reclaim both personal integrity and public possibility is the essence of American resistance, but it is not bound by America's borders. It has been taken up in struggles far from Concord, in languages and contexts Thoreau never knew, by people who understood what he did: that no authority is beyond challenge when it commands the violation of conscience, and few tactics are out of bounds in pursuit of justice. The test of our time is whether we will carry that legacy forward — not as an artifact of the past, but as a living principle for whatever comes next.

Josiah Jones and Henry Thoreau refused to bend to authorities that demanded the surrender of conscience, and both paid for it in the currency of resistance: their freedom. Between their stays in jail lies the transformation of the revolution of '75 into the nation's founding myth, a story recast to sanctify the very structures the original resistance would have opposed. By 1846, Thoreau could see that the men of '87 had not fulfilled the Revolution but instead replaced it, hardwiring injustice into the Constitution and clothing it in the language of permanence.

From that recognition came the resistance principle at the heart of *Civil Disobedience*: Ideas and values matter — perhaps more than anything else — and refusing to serve injustice is the starting point of any meaningful opposition capable of achieving the change it seeks. It is a principle born from the contradictions of the First Republic, sharpened by the failures of its institutions, and carried forward by those willing to do whatever it takes to defend the ground of conscience.

CHAPTER SEVEN

The Unbreakable Chain

Resistance Principle #7: When authority criminalizes conscience, individual acts of defiance must evolve into organized networks. The more total the system of oppression, the more sophisticated the resistance infrastructure required to defeat it.

BOSTON FEDERAL COURT, FALL 1851

Robert Morris was born in Salem, Massachusetts, the town of the Unconfessed. His father had been enslaved; his mother was born free. Infused with a deep, even environmental understanding of injustice, Morris studied law under a white Boston attorney and was admitted to the bar in 1847 — one of the first Black men in America to become a practicing attorney. But only four years later, he found himself on the other side of a trial as he sat at the defendant's table in the federal courthouse in Boston. Why? He had taken a stand against injustice, helping to deploy a clandestine resistance network that functioned to refuse the authority of the First Republic to return men and women to slavery. Just nine months earlier, Morris had helped rescue Shadrach Minkins from the same building, even the same room. Morris was part of a legal team representing Minkins, who had fled to Boston after escaping slavery in Virginia and then had been seized under the 1850 Fugitive Slave Act by federal marshals posing as customers at the coffeehouse where he worked. Morris and Minkins's other attorneys filed a writ of habeas corpus for Minkins's release from police custody, but they were denied. So Morris and two other Black activists took matters into their own hands, freeing Minkins from the custody of the marshals by force and spiriting him away.

Now Morris faced federal prosecution for that act — charged with violating the Fugitive Slave Act for his role in what Secretary of State Daniel Webster had branded "strictly speaking, a case of treason."

The courtroom that had witnessed Minkins's seizure now hosted Morris's trial. His defense attorneys, Richard Henry Dana, Jr., and John Parker Hale, faced a government determined to prove that resistance networks could be broken through prosecutions. The stakes were national. President Millard Fillmore had ordered these prosecutions to confirm that the North would submit to the enslavers' law. Southern papers demanded convictions. Webster's political future hung on enforcing the compromise he had helped craft. And across from Morris sat a jury that would decide whether the Underground Railroad's infrastructure could survive federal assault.

This wasn't Morris's first trial for his involvement in the Minkins rescue. The government's first attempt to convict him had ended in a hung jury when one juror refused to enforce the Fugitive Slave Act. Now, with Justice George T. Curtis presiding — the same federal commissioner who had issued the arrest warrant for Shadrach Minkins — prosecutors were confident they could secure a conviction that would cripple Boston's resistance network.

What they couldn't anticipate was that the trials themselves would expose exactly how sophisticated that network had become — and how deep its community protection ran.

Public reaction to the rescue of Shadrach Minkins in February 1851 was explosive, but the real revelation with national implications came in the trials that followed. When federal prosecutors indicted nine men for the rescue, they exposed something the government didn't want to acknowledge: The Underground Railroad wasn't a loose collection of good-hearted abolitionists who impulsively aided individual fugitives when the opportunities presented themselves. It was a sophisticated, clandestine resistance network that had been systematically defeating federal law enforcement for decades.

The numbers tell the story of the resistance organizing and resources that had been brought to bear. As many as one hundred thousand enslaved people made it out of slavery without getting caught because they were moving through a disciplined resistance infrastructure — one so effective that we still don't fully understand how it worked.

That operational secrecy wasn't an accident. It was the network's greatest achievement.

What these trials inadvertently revealed wasn't just the Underground Railroad's existence — it was the architecture of effective resistance itself, principles that transcend any single moment or movement.

The network succeeded through functional specialization that created operational efficiency beyond what individual heroics could ever achieve. Morris handled legal challenges, filing writs and mounting defenses. Hayden managed safe house operations from his Beacon Hill fortress. Scott provided logistics, moving people and resources. Coburn commanded security forces. Wright shaped public opinion through his newspaper. Each member had specific expertise, specific responsibilities, specific roles. This wasn't romantic improvisation — it was a disciplined organization where everyone knew their part and played it with precision.

But knowing your part didn't mean knowing everyone else's. The network's compartmentalization protected the whole operation from any single point of failure. When federal agents arrested Morris, he couldn't reveal routes he didn't know. When they questioned Hayden, he couldn't name contacts he'd never met. Each operator understood their role without exposing the complete network. The government couldn't roll up the entire infrastructure because no single arrest, no matter how significant, revealed all the connections. This was operational discipline.

The network's greatest weapon was what it refused to reveal. Even today, after decades of scholarship, after historians have combed through trial records and personal papers and newspaper accounts, we still don't know precisely how the Underground Railroad coordinated operations across hundreds of miles and thousands of participants. We know it worked — the results prove that — but the methods remain largely hidden. This enduring secrecy isn't a failure of the historical record. It's proof of resistance discipline that protected operations and operators alike, a silence so complete that it still guards the activists' secrets nearly two centuries later.

In the end results, not documentation, are the measure of success. The Underground Railroad didn't write reports or keep minutes or create organizational charts that prosecutors could seize. They delivered freedom — actual, permanent, life-changing freedom — and they did it again and again, year after year, despite the full weight of the First Republic trying to stop them.

The enslavers' regime put the network on trial and lost — not just in court, but in the larger battle for control. With lives and livelihoods on the line, the network held throughout the courtroom challenges. Aided by enough community support on juries to thwart convictions, trial after trial ended in hung juries or acquittals. Morris walked free. Hayden beat the charges. Scott was acquitted. Wright escaped conviction. By year's end, the government had secured nothing but humiliation.

Every acquittal proved that clandestine resistance could defeat federal authority when it combined sophisticated organization with disciplined secrecy. This wasn't luck. This was the predictable result when a resistance network is properly built and protected by its community.

That's the standard for effective resistance, then and now: not the stories we can tell afterward, but the concrete results we can deliver while the network operates. The Underground Railroad's greatest monument can't be found in any museum or historic tourist site. It's in the operational methods that remain hidden. The principles that the Minkins trial exposed — specialization, compartmentalization, operational security, results over recognition — aren't historical artifacts. They're the timeless architecture of resistance, as relevant today as they were when Robert Morris sat in that defendant's chair, knowing that Shadrach Minkins was already safe, beyond the reach of any federal marshal.

What made this network possible — what transformed it from a desperate scramble into a disciplined operation — was something the federal prosecutors couldn't touch: Minkins was safe in Montreal. He had reached Canada, where American law was powerless, where the Union flag meant freedom, where the First Republic could not follow.

The network hadn't just moved him from danger to danger within the same hostile system. It had delivered him to genuine sanctuary, beyond the reach of the republic that claimed to own him.

But sophisticated networks don't emerge overnight. The Underground Railroad's disciplined infrastructure and community protection were responses to an escalating threat — a federal law so extreme that it transformed scattered acts of individual conscience into organized, systematic resistance. And that transformation was only possible because there was somewhere to go.

The Northern Star: How Canada Became Freedom

Understanding the Underground Railroad requires understanding its endpoint. Resistance networks only function when they can reliably remove people from the reach of abusive authority — not just relocate them within the same system of control. The Fugitive Slave Act of 1793 had already demonstrated that "free" states offered no real sanctuary; federal law enabled those entrusted with it, such as George Washington, to abuse their authority by reaching anywhere within American jurisdiction to drag people back into bondage. What transformed isolated escapes into a sustained resistance network was the emergence of a genuine terminus: British territory where American slave law held no power.

For clandestine networks to scale up, they needed more than individual courage — they required that fixed point beyond American reach. Without it, the Underground Railroad would have been merely an internal relocation system, moving people from one precarious situation to another within the same hostile jurisdiction. As Ona Judge's interviewer reminded readers of *The Liberator* in 1847, she remained a fugitive in New Hampshire, forever under threat from Martha Washington's heirs.

That destination began to take shape beyond the Northern border, where Canada emerged as a haven through three decisive moments:

a legal breakthrough in 1793, wartime acceleration during the War of 1812, and legal ratification in 1819. Each step was driven by enslaved people themselves, whose resistance forced the law to catch up with the freedom they seized.

The first breakthrough came when one woman — Chloe Cooley — refused to submit.

What we know about Chloe Cooley has to be pieced together from what we know about her enslavers. She had been claimed as property by Benjamin Hardison, a patriot from Maine who was captured in the siege of Quebec at the end of 1775. Hardison liked Canada so much that he remained there after his release, becoming a major property owner — and an enslaver — in Fort Erie. At some point in the early 1790s, Hardison sold Chloe to Adam Vrooman, a white loyalist from New York. But Vrooman, like many enslavers in Upper Canada after the Revolutionary War, saw the beginning of the end of slavery there. Perhaps sensing that, too, Chloe had for some time engaged in day-to-day resistance, rendering her a troublesome property for Vrooman. So he decided to cash out to the only place that slavery's future could be depended upon – across the Niagara River in New York.

Upper Canada's 1793 Act to Limit Slavery emerged directly from Chloe Cooley's refusal to submit to Vrooman.

On March 14, 1793, Vrooman and two men tied Cooley with rope, forced her into a boat, and began dragging her across the Niagara River to sell her in the United States.

Cooley fought back. Her screams echoed across the water and reached Peter Martin, a free Black loyalist veteran who had served with Vrooman in the war against the patriots. Martin took the incident straight to Lieutenant Governor John Graves Simcoe — the same officer who had carried away Isaac Jefferson's family during the Revolutionary War, the same commander who had witnessed free Black communities fighting the patriots. Simcoe had seen enough. The result was the first legislation in the British Empire to limit slavery and halt its importation, passed only four months after Chloe was kidnapped.

The law's true impact wasn't in its carefully worded clauses but instead in the simplified, potent idea that spread through resistance networks: The British in Canada were taking a stand against slavery. The timing created a stark moral geography for anyone seeking freedom. In 1793, while the United States Congress passed the Fugitive Slave Act — legally extending enslaver power through slave catchers — Canada took a step to end slavery. Chloe might have disappeared forever into the slavery of the First Republic, but her legacy is safe in the freedom realized by so many in Canada.

The contrast created a fundamental shift in presumptions, regardless of legal specifics: In the United States, a Black person was presumed enslaved. In Canada, a Black person was presumed free. That distinction made all the difference.

If the Act to Limit Slavery of 1793 in Upper Canada had set a distant stage for change, the War of 1812 broadcast the divide between American bondage and British-held freedom in the starkest possible terms. For almost thirty years, the stories of the Black loyalists who had won their freedom by siding with the British during the Revolution had circulated through the slave quarters of the South. After a generation, those stories had hardened into legend, a political and geographical map to an alternative future. They constituted a usable past, a form of intellectual resistance that kept the hope of another world alive against a system designed to extinguish it.

The outbreak of war offered violent, tangible proof that another world might exist just beyond America's borders.

Enslaved people did not wait for formal invitations, abolitionist pamphlets, or British proclamations to understand and seize the moment. When British warships first appeared in the Chesapeake Bay in 1812 and 1813, they were met by a phenomenon for which they were unprepared. Under the cover of night, in stolen skiffs and dugout canoes, enslaved people in surprising numbers began escaping from the tobacco plantations of Virginia and Maryland, making their way to the British fleet.

On April 2, 1814, Vice Admiral Alexander Cochrane followed in Sir

Henry Clinton's strategic footsteps from 1779, issuing a proclamation to formalize the British policy of offering freedom to enslaved people who could reach their lines. Cochrane's offer gave a real choice to all those who might "be disposed to emigrate from the United States": either "enter into His Majesty's Sea or Land Forces, or be sent as FREE settlers to the British Possessions in North America or the West Indies."

Thousands took the deal. From Chesapeake plantations to Deep South cotton fields, they abandoned everything they couldn't carry and headed for British ships. They had learned to read the geopolitical moment better than most diplomats, and they had a resistance precedent to draw on — America's enemies were their potential allies, and wars created cracks in the system wide enough to slip through.

The exodus of some five thousand "Black Refugees" between 1812 and 1814 did more than any law to cement Canada's reputation as a sanctuary. Their presence renewed the promise that had drawn the Black loyalists a generation earlier, and the numbers created an undeniable reality. This was mass resistance reshaping the political landscape.

When thousands of newly freed people poured into Nova Scotia and Upper Canada, they didn't wait for official welcome committees or government assistance that would never come. Despite facing the familiar trinity of neglect, discrimination, and worthless land grants, they built what they had always built: community. They founded churches, opened schools, formed mutual aid societies. They created the social building blocks that survival demanded.

Those legions of free Black people were living, breathing advertisements for British superiority over American barbarism. Every church they built, every family they raised, every acre they farmed became evidence that the British system worked where the American experiment failed.

As a result, British officials found themselves trapped by their own rhetoric. You can't celebrate people as proof of British liberty on Tuesday and ship them back to American slavery on Wednesday. The contradictions were too obvious, the politics too messy. The 1793 Act Against Slavery had established a principle, but the presence of thousands of formerly enslaved people made the abstract concrete.

By 1819, the reality on the ground was forcing anyone responsible for enforcing the law into making choices. American enslavers and their agents were pursuing the thousands who had found freedom across the border. This created a crisis for Canadian courts and law enforcement: Whose authority applied? How far could the enslavers go? Moreover, from a geopolitical perspective, cooperating with US authorities would mean forfeiting a great propaganda victory. When Upper Canada's attorney general, John Beverley Robinson, was asked whether American bounty hunters could enter Canada to recover human property and whether Upper Canada should help stop them, the questions demanded definitive answers.

His response was clear: *no* to American slave catching and *yes* to Canadian protection of Black freedom.

Robinson's reasoning built directly on the Somerset Rule. Following English laws, Black people in Canada were people, not property, in any way, shape, or form. Therefore, "freedom of the person being the most important civil right protected by those laws, it follows that whatever may have been the condition of these Negroes in the Country to which they formerly belonged, here they are free."

Robinson went further, making Canadian courts the active guardians of Black freedom. Any attempt to interfere with the civil rights of Black people in Canada "would most probably call for, and could compel the interference of those to whom the administration of our Laws is committed." Not only couldn't the slave catchers depend on the help of Canadian authorities, but they would also be liable to prosecution for violating the civil rights of their targets.

It's worth asking how much of Robinson's opinion was shaped by his own place in resistance history, one stretching back to the world of Nancy Dixon. His father, Christopher, had been a student in Williamsburg at the College of William and Mary, just down Duke of Gloucester Street from where Nancy lived. In 1781, just after she went to the British lines, Christopher Robinson joined Simcoe's Queen's Rangers, taking a commission vacated when Charles Jones — Thoreau's great-uncle — was killed in battle days before. The loyalist networks that scattered to Canada after their defeat had positioned their children to reject American authority entirely. While Robinson would, a decade later, refine his holding to exclude self-emancipated Black people subject to formal extradition because they were also accused of a crime, the basic principle remained what *Somerset* had established in 1772, that all Black people were presumed free and entitled to the same protection of the law as anyone else.

Then came 1833 and the British Parliament's Slavery Abolition Act, which declared slavery illegal throughout the entire British Empire, effective August 1, 1834. The news traveled fast — faster than most official dispatches — carried by ship captains, newspaper editors, and the underground information networks that already connected Black communities across the Atlantic world.

For Canada, there wasn't much practical impact. By 1833, slavery had largely disappeared from British North America — the 1831 census recorded only a few hundred enslaved people in all the provinces combined, most of them elderly or already transitioning to freedom under various provincial laws.

But for the hundreds of thousands still in chains south of the border, the Abolition Act was a thunderclap. Here was the clearest possible proof that freedom was not a utopian dream but a legal reality, one that began the moment an enslaved person crossed an invisible line on the ground. No longer could enslavers seek to dissuade people from fleeing northward to emancipate themselves by dismissing Canada as a cold, distant refuge where freedom was uncertain. Now it was a place where the British Crown itself guaranteed that bondage was not just illegal but impossible.

The news rippled through enslaved communities with electric speed. Kitchen conversations, Sunday gatherings, and late-night whispers in quarters carried the same wondrous message: Slavery was dead in every territory flying the Union flag. For people whose entire lives had been defined by the supposedly permanent fact of their bondage, this was revelatory intelligence. Freedom wasn't just possible — it was waiting, protected by the world's most powerful government.

By 1837, that guarantee had been tested and proved. When a group of Kentucky enslavers arrived in Niagara, demanding the return of a man named Solomon Moseby, Canadian authorities didn't just refuse — they mobilized to protect Moseby. A crowd of hundreds of Black residents and white allies surrounded the jail where Moseby was being held while lawyers argued his case in court. The message was unmistakable: Canadian freedom was real, and it would be held.

Beyond just creating a destination, the Abolition Act also established an external base where resistance could operate openly. This was the crucial missing piece that transformed individual escapes into a coordinated network. When Henry Bibb began publishing *The Voice of the Fugitive* from Windsor, Ontario, he wasn't hiding in someone's basement — he was operating a newspaper that openly coordinated escape routes, published detailed intelligence about safe passages, and raised funds for clandestine operations. From Canadian soil, Bibb could do what no one south of the border dared: advertise resistance.

This reliable terminus gave the Underground Railroad its essential character as a resistance network. Like the escape routes that moved downed pilots and Jews beyond Nazi reach, it worked because it actually removed people from the sphere of abusive authority. For the networks that would emerge to guide people to freedom, there was no ambiguity about the goal — Canada wasn't just a hiding place, it was a new home.

The Building Pressure: From Constitution to Crisis

Understanding how the Underground Railroad became necessary requires understanding the escalating conflict between an expanding slave regime and the growing resistance to it. From the moment Washington signed the Fugitive Slave Act of 1793, establishing federal machinery to hunt down people like Ona Judge, the battle lines were drawn. What followed over the next half century was a steady intensification of that conflict as each act of resistance met a more brutal response, each compromise proved more morally bankrupt than the last.

Black resistance, especially the self-emancipation of enslaved people during the Revolution, presented a practical challenge and moral conflict for Thoreau's "men of '87" — the architects of the Constitution. Madison himself argued at the Virginia ratifying convention that the Constitution's fugitive-slave clause was a direct response to Black loyalists escaping with the British. This federal power to reclaim Black people who had freed themselves was not inherited from the Confederation or British rule; it was a radical new assertion of federal authority designed specifically to deny freedom to Black people while supposedly securing liberty for white people.

The pattern of federal overreach was set early. When Pennsylvania's gradual abolition law threatened to free the Washingtons' enslaved people, the first president didn't respect the law — he conspired to evade it through illegal rotations. When Ona escaped anyway, he deployed federal officials in a personal vendetta to reclaim her. That wasn't an isolated incident but instead a preview of how the enslavers' republic would operate: using federal power to protect slavery while claiming to respect states' rights, deploying legal machinery while operating outside the law.

The Hartford Convention of 1814–15 marked a recognition of this betrayal. Men who had been part of the genuine resistance against British authority in New England in the 1770s were now organizing resistance against American authority that served the enslavers. And they brought credibility to that fight. Samuel Ward had served as an officer in the 1st Rhode Island Regiment through much of the Revolutionary War. Nathan Dane had written and introduced the ban on slavery that made it into the Northwest Ordinance of 1787. William Prescott's father had distinguished himself at Bunker Hill. And Harrison Gray Otis was the nephew of Mercy Otis Warren, a staunch patriot and member of the Anti-Federalist resistance against the original Constitution. In their eyes, there was no time to lose for "mighty efforts to rescue from ruin, at least some portion of our beloved country." Their primary target? The three-fifths clause had given the enslavers control, inflating their representation enough to dominate presidential elections and maintain their grip on the executive branch for twenty of the republic's first twenty-four years. Of the seven amendments to the Constitution that the Hartford Convention proposed, erasing the three-fifths clause was at the top of the list. But it failed.

Thirteen years later, in 1828, news of Andrew Jackson's landslide victory in his rematch with incumbent John Quincy Adams engulfed the country in a wave of American patriotism, solidifying a populist sentiment that the hand of God was seemingly involved in directing the affairs of the United States. The powerful infusion of nationalism interrupted, and not for the first time, any discussion that the founding documents could be touched. Enslavers, including Jackson, would go on to control the White House for thirty-three of the next forty-seven years, and the Supreme Court for the entire period, until the Civil War.

In just five years, the Missouri Crisis revealed how completely the enslavers had captured the federal government. When Missouri applied to enter the Union as a slave state, the enslavers didn't argue the merits — they threatened the Union. Henry Clay, an enslaver himself, dressed up his first surrender as a "compromise" to just hand them what they wanted: Missouri as a slave state, a line across the continent promising slavery's expansion, and the precedent that the Constitution's survival mattered more than the Declaration's promises.

Jacksonian America was marked by an acceleration of the country's slide into nationalist mythology. The country's emerging narrative of itself followed a divinely inspired "manifest destiny" to spread democracy — insofar as white, male America was willing to allow it — across the continent. At the same time, the exclusionary republican political institutions created by the founders were being rebranded, without any change to their structure or function, as key elements of an American identity, rooted in the sort of democracy that would have churned James Madison's stomach.

Alexis de Tocqueville observed the evolving version of America in the early 1830s, noting that the mythology was dramatically shaping how white, male Americans saw themselves — and didn't see how their view was at odds with their political reality. As American democratic political culture evolved into a shield for its anti-democratic political institutions, and its entrenched abuse of the authority it claimed from the consent of the governed, meaningful change was pushed into a practical impossibility. The performance of American democracy, projecting an image of equality, drowned out any chance of making either a reality.

In 1834, when British abolition exposed American slavery's isolation on the world stage, American intellectuals doubled down on exceptionalist mythology. George Bancroft began publishing his *History of the United States* that same year, proclaiming that Americans had "the precedence in the practice and the defence of the equal rights of men." The louder America declared itself the world's beacon of freedom, the more aggressively it was restricting who could access that freedom — and the more people noticed the glaring gap between rhetoric and reality.

The response from Capitol Hill was the gag rule — a blanket ban on even hearing anti-slavery petitions. John Quincy Adams, who reentered Congress as a representative from Massachusetts after losing the presidency to Jackson, recognized it for what it was: "the first step on the part of the slave power to extend their dominion over the free states." His eight-year fight against it was about whether the Constitution could survive as anything more than a slaveholders' charter.

The 1837 murder of Elijah Lovejoy crystallized the reality of America's dominant political culture. The abolitionist editor was shot down by a pro-slavery mob while defending his fourth printing press in Alton, Illinois. The resistance press itself was being silenced by mob violence that the state refused to stop.

In 1842, the Supreme Court delivered *Prigg v. Pennsylvania*, striking down state protections for free Black people and ruling that federal authority over slavery was absolute. Justice Joseph Story's decision made clear that the Constitution's slavery clauses were active commands that every state and citizen must obey.

William Lloyd Garrison embodied the growing recognition that the Constitution itself was the enemy, literally burning copies while arguing that it was the embodiment of the enslavers' republic. The American Anti-Slavery Society proclaimed, LET THE CONSTITUTION PERISH. Garrison echoed with NO UNION WITH SLAVEHOLDERS.

The Mexican-American War brought these contradictions to their breaking point. Here was the enslavers' republic deploying federal armies not to defend liberty but to expand bondage, stealing half of Mexico to create new slave states. When Thoreau asked whether the Constitution was "not worth looking at," the war provided his answer.

All of this pressure — the closing of every peaceful avenue for change, the expansion of slavery through war, the silencing of opposition — created the conditions for the Underground Railroad's transformation. Canada stood as the constant counterpoint, the proof that another way was possible, the destination that made resistance real rather than symbolic.

The Invention of the Underground

As the story was later told — and like so many Underground Railroad stories, we can't be certain when the telling began — Tice Davids broke the surface of the Ohio River, gasping for air in the September twilight of 1831. Behind him, his enslaver was searching the northern bank in the dusk, baffled. Davids had been just ahead of him, swimming desperately across the river. The enslaver had watched him struggle against the current, had seen him reaching the Ohio shore. But when the enslaver's small boat finally touched the bank, Davids had vanished.

"He must have gone off on an underground road," the frustrated enslaver reportedly complained in nearby Ripley, Ohio.

Whether he really said this, or whether the story was invented years later when people needed an origin myth for a name already circulating, hardly matters. The phrase captured something true: the bewilderment of enslavers confronted by a network they couldn't see or stop.

What we do know is that by the 1830s — just as British abolition was making Canada's freedom absolute and unquestionable — the whispered networks that helped people like Davids disappear were being called the Underground Railroad. The name captured both its invisible nature and, crucially, its modern efficiency. The timing wasn't coincidental. America's first actual railroad, the Baltimore & Ohio, had begun operations just the year before. The machine age was transforming how Americans understood speed and systems. This clandestine network that could make human beings vanish and reappear hundreds of miles away — most of them ultimately in Canada — seemed to operate with the same mechanical precision as those new iron roads. Conductors, stations, passengers, tracks — the terminology wasn't just metaphor. It was a declaration that this resistance network was as sophisticated, as modern, and as unstoppable as any technology the industrial age could produce.

But in its first incarnation, the Underground Railroad wasn't anything like a railroad at all — it was barely even organized. It was, instead, a series of individual moral decisions that happened to intersect, all pointing toward the North Star and the freedom it promised.

The earliest seeds were planted by the Quakers, whose testimony against slavery had crystallized during the revolutionary era. Pennsylvania Quakers continued their pronounced push for abolition in the months following independence to create the first organized assistance networks based on their own highly organized avenues. The Pennsylvania Abolition Society, founded in 1775 and reorganized in 1784, established legal aid committees for fugitives and maintained safe houses in Philadelphia. By 1786, Quakers in Delaware, Maryland, New York, and New Jersey had created similar societies, loosely connected through correspondence and traveling ministers.

But the real infrastructure came from free Black communities. In Philadelphia, Richard Allen's Mother Bethel AME Church, established in 1794, wasn't just a spiritual sanctuary. Its basement was used to hide fugitives like Ona; its congregants served as guides along escape routes, and its ministers carried coded messages between cities. Similar networks emerged wherever free Black communities took root — Boston's African Meeting House, rising in 1806; New York's Abyssinian Baptist Church, founded in 1808; Baltimore's Sharp Street Methodist Church, established in 1787 and rebuilt in 1802. These were more than churches. They were fortresses of freedom, communication hubs, and training grounds for resistance.

The early network operated on a logic of protective obscurity. There were no membership rolls, no meetings, no organization charts. You knew who you knew, and that was enough. Knowledge stayed within compartments — a conductor in Philadelphia might know the next station in Wilmington but nothing about what happened after that. Everything depended on plausible deniability. A fugitive might appear at your door, sleep in your barn, and disappear before dawn. You could honestly say you never "harbored" anyone — they simply passed through. The law required intent to violate it, and intent was hard to prove if everything happened in shadows and silence.

Most important, the network was reactive, not proactive. Nobody was recruiting fugitives or encouraging escape. When someone appeared seeking help, conscience responded. It was humanitarian aid, not organized resistance — at least, that's what everyone could tell themselves.

But this changed with every fugitive who succeeded. Each escape was a proof of concept. Word traveled back through the enslaved communities along paths as invisible as the railroad itself. There was a way out. There were people who would help. And there was a place — Canada — where freedom was real and permanent. What the enslavers called "theft" of their "property," the network called testimony — living proof that the enslaved were not property but people, capable of choosing freedom when given the chance.

By the 1840s, the network had evolved from scattered acts of conscience into something more systematic. Routes were becoming established, all converging on the same destination. The promise of British protection, proven during the Revolution, reinforced during the War of 1812, and made absolute by the Abolition Act of 1833, had created not just hope but a concrete goal. Canada wasn't a maybe — it was a certainty.

The Compromise That Compromised Everything

The Fugitive Slave Act of 1850 was a declaration of war on the conscience of every American. To understand its effect, we have to understand its precision. This was part of another one of Henry Clay's great compromises, which were designed to hold the Union together by finding ways to ensure the perpetuation of slavery. Under this new compromise, which followed his previous Missouri Compromise of thirty years prior, California would enter the Union as a free state, but in exchange, the entire machinery of the First Republic would become an engine of slave catching.

The evil was in the details. There would be no jury trials — special commissioners, not real judges, would decide freedom or slavery in summary proceedings. The accused couldn't even speak in their own defense. The system was rigged from the start — commissioners earned ten dollars for ruling against freedom, five dollars for ruling in favor. It was a bribe written into law. Any citizen could be deputized on the spot to assist in capture, and refusal meant six months in prison and a thousand-dollar fine. The law reached backward through time — it didn't matter if you'd been free for twenty years. You could be seized and "returned" to an enslavement you'd never known.

But the law's authors made a fatal miscalculation. They could close every door within the United States, but they couldn't close the border with Canada. They could make every American a potential slave catcher, but they couldn't make the British comply. The North Star still pointed to freedom.

US Senator William Seward of New York rose to make the case in his first speech to Congress. He laid out the reality facing the country. The framers embraced slavery, it is true, and embedded it in the Constitution. But the expansion of that power was governed by a "higher law than the Constitution." There was a moral law that set all of the compromises that gave in to slavery as "radically wrong and essentially vicious." Slavery would end, one way or another, and the abusive authority of enslavers could divide the Union, let it come, but in the Union's fracture, the enslavers' republic would see its own demise.

Lydia Maria Child's *National Anti-Slavery Standard* built on Seward's ideas to draw the obvious resistance parallel: "If the American revolutionaries had excuse for shedding one drop of blood, then have the American slaves for making blood flow 'even unto the horsebridles.'" But Daniel Webster, the same man whom Thoreau had scorned for his moral cowardice, defended the Compromise of 1850 as the price of union. He took three hours on the floor of the US Senate to defend it. He attacked the opponents of slavery, insisting that respect for slavery in the South, participation in the return of fugitive slaves, and support for the Union were all joined together. Better to sacrifice conscience, Webster argued, than risk disunion.

The response to Webster's logic was immediate and visceral. When the Fugitive Slave Act of 1850 took effect on September 18, it transformed the nature of American resistance overnight. What had been a network of individual conscience became, by necessity, organized opposition with a clear goal: get people to Canada before the slave catchers could stop them.

The Invention of Vigilance

Within days of the Fugitive Slave Act's passage, Boston's Black community convened at the African Meeting House to decide what to do about it. The answer was vigilance — organized, armed, and unapologetic.

Lewis Hayden presided. He was himself a fugitive from Kentucky, had come north through the Underground Railroad, and knew exactly what Canada meant to the people in that room. He also knew what it meant to stay and fight. William Cooper Nell read aloud a statement condemning the law, invoking the Revolutionary Fathers and their resistance to the constructed fiction of British tyranny. Nell was already at work on what would become the first serious histories of Black Americans in the Revolution, and he was building something here — a claim on patriot identity that would become central to abolitionist strategy.

But the men assembled that night had practical matters to settle. They acknowledged the reality of Canada — "the mane of the British Lion affords a nestling place to our brethren in danger from the claws of the American Eagle" — but they did not want that escape route to become an excuse. They were walking a fine line: building the infrastructure of vigilance to protect the enslaved who fled north, while insisting that America itself could be redeemed. So even as they organized safe houses and lookouts and networks, they resolved to caution enslaved people against "leaving the soil of their birth, consecrated by their tears, toils, and perils," because they could yet make America "truly 'the land of the free and the home of the brave.'"

The Fugitive Slave Act had left them no choice but to adopt the tactics of the patriots of 1775 in their battle against the men of 1787.

A few weeks later, an even larger crowd crammed into Faneuil Hall and formed the Boston Vigilance Committee. It wasn't your grandfather's abolition society. Non-resisters, like abolitionist William Lloyd Garrison, who had attended the African Meeting House gathering, were to be left behind. This was organized resistance with an architecture designed for war. An executive committee of eight members could authorize emergency action without consultation. A legal committee of lawyers stood ready to file writs and challenge proceedings at a moment's notice. A finance committee raised thousands of dollars in its first year — real money for real operations. An intelligence network monitored ships, hotels, and railways, tracking every suspicious visitor from the South. Safe houses spread across a dozen towns stretching to the Canadian border, each one a link in an increasingly visible chain.

This was a parallel resistance institution, created not to reform a corrupt system but to defeat it by moving people beyond its reach — to Canada.

When danger approached, church bells would ring in sequence, spreading the alarm faster than any telegraph. Similar committees sprouted in Philadelphia, New York, Syracuse, Detroit, Cleveland, and Chicago. They shared intelligence through coded letters, coordinated routes through trusted intermediaries. They began to operate less like a charity and more like an intelligence service at war with the federal government.

The network was tested immediately when two bounty hunters from Georgia appeared in Boston to seize William and Ellen Craft, who had freed themselves from slavery through an audacious escape and spent two years telling their story to anti-slavery audiences. In November 1850, they were staying in Lewis Hayden's home when the slave catchers arrived with warrants.

But the underground was ready. The Crafts were moved between safe houses while the hunters were personally hounded, arrested repeatedly for slander and conspiracy. They couldn't find a local official to serve their warrants. Hayden booby-trapped his front door with explosives. The slave catchers realized they faced not individuals but an entire resistance infrastructure and retreated to Georgia empty-handed.

But everyone knew the limits of resistance within American jurisdiction. When the Crafts' former enslaver complained to President Fillmore, who authorized military force to return them to slavery, the only answer was escape from the republic's reach. They fled to England, not Canada, but the principle was the same: British territory meant freedom.

And then came Shadrach Minkins on that cold Saturday morning in February 1851. Looking up at the skyscrapers of the Financial District today, within sight of the Old State House, it would be hard to conjure the drama of that day. Minkins had escaped from Norfolk, Virginia, and followed the underground network to Boston, working as a waiter in the Cornhill Coffee House when federal agents seized him.

The resistance struck immediately. Robert Morris and others burst into the courthouse, grabbed Minkins, and rushed him into a waiting carriage. In two weeks, Minkins would be safe in Montreal — having traveled the tested route from Beacon Hill to Cambridge to Concord to Leominster, and from there to Canada, where American law couldn't touch him.

The transformation was crystallized in the person of Harriet Tubman. In the first months after her escape, she had made two careful journeys to lead family members north, moving in shadow and silence. After 1850, she became something else entirely — a general conducting military operations in enemy territory. She carried a pistol and wasn't afraid to point it at wavering fugitives who might turn back and compromise the entire network. "You'll be free or die," she reportedly told them, and she meant it.

Tubman studied weather patterns like a meteorologist, memorized train schedules like a station master, and maintained a network of operatives from Maryland to Ontario that would have impressed any spy service. In ten years, she made thirteen trips and never lost a single passenger. Every one of them reached genuine freedom in Canada.

Frederick Douglass called this transformation the "upperground railroad" with characteristic precision and growing frustration at its increasing visibility. The network was becoming increasingly public, deliberately confrontational, almost daring the federal government to stop it. But it could afford this visibility because its success didn't depend on hiding within America — it depended on reaching Canada.

Blood in Boston: The Burns Affair

Anthony Burns was twenty years old when he made a mistake that would accelerate clandestine resistance into armed conflict. Free in Boston for two months, working in a clothing store on Brattle Street, he wrote a letter to his brother, who was still enslaved in Virginia. It was an act of love that became an act of war. His enslaver, Charles Suttle, intercepted the letter and came north to reclaim his "property."

On May 24, 1854, Burns was arrested on a fabricated charge of theft and locked in the federal courthouse. Within hours, handbills appeared across Boston, printed in the offices of *The Liberator* and distributed by boys who ran through the streets: THE KIDNAPPERS ARE HERE!

What followed was the largest show of resistance to federal authority between the Revolution and the Civil War, a week that would cost the government a fortune and the Fugitive Slave Act its last shred of any perceived legitimacy.

By May 26, thousands surrounded the courthouse, their anger palpable in the spring air. The Vigilance Committee's lawyers — Dana and Morris, both of whom had been tried for Shadrach's escape, and Charles Ellis — filed for that ultimate instrument of freedom, habeas corpus. Commissioner Edward Loring, who also happened to be a Harvard Law lecturer, denied it with barely a glance at their arguments.

The next evening, on Saturday, May 27, the ghosts of the American Revolution assembled in Faneuil Hall when Theodore Parker took to the podium. Seventy-nine years before, in 1775, his grandfather had stood on the green in Lexington in command of the patriot militia that turned out the morning of April 19. Captain John Parker looked out at the British troops that had aligned against them and was remembered to have turned to his men to say, "If they mean to have a war, let it begin here." His grandson had the same gleam in his eye that night in 1854 as he looked over the crowded room.

Parker opened up a brutal speech that fired a terrible volley into the packed chamber, invoking the American Revolution against the Constitution and the evil that it promoted. The Constitution had established "the slave law" that erased Boston and its history, turning it into "a north suburb of the city of Alexandria," enabling the hand of Virginia to reach into Massachusetts to send a man into slavery forever. The entire architecture of the First Republic — the president, the Supreme Court, Congress, every federal agent — was in the service of the slave law.

But, Parker insisted, there was another law, a law that had once governed people in the time of their parents and grandparents. "There was a Boston once," he pronounced, a town full of people that declared that laws that were not just were not laws that deserved to be obeyed. Unjust laws were not laws at all. That was the Boston of the patriot revolutionaries, men such as his grandfather and the Adamses. What did they do on a similar night in December 1773 when faced with the question of abusive authority, in a meeting just like theirs, held only a few blocks away in the Old South Meeting House? What was their resolution? Those patriots chose to go "behind a wicked law to enact absolute justice."

Parker then paused. The audience was with him, in that moment between that first revolution and the beginning of their own. He then leaned into them. "I love peace," he stated. "But there is a means, and there is an end; liberty is the end, and sometimes peace not the means towards it." His audience responded with thunderous applause, priming him for the final push to direct resistance.

"Now I want to ask you: what are you going to do?"

A voice cried out, "Shoot, shoot!"

Outside the hall, the resistance moved from rhetoric to kinetic action. A group led by Lewis Hayden and Thomas Wentworth Higginson didn't wait for a vote; they assaulted the courthouse doors with a battering ram. The attack failed tactically — a federal deputy was killed, the rescuers were beaten back, and the prisoner remained in chains — but it succeeded in forcing the federal government to reveal its true nature.

President Franklin Pierce, sitting in Washington, made a decision that would haunt the republic. He ordered marines to Boston. Then cavalry. Then artillery. By May 28, Boston was an occupied city. The cost was staggering and climbing — estimates range from forty to one hundred thousand dollars, just to hold one twenty-year-old man.

June 2 brought the final act of this tragedy. The rendition became a funeral march for American law. Thousands — some witnesses said tens of thousands — lined the streets as Burns was marched to the harbor. Every building was draped in black. A coffin labeled LIBERTY hung from a window on State Street. American flags flew upside down or were covered in black crepe. The crowd pressed so close that troops affixed bayonets, turning State Street into a tunnel of steel.

It took somewhere between fifteen hundred and two thousand armed men to return one twenty-year-old to slavery. The federal government had won the battle but lost the war. The spectacle of military occupation to enforce slavery destroyed the Fugitive Slave Act's legitimacy forever. No fugitive would successfully be returned from Boston again, though not for lack of trying. Commissioner Loring would lose his position at Harvard. And Anthony Burns? Northern supporters would purchase his freedom within a year for thirteen hundred dollars — a fraction of what the government had spent trying to keep him enslaved.

The lesson was clear: Within American territory, the First Republic could still abuse its authority, but against organized, effective resistance, the cost might be more than it could bear.

The Economics of Revolution

The Burns case exposed a critical vulnerability that the vigilance committees would exploit ruthlessly: Enforcement was economically unsustainable. At its core, all resistance makes authority pay a price for abuse. Resistance makes it pause and recalculate whether the abuse is worth the price. Sometimes that is measured in dollars, which is a much easier burden to bear than losses in lives. But that single rendition of Anthony Burns cost the federal government a fortune — the equivalent of millions in today's money. The federal government could afford maybe one of those cases, perhaps. But not many, if any, more. The mathematics of resistance had shifted decisively.

The vigilance committees understood this and developed a strategy of economic warfare that would have impressed any military strategist. Legal delays required housing and feeding federal marshals for weeks at city expense. Mass demonstrations required expensive military deployments that Congress would have to fund. Property damage during rescue attempts generated bills that cities would forward to federal authorities. Boycotts destroyed businesses that cooperated with slave catchers, making collaboration economically ruinous.

But the resisters also created an alternative economy. The Underground Railroad was expensive — bribes for ship captains who would hide fugitives in cargo holds, rail tickets purchased under false names, safe house maintenance in dozens of cities, legal fees for the constant court battles. The various vigilance committees raised and spent thousands of dollars each year — funded entirely by voluntary contributions, benefit concerts that packed halls, and church collections that emptied pockets every Sunday. When multiplied across dozens of cities, the Underground Railroad represented a massive redirection of capital from the formal economy to the resistance economy.

And the goal of all this expenditure was clear: get people out of the First Republic. Fundraising appeals could cite specific costs — ferry fare across the Detroit River, passage across Lake Ontario, a berth across the Atlantic, initial settlement funds in Toronto or London or Nassau. Donors knew exactly what their money was purchasing.

The Architecture of Liberation

By 1855, the Underground Railroad had evolved into something unprecedented in the history of resistance: a transcontinental, even transatlantic, network operating in open defiance of federal law, with routes as complex as any railroad timetable.

The Eastern Corridor ran from Maryland through Philadelphia and New York to New England and Canada. This was the oldest route, developed over decades, with stations every ten to twenty miles and multiple alternative paths for when one became too dangerous. Conductors knew every creek bed that could hide footprints, every sympathetic farmer who would look the other way, every bridge where federal marshals might wait. The final push was through Vermont or Maine into Quebec, or across Lake Champlain or the St. Lawrence River.

The Central Corridor stretched from Kentucky through Ohio and Indiana to Detroit and across to Ontario. This became the highest-traffic route — Ohio was so active that it earned the nickname "the trunk line." Thousands passed through the state, though exact numbers remain impossible to verify. Detroit became the crucial gateway — one mile across the Detroit River lay Windsor and freedom. The city's Black community, led by figures like William Lambert and George DeBaptiste, operated what they called a Secret Order that moved fugitives across the river with military precision.

The Western Corridor ran from Missouri through Iowa to Chicago and then to Canada, crossing territories where pro-slavery forces were strong and violence was common. Chicago became a major hub, with fugitives moving north through Wisconsin to cross into Canada via the Great Lakes.

But there were also routes that historians have only recently begun to document. Maritime networks used Black sailors and sympathetic captains to move fugitives from Southern ports to Boston, New York, and Philadelphia. Ship records suggest mysterious "crew members" who appeared in one port and vanished in another, never to sail again. The Mexican Route ran from Texas through Mexico, where slavery had been abolished in 1829 and authorities refused American demands for extradition. Some fugitives continued to Veracruz and sailed for Haiti or other Caribbean islands. The Florida Keys Network relied on

Bahamian fishermen and wreckers to spirit fugitives to the Bahamas, that home of so many Black loyalists — such as Nancy Dixon and her daughter — where slavery had been abolished in 1834 and where the Union Jack meant freedom.

The Psychology of Transformation

The Fugitive Slave Act achieved something its authors never intended: It made resistance respectable. Before 1850, helping fugitives was the province of radicals and outcasts, people already on society's margins. After 1850, it became a mark of moral courage that even the most respectable citizens wanted to claim.

Consider Levi Coffin, the man who would be called the President of the Underground Railroad. A Quaker merchant in Indiana, Coffin had quietly helped fugitives since the 1820s, working in shadow and silence. After 1850, he went public, openly declaring his house a station and daring authorities to stop him. His Newport home became so well known that fugitives would simply ask for "the house of the Quaker" and be directed there by people who knew exactly what they were facilitating. Coffin could afford this openness because his passengers weren't staying — they were going to Canada.

Or witness the evolution of resistance in Oberlin, Ohio. In September 1858, when fugitive John Price was seized near Oberlin College, the entire town rose as one. Students abandoned their classes, professors their lectures, townspeople their shops. Black and white together, they surrounded the hotel where Price was held. They broke down the door with improvised battering rams, carried Price away in triumph, and sent him to Canada within hours.

When thirty-seven rescuers were indicted for violating the Fugitive Slave Act, hundreds more came forward to demand they, too, be arrested. The trials became a circus that the government couldn't control. The few who were convicted were treated as heroes in jail, receiving constant visitors, gifts, and letters of support. The government dropped most charges and tried to forget the whole embarrassing affair. They could prosecute the rescuers, but they couldn't get John Price back from Canada.

Thoreau's admonition that "under a government which imprisons any unjustly, the true place for a just man is also a prison" was becoming an object lesson.

From Canadian soil, formerly enslaved people could operate openly in ways impossible within the United States. Henry Bibb's *Voice of the Fugitive* from Windsor, Ontario, wasn't hiding its operations — it published routes, raised funds, coordinated escapes. Mary Ann Shadd Cary's *Provincial Freeman* in Toronto provided another platform for open resistance. These newspapers reached back into the United States, carrying intelligence and encouragement to those still enslaved, proving that freedom wasn't just a dream.

The Mythology of Memory

Here's where the story of the Underground Railroad becomes complicated in ways that tell us something essential about resistance history. After the Civil War, when slavery was safely abolished and the Underground Railroad was no longer needed — or dangerous — something peculiar happened. Suddenly, everyone had been part of it.

Houses across the North sprouted secret rooms that had "hidden fugitive slaves." Every old barn had a concealed space, every church basement a secret tunnel. Prominent citizens who had been conspicuously silent during the actual operation of the Underground Railroad now told elaborate stories of their midnight adventures helping fugitives. The number of people claiming to have been conductors would have required a network larger than the actual railroad system of the 1850s.

This phenomenon isn't unique to America. After World War II, a similar mythology emerged in France. By 1946, to hear the stories, virtually every French citizen had been in the Resistance. The collaborators, the attentistes who simply waited to see who would win, the millions who had simply tried to survive — they all vanished from memory, replaced by a nation of heroic resisters. It took decades for historians like Robert Paxton to puncture this myth, revealing that actual French Resistance members were a tiny minority, that most French citizens had cooperated with or tolerated the Vichy regime, and that the mythmaking itself served a political purpose in reconstructing French national identity after the shame of occupation.

The same process transformed the Underground Railroad from a dangerous, limited network into a vast, safe, and retrospectively popular movement. Walk through any nineteenth-century neighborhood in the North today and you'll likely be shown a house with a "hiding place" for fugitive slaves — a small room, a root cellar, an odd closet. The current owners will tell you with pride about their house's role in the fight for freedom. Never mind that the geography makes no sense, that no documented route passed that way, or that the supposed hiding place was actually built in the 1870s. The story has become more important than the history.

This isn't harmless mythology. It obscures the actual courage required to participate in the real Underground Railroad. If everyone was part of the resistance, then no one risked anything. If every house was a station, then hiding fugitives wasn't dangerous. The multiplication of mythical participants diminishes the sacrifice of actual participants. Lewis Hayden really did keep kegs of gunpowder in his basement, ready to blow up his house rather than let slave catchers take the fugitives he was hiding. Harriet Tubman really did risk capture and death nineteen times. The Coffins really did face constant surveillance and threats. These weren't common acts by common people — they were extraordinary acts by people who chose to risk everything when most of their neighbors chose to risk nothing.

The mythmaking also obscures a harder truth: Most Northerners, even those who opposed slavery in principle, did nothing to help fugitives in practice. They might vote for anti-slavery politicians, attend anti-slavery lectures, even donate to anti-slavery causes. But when a fugitive needed shelter, when a slave catcher needed to be confronted, when the federal marshal came to town, most people found reasons to look away. The actual Underground Railroad succeeded not because of widespread support but despite widespread indifference.

Consider the mathematics. Modern historians estimate that between thirty thousand and seventy thousand people escaped slavery through all routes between 1830 and 1860 — perhaps one hundred thousand at the absolute maximum. That's out of nearly four million enslaved people. The Underground Railroad, for all its heroism and importance, helped perhaps 1 or 2 percent of enslaved Americans reach freedom. This isn't to diminish its achievement but rather to clarify it. The Underground Railroad mattered not because it emptied the South of enslaved people but because it proved that resistance was possible, that the system could be defied, that some Americans would risk everything for justice.

And crucially, most of those who did escape ended up in Canada. Fugitive slaves founded towns like Buxton and Dawn in Ontario. The British Methodist Episcopal Church, the True Band societies, the Canadian Anti-Slavery Society — these institutions were built by and for people who had escaped American slavery. When the Civil War began, many of these Canadian refugees returned to fight — the 54th Massachusetts Infantry included men who had found freedom in Canada and came back to destroy the system that had enslaved them.

The proliferation of false Underground Railroad stories serves what we might call performative allyship — the desire to claim participation in righteousness without having borne its costs. It's the same impulse that leads people today to insist their ancestors didn't enslave people (when records suggest otherwise) or that their family "was always on the right side of history" (when history suggests almost no one was). We want the moral credit for resistance without the moral reckoning of complicity.

This matters for how we understand resistance. Real resistance is rare, dangerous, and usually unpopular in its own time. The people who hid fugitives in the 1850s weren't celebrated — they were criminals. The lawyers who defended fugitives weren't respected — they were traitors to their race and class. The towns that rescued fugitives weren't heroic — they were lawless. Only later, after the danger passed and the outcome was decided, did resistance become respectable, even fashionable.

The Underground Railroad's true history — as opposed to its mythology — teaches us to be skeptical of retroactive heroism. When everyone claims to have been part of the resistance, we should ask: Where were you when it mattered? When the risk was real? When the cost was high? The answers, then and now, are usually uncomfortable. Most people, most of the time, choose safety over justice, comfort over courage, the familiar over the right. This isn't a condemnation — it's human nature. But it makes the choice of those who chose differently all the more remarkable.

From Railroad to Army

By 1856, the Underground Railroad wasn't just moving fugitives — it was building an army. The same networks that carried people to freedom began carrying something else: weapons. Rifles labeled as TOOLS or MACHINERY moved along familiar routes. The same safe houses that hid fugitives began hiding crates bound for Kansas, where the question of slavery was being decided by force.

John Brown understood this transformation better than anyone. When he visited Boston in 1857, he didn't just meet with abolitionists over tea — he met with the Underground Railroad's radical resistance wing. Lewis Hayden gave Brown money and promised men. Thomas Wentworth Higginson, bloodied in the Burns rescue, pledged support and strategic advice. These weren't pacifists anymore — they were revolutionaries who had learned through experience that freedom required force.

But Brown also went to Canada. In May 1858, he held a convention in Chatham, Ontario, with fugitive slaves who had found freedom there. He didn't just want their support — he wanted their military experience. Many had fought their way to freedom. They knew Southern terrain, Southern tactics, the Southern mind. Brown's "Provisional Constitution" was ratified not in Boston or New York but in Canada, by people who had already proved that they would fight for freedom.

The Upperground Revolution

Frederick Douglass used the term *upperground railroad* with frustration — too many abolitionists were publicizing their work, endangering operations. But he also recognized a deeper truth: The Underground Railroad had evolved from a clandestine network into an open insurrection against federal authority.

By 1860, the transformation was complete. Tens of thousands of fugitives had found freedom through the network. Thousands of federal violations had gone unprosecuted because conviction was impossible when entire communities supported the accused. Millions of dollars in what the South called "property" had been liberated with impunity. Multiple states were in open defiance of federal law, their officials refusing to cooperate, their citizens proud of their resistance.

The Underground Railroad had achieved more than individual salvations — it had created a crisis of legitimacy for the federal government itself. When South Carolina seceded in December 1860, it cited the North's refusal to enforce the Fugitive Slave Act as a primary cause. But what really terrified the South was Canada — a place where tens of thousands of formerly enslaved people lived free, prospered, and, worst of all, provided living proof that Black people were fully capable of freedom, education, and self-governance. The Underground Railroad hadn't just resisted an unjust law — it had effectively nullified it.

The Verdict of History

Robert Morris walked out of the federal courthouse a free man. Again. The government's second attempt to convict him had collapsed just like the first — another hung jury, another failure to break the network. Richard Henry Dana, Jr., and John Parker Hale had defended him brilliantly, but the real defense came from something deeper: a community that refused to convict its protectors.

The Minkins trials had been meant to decapitate Boston's resistance infrastructure. President Fillmore and Secretary Webster had demanded convictions that would prove that federal authority could crush the Underground Railroad. Instead, trial after trial exposed the government's impotence. Morris acquitted. Hayden walking free. Scott vindicated. Wright untouchable. Nine men charged, zero convictions. The network had held.

But the trials revealed something more profound than legal victory. Under the pressure of federal investigation, with grand juries probing and prosecutors threatening, the Underground Railroad's true architecture had briefly become visible. Not the mythology that would later grow around it — those endless secret rooms and hidden tunnels — but the actual machinery of organized resistance: specialized roles, compartmentalized knowledge, operational security so tight that even today we can't fully reconstruct how it worked.

The government had put clandestine resistance on trial and lost. Every acquittal sent the same message: When a network combines sophisticated organization with community protection, federal authority becomes a paper tiger. The Fugitive Slave Act could make every citizen a potential criminal, but it couldn't make them comply. It could demand universal participation in slavery's enforcement, but it couldn't overcome organized refusal.

But the more resounding victory was that Shadrach Minkins was in Montreal, beyond the reach of American law forever. That's what the trials couldn't change — Canada existed, it was free, and the Underground Railroad could get people there. The network's success wasn't measured in legal victories but instead in lives saved, families reunited, freedom achieved in a place where it was real and permanent.

This was the Underground Railroad's greatest lesson, one that transcends its historical moment. Resistance isn't about individual heroics or spontaneous uprising. It's about the patient work of building infrastructure that can survive repression. It's about creating networks that protect both operations and operators. It's about maintaining discipline when the state tries to break you through prosecution, infiltration, or terror. And crucially, it's about having a genuine sanctuary — a place where authority cannot reach — that makes the entire network possible.

The principles are timeless because authority's playbook rarely changes: Make everyone complicit in injustice. Criminalize conscience. Demand that citizens become enforcers. Use spectacular force to create fear. Prosecute leaders to decapitate networks. The Fugitive Slave Act deployed all these tactics, and the Underground Railroad defeated them all — not through violence or revolution, but through disciplined, organized, clandestine resistance that moved people to a place where federal law couldn't follow.

Morris and his codefendants had won more than their freedom. They had proved that resistance networks, properly built and protected by their communities, could nullify the authority of the state itself. The Underground Railroad hadn't just moved bodies to freedom; it had created a crisis of legitimacy that would help precipitate the final conflict over slavery.

CHAPTER EIGHT

Arming the Hosts of Freedom

Resistance Principle #8: Whatever it takes.

ST. LOUIS, JULY 1856

A little office led into a little, dark room, beyond which was a little kitchen, which led into a dirty, open yard. Brick and iron walls rose twenty feet into the unforgiving heat of a summer sky. Without those walls, the Mississippi River would have been in sight. The sounds of river boats — steam whistles, calliope music, churning paddlewheels — could probably be heard.

But the boats, the water, the breeze winding through all the new buildings that crowded the St. Louis riverfront since the Great Fire of 1849 — none of that mattered to the two dozen people in that dirty yard. Most were under fourteen.

A "large, lounging" slave trader pulled three girls — sisters — into the office, all wearing "dirty pink frocks." They were eleven, nine, and seven. Barefoot. Faces of "black marble."

A well-dressed man — a gentleman, a member of the city government — had asked the slave trader for "a good article of a small girl." These three were from Virginia, sold south, now readied to be sold again, if not there in Missouri, then on to Mississippi.

"What's that on her cheek?" the gentleman asked, gesturing to a scar on the face of the oldest girl, Martha.

"Somebody's whacked her chops, most likely," said the slave trader.

"Girl is sound, I suppose?" inquired the gentleman.

"Strip her naked and examine every inch of her, if you wish," responded the slave trader.

The girls' faces remained impassive — black marble. Then the youngest, Sue, shed one slow tear. Then she turned to the wall and broke down. The sobs cascaded. The gentleman — a pillar of his community — looked uncomfortable and turned away. The slave trader became annoyed and gave Sue "an ominous look."

"I wish I could stay with my mother," Martha told the gentleman.

"Nonsense," proclaimed the slave trader. Their mother was still in Virginia. There, she was called "servant" and "person" by those who claimed to own her. But soon, the slave trader said, she would be sold, too. To the Deep South, where they had no patience for polite euphemisms for property. It was the land of "'Negroes' or 'Niggers.'" The girls should forget their mother.

The gentleman counted out seven hundred dollars and took her away from her sisters. The slave trader was happy with the transaction. He'd have to "shut up shop pretty quick" if he gave any thought to keeping families together. No, "take 'em as they come" and sell them on.

That was the nature of life in America in 1856, but a learned, eloquent, passionate thirty-three-year-old New England minister who watched it all didn't think it had to be. Thomas Wentworth Higginson was a Harvard graduate who left a Unitarian pulpit to fight slavery with his words. Nearly every other country in the Atlantic world had ended slavery by then. Just not the United States.

Higginson personally knew Harriet Beecher Stowe, whose *Uncle Tom's Cabin* painted the reality of slavery for Americans who would never be close to its horrors; Frederick Douglass, whose speeches were so important to the abolitionist cause; and Harriet Tubman and her inspiring example. He'd also met and heard testimonials from countless Black fugitives and had helped some of them get to safety. He even had a scar on his chin from a saber blow he'd endured trying to rescue a person who had escaped slavery from the custody of a federal marshal in Boston.

On his way in 1856 to witness the battlegrounds in Kansas where pro- and anti-slavery forces were fighting years before the Civil War, Higginson had sought out that slave trader in St. Louis to see the reality of the brutality for himself, far away from the cravats and cocktails of Boston's genteel parlors. He had seen the work of the Underground Railroad in New England, but he later recalled, "I wanted to see something above the ground." But three small girls in dirty pink frocks — their marble-like countenance broken by sobs and the quiet plea for a mother — changed something inside him.

Higginson was already a passionate abolitionist, but the fate of Martha, Sue, and their unnamed sister turned his anger into rage, and his rage then turned to resolve. Cool, resigned resolve.

Higginson determined there and then that slavery must end, even if the republic — the First Republic — must end. James Madison, now dead for twenty years, and his insistence that the good of the Union was worth accepting the evil of slavery, must finally be buried. The disease of bondage, Higginson maintained, is "too deep to cure without amputation."

From that moment forward, his motto would be: "Peacefully if we can, forcibly if we must."

Higginson wasn't alone in reaching such terrible clarity. Across the North, a small but influential group of abolitionists was arriving at the same conclusion through different paths — some through moral philosophy, others through political pragmatism, still others through direct experience of revolutionary violence. Thomas Wentworth Higginson, Samuel Gridley Howe, Theodore Parker, Gerrit Smith, George Luther Stearns, and Franklin Sanborn would come to be known as the Six — John Brown's inner circle, his financiers, his coordinators, his accomplices. None of them was quiet or obscure. Smith was one of the wealthiest men in America and had run for president three times. Howe was a revolutionary who had helped topple regimes in Greece and France and been imprisoned for helping Polish revolutionaries, all before he turned thirty. Higginson and Parker thundered so loudly against the enslaver power of the republic that they earned death threats from the deepest South.

What remained hidden was how far they were willing to go.

By 1856, none of the Six were naive about violence. They had already crossed that line. They had supported armed resistance in Kansas for years, sent rifles knowing what they'd be used for. Higginson had taken that saber slash to the face trying to rescue Anthony

Burns from federal custody. They had watched every peaceful avenue close: The Fugitive Slave Act turned the entire nation into a hunting ground; Kansas bled. Charles Sumner, an anti-slavery senator from Massachusetts, was beaten nearly to death on the Senate floor in the wake of his "Crime Against Kansas Speech" in which he criticized the Kansas–Nebraska Act and denounced the "Slave Power." The republic perverted every pretension about liberty to protect and expand slavery. The Six were comfortable men, establishment figures with everything to lose, and they had accepted that tactical violence was necessary.

The Closing Doors

For twenty years, the Underground Railroad had been American resistance at its most sophisticated and its most perilous. As it evolved from the first days of the republic into the organized juggernaut of the 1850s, it was the first point of interruption in the resistance to the republic, where protest and political opposition stepped outside the law into necessarily clandestine action. By 1856, the network taxed the enslavers' patience, drained federal resources, made the Fugitive Slave Act look impotent. Every person who reached Canada was a victory.

But it was triage in a hemorrhaging nation. The Underground Railroad saved individuals while the system manufactured slavery — four million people would be in bondage by 1860, and the number would just keep growing. Every year, more people were born into slavery than escaped from it. Every session of Congress expanded slavery's territory. Every Supreme Court decision strengthened slavery's grip. You could save people forever — the abolitionists would, and did — but bleeding wasn't going to stop. That's why Higginson didn't want to see what was happening underground on his trip west. The Underground Railroad would never move fast enough to matter. It could address slavery's symptoms forever without touching the disease.

Compromising Northern moderates had handed enslavers the Kansas–Nebraska Act in 1854, tearing up the Missouri line, a boundary to the practice of slavery that even slaveholders had come to recognize. When armed Missourians poured across the Kansas border to steal elections at gunpoint, federal officers certified the theft as democracy in action. Two years later, Charles Sumner — towering, colorful, forty-five years old, an anti-slavery resister — spent five hours documenting the "Crime Against Kansas." How border ruffians overthrew popular sovereignty through murder and terror. How this violence merely extended slavery's essential logic. How the same brutal force that held millions in bondage now crushed republican government itself. He singled out South Carolina's Andrew Butler, mocking his pretensions to chivalry while taking "a mistress . . . who, though ugly to others, is always lovely to him . . . the harlot, Slavery."

Two days later, as Sumner sat at his desk on the floor of the Senate, Butler's cousin Preston Brooks entered the chamber with a light cane — the kind used to discipline dogs — and beat him until Sumner lurched about the chamber trying to shield himself from Brooks's blows. Blood streamed down his face while another congressman prevented at gunpoint anyone from coming to Sumner's aid. Brooks walked calmly out of the chamber. The House failed to censure him. Southern newspapers sent him replacement canes. The state had not failed to maintain its monopoly on legitimate violence — it had just expanded it, outsourcing violence to slavery's champions and throwing them parades when they used it.

Then came *Dred Scott* in 1857. Roger Taney's Supreme Court declared that Black people had no rights that white people were bound to respect, that Congress never had the power to restrict slavery anywhere, that the founders always meant for things to be this way. Even when free-state settlers finally won democratic majorities in Kansas, President Buchanan and his congressional allies tried to force slavery on them through the fraudulent Lecompton constitution. And Abraham Lincoln — the great anti-slavery hope of 1858 — stood on debate stages against Stephen Douglas, promising that he'd never touch slavery where it existed, only prevent its expansion. He explicitly disavowed racial equality and pledged to enforce the Fugitive Slave Act. That was as far as electoral politics could reach.

Every permitted channel — closed. Every institution — compromised. The enslavers hadn't just captured the government; they'd become it. They controlled the House, which wouldn't censure attempted murder. They controlled Taney's Supreme Court, which declared millions without rights. They controlled the Senate, where the Slave Power held veto over all legislation. They controlled legitimate violence — the army that enforced expansion, the marshals who hunted fugitives, the legal right to kill — while their opponents were told to respect process, obey law, trust elections that Missouri proved could be stolen at gunpoint. The monopoly on force belonged entirely to slavery, wielded through federal power. By 1858, only fools and collaborators still believed in peaceful abolition. The moderates knew the truth; they just preferred their committee seats to saying it out loud.

The question the Six faced wasn't whether violence was morally justified. The whip, the auction block, the federal army deployed to return one man to bondage — this was systematic, generations-long violence that made compliance into complicity. The question was whether they could carry the moral weight of acting on that necessity to provoke a rupture. Could they support destruction to its ultimate expression and own it?

The Six faced a specific proposal from John Brown in 1858: move the war from Kansas to Virginia. The record remains murky about who knew what and when. What is known: The Six had already helped arrange for rifles and violence on the prairie. Now Brown wanted to raid the federal arsenal at Harpers Ferry, arm enslaved people, establish guerrilla positions in the Appalachian Mountains. But they understood that the real objective wasn't holding territory or even freeing more than a few enslaved people. It was strategic provocation — forcing the federal government to mobilize against anti-slavery forces, making Northern moderates choose sides, destroying the fiction, maintained for seventy years, that slavery could be tackled through democratic means. Brown was offering them the chance to light a fuse that would explode the entire political order.

You cannot endorse such violence while maintaining distance from its consequences. You cannot enable an insurrection through intermediaries and keep your Boston respectability. You cannot make Brown's raid a reality and then act surprised when federal marshals show up at your door. The choice was absolute: Either you cross that line completely — accept that you're now an insurrectionist, own whatever bloodshed follows, carry it the rest of your life — or you admit that you're not ready for what defeating slavery actually requires and walk away.

What Brown was proposing was the test of whether thirty years of hidden resistance could transform into open confrontation. Not whether to break unjust laws — they'd all done that through the Underground Railroad — but whether to force a public reckoning through violence that would inevitably result in death. Not defensive violence to protect individual fugitives, but offensive violence to attack the system itself.

Higginson had that capacity. He could carry that burden, and he knew it. Parker had it — preserving his grandfather's musket, dying of tuberculosis, he had nothing left to lose and everything to prove about whether his years of preaching violence as necessary meant anything when the moment arrived. Howe carried it with him, having been on the battlefields of two revolutions and having treated their casualties. And Sanborn, the youngest, always in the company of vital men and women, hoped he had it.

The others would give their answers in the months ahead — answers that would reveal who they truly were when theory became reality.

The group that secretly organized John Brown's raid on Harpers Ferry never called themselves the Secret Six. That designation came later, from historians seeking a tidy label for a conspiracy that participants themselves were careful not to name. But the men involved did refer to themselves collectively as the Six and later, with dark humor after the raid's failure, as the six Peters, alluding to the biblical apostle who denied Christ three times. These weren't just casual references. They suggest a group that understood itself as a coherent entity, bound by shared purpose and mutual risk.

They knew each other well before Brown entered their lives. They had worked together on various reform causes — temperance campaigns, women's rights advocacy, an impressive portfolio of moral improvement projects that sparked activism in a tumultuous time. But what bound them, what made them conspirators rather than merely collaborators, was their strenuous opposition to slavery. They had been compatriots in that cause for years: supporting the Underground Railroad, aiding refugees from slavery, and — as tensions between North and South ratcheted up during the 1850s — backing increasingly direct action. By the time they began funding and organizing Brown's operations in Kansas, they had already crossed lines together. Sending Sharps rifles to free-state settlers was not humanitarian aid. They didn't purchase crate after crate of the latest in breech-loading weapons so that anti-slavery forces could display them over their fireplaces.

At first glance, the six men who made John Brown's raid possible seem remarkably similar: establishment Northeasterners, educated, prosperous. But to assume an ideological uniformity is to mistake the passion of the times and the seriousness of the issues that consumed them. These were not men following a shared script. They came from different backgrounds, held different temperaments, arrived at abolitionism through different routes. Yet they all reached the same conclusion: Violence was not merely justified but necessary as a tool of resistance. To understand why that convergence happened — why men of such privilege and position chose to organize, plan, argue, mediate, raise funds, and procure weapons to make armed insurrection possible — we need to understand how each of them got there. And we need to understand why others, in similar positions with similar privileges, did not.

When the Oppressed Cannot Provoke

Black resistance was born with the first enslaver. It matured, evolved, and deepened as the First Republic expanded its abuse. Armed escapes, organized rescues, community self-defense networks — these operated openly enough that everyone knew they existed. When Margaret Garner killed her daughter rather than see her returned to slavery in 1856, when the Christiana Resistance in 1851 resulted in an enslaver's death, when Harriet Tubman carried a pistol and pointed it at anyone who might turn back and compromise the network, Black resistance wasn't debating the morality of violence. That question was settled, if it had ever needed to be asked.

But escalating to strategic provocation — deliberately initiating violence designed to force a crisis of authority — was a calculation Black resisters had learned they could not make. Not from lack of courage or understanding. The First Republic had taught them through blood what happened when enslaved people or free Black communities initiated strategic violence.

Denmark Vesey's 1822 conspiracy in Charleston never got past the planning stage. Betrayed before it began, crushed, with thirty-five Black men executed and the city's Black population subjected to waves of surveillance and repression that lasted decades. Nat Turner's 1831 rebellion in Southampton County, Virginia, actually succeeded in killing nearly sixty white Virginians before militias and mobs killed more than twice that many Black people in retaliation — most of them uninvolved in the uprising. Turner's rebellion lasted two days. The reaction reshaped Southern slavery for a generation. Every enslaver state tightened its codes, increased patrols, criminalized teaching enslaved people to read, and made conditions infinitely worse to prevent such an uprising from happening again.

The pattern was clear: Oppressive regimes expect violent insurrection from the oppressed, and they can absorb it. Vesey never got the chance to find out — his plot was betrayed by enslaved men who made an impossible calculation, that their odds were better with the system they knew than with a rebellion that might fail. Turner got further, but his defiance was contained and used as justification for even harsher control. Strategic provocation from the oppressed didn't create a crisis for the system; it created justification for more repression. The First Republic could weather that kind of insurrection. It had been built to.

From Vesey and Turner, Black resistance learned that without scale — without broad allyship from those outside the oppressed population — violent revolt could never go far enough. Different strategies emerged from that understanding.

Historian Kellie Carter Jackson frames it precisely: Violence among Black abolitionists became "a political language and a means of provoking social change." Not insurrection for insurrection's sake — that got you killed and your community crushed. But tactical violence, protective violence, violence that forced white Northerners to watch the machinery of slavery operate in their own streets. Violence that made the comfortable uncomfortable.

Frederick Douglass and William Nell took a different path. They turned to moral suasion — the belief that you could convince white America, through argument and evidence and sheer rhetorical force, that Black Americans deserved a share of the founding principles. But they understood something the white abolitionists could afford to ignore: Black resistance that looked like it rejected American nationalism would be crushed. The pageant of patriotism was a gatekeeper. You had to claim a share of it — the Constitution, the Revolution, the mythology itself — or you didn't get through.

At the African Meeting House in Boston in the fall of 1850, Nell reached for language that might move white allies. He compared the refusal of revolutionary patriots to "submit to a three-penny tax" to the struggle against "the system of American slavery, the vilest ever saw the sun." He named James Fayette and Prince Whipple, Black men who had fought for America's independence. And then he landed on the name that would carry furthest: Crispus Attucks, "the first martyr" —

killed at the Boston Massacre, a Black man who bled for the republic before there was a republic to bleed for. Nell was no longer just writing history. He was deploying it.

It was a powerful argument: we were there at the beginning, we paid the price, we earned this. But the mythology Nell was claiming had already been built on erasure. The Black loyalists who had looked at the Revolution and made a different calculation — who fought *against* the founding because the British were offering freedom and the patriots weren't — had been scrubbed from the record before Nell was born. He couldn't tell their story because he didn't have it. The nationalist project had buried them so thoroughly that the only Black revolutionary history available was patriot history. Nell worked with what he had.

This wasn't weakness. It was strategic brilliance under impossible constraints. White abolitionists could debate disunion from positions of relative safety, could burn Constitutions and declare no union with slaveholders without risking their lives or their community's survival. Black Americans had no such luxury. Reject the nationalist mythology entirely and you guaranteed failure. But claim it, and you had to bury the ancestors who had refused it.

Douglass was threading his own needle. He'd built his public career on constitutional patriotism, on the argument that the founding documents — properly read, honestly applied — already contained the seeds of Black liberation. It was a bet on persuasion, on the possibility that white America could be shamed into living up to its own stated principles. But by the 1850s, Douglass could see that moral suasion wasn't working, that the Slave Power was winning, that the Constitution's promises meant nothing if the people interpreting it wanted them to mean nothing. Violence was probably necessary. He knew that. The problem was who would wield it. Black insurrection invited massacre — Turner had proved that. For violence to crack the system rather than justify its intensification, white hands would have to be on the weapons. Or at least, white bodies would have to be in the line of fire alongside Black ones.

William Still and Harriet Tubman took yet another path: clandestine action. They did not confront slavery openly but instead undermined it through the secret script — safe houses, coded signals, routes north. The Underground Railroad operated as sophisticated military infrastructure with intelligence networks, operational security, and armed protection when necessary. Lewis Hayden rigged his Boston house with explosives rather than let slave catchers take William and Ellen Craft. Violence was possible in their work, even expected. But it was always defensive, always reactive. All of them knew provocation, at least by them, had to be avoided.

The Black men who had already joined John Brown in Kansas represented a different calculation. But even their choice fit the same logic. They joined an operation led and organized by white men — violence that would not be read primarily as slave rebellion, that carried different structural implications because of who led it.

When white establishment figures initiated strategic violence against slavery, the system faced a crisis it couldn't suppress through massacre. That wasn't about moral courage — the question was never whether Black resistance understood that violence was necessary or had the courage to use it. The question was structural capacity: Who could initiate strategic provocation in ways the system couldn't simply crush and contain?

Black resistance understood what Douglass articulated clearly in refusing Harpers Ferry — that strategic provocation required allies external to the demographic the system protected. Not because Black people needed white permission or validation, but because power dynamics meant that only certain people could make strategic provocation work without inviting genocide.

The Underground Railroad could not have scaled without white abolitionists willing to harbor fugitives, transport refugees, provide funds and safe houses. That collaboration was illegal, was dangerous, and saved thousands of lives. But it still worked within the logic of symptom management. It addressed the brutality of slavery by helping individuals escape it. It did not threaten the structure that made slavery legal, profitable, and politically entrenched — especially not as the 1850s revealed the enslaver power expanding its hold on the country. The system could tolerate the Underground Railroad. It prosecuted participants when it caught them, but the network itself did not pose an existential threat to slavery's continuation.

The Six crossed that line. They were not content to help people escape. They were not satisfied with moral witness or political advocacy. They concluded that slavery could not be ended through law or persuasion; the Slave Power had so completely corrupted the republic's institutions that only force could break it. If that force were initiated by the enslaved alone, the system could dismiss it as criminal rebellion to be crushed. When the Six organized armed insurrection against federal authority, they built on Black resistance to transform the fight into something the system could not absorb. Higginson stated the case clearly: "The conflict with Slavery is not reform, it is revolution."

That's the resistance dynamic: Structural change requires resistance to expand beyond those directly suffering the abuse. When the comfortable decide that the system itself must fall, they can provoke in ways the oppressed strategically should not. The moment establishment figures decide that the cost of preserving the system outweighs the cost of opposing it marks the turning point from symptom management to structural threat. That calculation — what one is willing to lose and what one's position allows one to accomplish — defines the boundary between addressing symptoms and forcing systemic crisis.

Yet it was not simply a matter of accepting violence as necessary. The Six had already crossed that line in Kansas. What made Harpers Ferry different was its intent. Brown's plan was not to win votes or territory, but to ignite collapse. That was the strategic threshold — the deliberate raising of stakes until the system could no longer absorb the resistance without breaking. The Six understood that difference. Supporting violence in Kansas cost them little. Supporting Brown meant risking everything — their freedom, their reputations, their moral standing, even the stability of the nation itself. But that was the point. Not whether violence was justified, but whether they were willing to become its authors.

The Possibilities of Privilege

The Six have been portrayed in standard histories as a unified, even closed, group — wealthy financiers of John Brown, radical abolitionists bound by shared theology and philosophy. That treatment distorts the picture. Taken together, the six men who would make Harpers Ferry possible shared almost nothing except privilege and the conclusion that the republic needed to be destroyed to save it.

Of the six, only two — George Luther Stearns and Gerrit Smith — had significant financial resources. Stearns was a successful Boston manufacturer. Smith was one of the wealthiest men in America, a New York land baron who had run for president three times. They wrote the checks that made Brown's operations possible.

The other four — Thomas Wentworth Higginson, Samuel Gridley Howe, Franklin Sanborn, and Theodore Parker — couldn't write those checks. What they possessed instead was a different kind of wealth: New England establishment privilege born of Harvard Yard and Congregationalist meeting houses and the lived legacy of American patriot resistance, still vital seventy years after the Revolution. Their contribution was social and cultural capital — voices and networks that unlocked resources that money alone couldn't access. They recruited young men from establishment families. They solicited funds from ministers and reformers and philanthropists who trusted their judgment. They created the moral permission structure that made armed insurrection not just acceptable but also celebrated in certain Northern circles. Higginson could make violence sound righteous. Parker could thunder from his pulpit to thousands every Sunday. Sanborn could coordinate operations across Massachusetts. Howe's revolutionary credentials gave him authority no amount of money could buy.

What bound them was their shared understanding of abusive authority. They had watched every peaceful avenue close — the Fugitive Slave Act; Kansas; the beating of Sumner, one of their own; Roger Taney declaring it a founding principle that Black people had no rights that white people were bound to respect. They understood that the Slave Power had corrupted the republic's institutions so completely that reform was structurally impossible and that ending slavery would require the republic's destruction.

But they reached that moment through completely different paths. They needed different moral frameworks to sustain the choice they were making — frameworks capable of bearing the permanent weight of enabling violence, of accepting that people would die because of their decisions. Without such grounding, they would have been like so many other abolitionists who opposed slavery in opinion, in faith, but did nothing that actually threatened it.

They were six men from different backgrounds who had independently reached the same terrible conclusion and found one another because that conclusion was rare enough that those willing to act on it needed allies. What they built together was not ideological consensus but instead operational coordination — a network that could move money, weapons, men, and information in service of forcing the crisis they believed was necessary. They were the hub of resistance, not the entire wheel.

Understanding who they were individually matters for understanding what they contributed to making the raid on Harpers Ferry — and the last phase of resistance to the First Republic — possible.

The Moral Authority

Thomas Wentworth Higginson was born into exactly the kind of privilege that mattered in 1850s New England. Cambridge, 1823. Harvard College, then Harvard Divinity School. A Unitarian pulpit. A family history that included the Revolution — not the mythologized version but the lived experience passed down through a grandfather who had served in the Continental Congress. The kind of establishment credentials that meant when he spoke, other establishment figures listened, even when they disagreed.

He'd left that pulpit in 1847 because he couldn't reconcile preaching about justice while doing nothing that actually threatened injustice. Higginson needed action, not just contemplation. By his early thirties, he'd settled in Worcester as a minister, married, riding the lyceum circuit giving anti-slavery, temperance, and women's rights speeches, and growing increasingly convinced that moral suasion accomplished nothing.

The war with Mexico and then the Fugitive Slave Act of 1850 clarified things. Higginson wrote editorials warning that anyone who came hunting fugitives in his town should expect armed resistance. But writing wasn't acting. And he joined Worcester's vigilance committee.

April 1851 taught him what resistance actually required. Thomas Sims, a twenty-three-year-old bricklayer from Savannah, had been captured in Boston under the new federal law and was being held in the courthouse. Higginson caught the afternoon train to Boston.

What he found at the Boston Vigilance Committee meeting struck him as "a set of men, personally admirable, yet less fitted on the whole to undertake any positive action." William Lloyd Garrison stood drafting newspaper copy for the next issue — more interested, Higginson thought, in "the purifying of a nation" than "the rescue of an individual." Free Soil politicians worried that violence would cost them votes. Almost nobody was prepared to actually break Sims out. The committee had become "a disorderly convention, each man having his own plan or theory," when what the moment demanded was "the most unflinching unity in action."

At least that was true of the white abolitionists.

Lewis Hayden was ready to fight. A Black committee member who'd escaped slavery in Kentucky, Hayden had been sold by his enslaver — a minister — for a pair of horses. When Higginson said that Boston's Black community should step up, Hayden agreed immediately. Then he pulled Higginson aside with harder news: Many fugitives and free Black people had already left for Canada. The community that might have fought for Sims had already calculated the cost and chosen survival. "What is to be done must be done without them," Hayden told him.

That conversation changed how Higginson understood resistance. Here was Hayden, a man who would lose everything if the rescue failed — his own freedom, possibly his life — and he was prepared to risk it anyway. The white abolitionists who faced nothing more than fines or brief imprisonment were the ones urging caution. The comfortable chose their comfort. The Black man who faced the loss of everything chose to act. Hayden had what Higginson recognized as the "practical grit" that all of Garrison's subscribers lacked.

Higginson and Hayden developed a plan with the Reverend Leonard Grimes, another Black minister. Sims would jump from his third-floor window onto mattresses, then escape by carriage. Direct, achievable, dependent on maintaining security and complete commitment.

But the plan was discovered. Hours before it could happen, Higginson watched workmen install bars across Sims's window. At dawn, federal marshals and three hundred police marched Sims through Boston streets to the docks. They shipped him back to Georgia, where he was publicly whipped before being sold to Mississippi.

"It left me with the strongest impressions of the great want of preparation, on our part, for this revolutionary work," Higginson admitted afterward. The failure revealed two things. First: The vigilance committee wasn't prepared for revolutionary work. Too many members were "non-resistants, irresolute & hopeless visionaries" who treated resistance as moral theater. They wanted to witness against injustice, not actually disrupt abusive authority. Second: Black resistance was already at the vanguard. White abolitionists weren't going to lead this fight. Black activists like Hayden had been doing the work for years. What they needed were allies from outside their community — people whose participation would change how the system responded.

Three years later, as we've seen, Anthony Burns gave Higginson the chance to apply those lessons. Another fugitive captured, another federal courthouse, another vigilance committee meeting that accomplished nothing. That time Higginson didn't wait for consensus. With Hayden, he bought a dozen axes and hid them outside the courthouse. As a protest meeting filled Faneuil Hall and Theodore Parker thundered to the crowd, Higginson extinguished the gas lamps around the courthouse and waited in darkness.

When the crowd surged toward the square around 9:30 P.M., Hayden appeared with a fourteen-foot wooden beam liberated from a nearby construction site. Higginson grabbed one end as a battering ram; a Black man he knew only as Pennington grabbed the other. They ran up the courthouse steps and smashed through the door, making just enough room for one person to enter at a time.

Hayden went through first. Pennington followed. Higginson was right behind them.

Inside, they faced half a dozen officers with clubs. More marshals upstairs were frantically distributing pistols and taking defensive positions. Burns was locked in a cell with iron bars and half a dozen armed guards; there was no quick rescue to be had. In the chaos, a pistol shot caught one federal guard in the groin. Another round hit a marshal in the arm. Reinforcements charged into the square and began making arrests.

In the fighting, a saber blade caught Higginson across the chin, opening a gash that would leave a permanent scar. He didn't feel it in the moment. Only later, when he'd escaped to a friend's house and the wound was bandaged, did he realize that he'd been cut. The next day, he spoke at city hall, face bandaged and arm in a sling, to more than a thousand people about what they'd attempted and why.

Burns was returned to Virginia. Federal marshals deputized the local militia to escort him to the docks. It cost the government a fortune to return one man to slavery, but the affair radicalized thousands who'd been indifferent. More important for Higginson, it confirmed what he'd learned from Sims: Who'd gone through that door first mattered. Not the Harvard-educated minister but Hayden and Pennington — Black men who understood that this fight was theirs, who'd been leading it all along. "The experience was of inestimable value to me,"

Higginson reflected later, "for it removed once and for all every doubt of the intrinsic courage of the blacks."

Higginson wore his scar with pride. It marked the moment he'd stopped talking about resistance and started doing it. Four days after the failed Burns rescue, face still bandaged, he delivered a sermon, which he called "Massachusetts in Mourning," to his Worcester congregation. Some still hoped for a peaceful resolution — petitions for the Fugitive Slave Act's repeal were gathering thousands of signatures. Higginson had no patience for that.

"I am glad to be deceived no longer," he declared. "I live under a despotism." The republic had essentially declared martial law in Boston to return one man to slavery. Peaceful channels were closed. "Under the influence of Slavery, we are rapidly relapsing into that state of barbarism in which every man must rely on his own right hand for his protection," he told his audience. The social compact was at an end. "May we gain iron in our souls," he concluded.

The lesson cemented Higginson's contempt for Garrisonian pacifism. Non-resistance wasn't a principled position — it was a luxury afforded to people who'd never faced slavery themselves and could afford to counsel moderation. Moral suasion provided cover for inaction, allowed people to claim anti-slavery credentials without accepting risk. The movement didn't need more speeches or editorials. It needed people willing to break down doors and take saber slashes to the face.

By 1856, after Kansas and St. Louis, Higginson had reached his final position. The disease was systemic. It required amputation. The republic would have to be destroyed to save it. Peaceful methods if possible, force if necessary.

What Higginson brought to John Brown's operations wasn't money. It was privilege coupled with passion. His Harvard credentials opened doors. His pulpit gave him platforms to make armed resistance sound like righteous necessity rather than criminal violence. He recruited young men from good families to fight in Kansas. He coordinated weapons purchases — visiting Boston gun shops to buy Sharps rifles twenty at a time, then coming back days later for another twenty.

He activated Worcester's networks, convinced others to write checks, created the social infrastructure that made insurrection thinkable.

By 1859, Higginson had concluded that ending slavery required more than tactical violence for limited goals. It required strategic provocation designed to force a national crisis the system couldn't contain. Violence that was expected to fail tactically but succeed strategically by compelling people to choose sides and making slavery's continuation structurally impossible.

Theodore Parker was the closest thing Higginson had to an ideological twin. Lexington-born and thirteen years older, Parker had worked his way through Harvard College before going on to the divinity school. A Unitarian minister with a pulpit, like Higginson. And like Higginson, Parker's theology had gotten him into trouble with the establishment he was supposed to represent.

Parker's embrace of German higher criticism, religious rationalism, and transcendentalism made him controversial even among Unitarians who prided themselves on open-mindedness. His questioning of biblical authority, his willingness to treat Scripture as human document rather than divine revelation, got him branded a heretic by his ministerial peers. But the controversy only increased his following. By the mid-1850s, Parker preached to seven thousand people every Sunday at the 28th Congregational Society in Boston — the largest regular congregation in the city. When Parker spoke, establishment Boston listened, even when they hated what he said.

Parker brought moral authority on a scale that no other abolitionist could match. Parker didn't just oppose slavery — he preached that ending it justified force, that peaceful avenues had closed, that God demanded action not witness. Thousands of respectable New Englanders heard that message every week and began to think thoughts they'd previously dismissed as extreme.

Parker's radicalism wasn't just theological. His grandfather had commanded the Lexington militia on April 19, 1775, and supposedly told his men as British troops aligned against them, "If they mean to have a war, let it begin here." Parker kept two of his grandfather's weapons in his study: the musket that Captain Parker had carried into battle at Lexington and the musket that he'd taken off a British soldier that day. Visitors expecting books and theology also found firearms. When Parker wrote to President Fillmore, protesting the Fugitive Slave Act, he made the connection explicit: "There hangs in my study . . . the gun my grandfather fought with at the battle of Lexington . . . and also the musket he captured from a British soldier on that day. If I would not peril my property, my liberty, nay my life to keep my parishioners out of slavery, then I should throw away these trophies, and should think I was the son of some coward and not a brave man's child."

Parker wasn't using his grandfather as metaphor. He was following his example. He led the Boston Vigilance Committee, organizing resistance to the Fugitive Slave Act — coordinating protection for refugees from slavery, obstructing federal slave catchers. And he armed himself. Parker carried a pistol. Had for years. By the time he leaned into Brown's purposes, Parker had already decided that violence was legitimate.

In 1854, during the Burns crisis, Parker asked the crowd at Faneuil Hall what they were going to do. When someone shouted, "Shoot, shoot," Parker let the moment build before Higginson and Hayden went to work with their battering ram. Parker noticed that Anthony Burns was marched to the ship over the exact spot where Crispus Attucks had fallen during the Boston Massacre. Same ground, same resistance. He told Samuel J. May: "The American Republic is the child of Rebellion; the national lullaby was 'Treason.'"

In March 1858 at an event in Faneuil Hall commemorating the Boston Massacre, Parker shared the platform with William Nell and John Rock. He predicted that "slavery will not be exterminated at one blow, and . . . black men will do their part." The next day, he agreed to raise money for Brown's plan. When he later called Brown "one of the noblest New England patriots" whose heroism recalled "the times of the Stamp Act," he was connecting Brown's violence, and his work in support of it, directly to his grandfather's resistance.

Parker's reach extended beyond Boston. He blended theology with radical patriotism rooted in the Revolution's promise. By the early

1850s, a young Illinois lawyer named Abraham Lincoln was reading Parker's sermons. Parker's declaration that America was founded on "a government of all the people, by all the people, and for all the people" particularly resonated with Lincoln — language Lincoln would later adapt for his Gettysburg Address.

Parker and Higginson had both discovered that transcendentalism — with its emphasis on individual conscience and higher law — could bring you to the edge of accepting violence but couldn't carry you across. The philosophy dissolved into abstraction when confronted with the practical question of forcing change. They both turned to something older: Stoicism blended with Christian moral philosophy. Frameworks that could accommodate permanent moral weight without demanding impossible purity, that acknowledged tragedy without collapsing into relativism, that understood you could be justified and still carry the burden.

Parker had done that philosophical work years before Brown came asking for guns. In his 1850 sermon "The Function and Place of Conscience," he argued that conscience operates above law — that when human law contradicts divine law, conscience compels disobedience. But Parker went further than most ministers, thinkers, and every politician. Consistent with Thoreau, he argued that passive disobedience wasn't enough when confronting systematic evil. If slavery was sin — and it was — then Christians had a duty not just to refuse participation but also to actively work for its destruction. By whatever means necessary.

What Parker contributed operationally was his pulpit and the networks it connected to. His massive congregation meant thousands of potential supporters — donors, recruits, people who could be activated when needed. His theological credentials gave him authority with exactly the audiences that mattered: educated, establishment New Englanders who might contribute to armed resistance if it came with proper moral sanction. When Parker preached that violence was Christian duty and carried a pistol to prove his conviction, it wasn't fringe radicalism. It was respectable theology from one of Boston's most prominent ministers.

By 1859, Parker was dying. Consumption was destroying him. He'd left for Italy, hoping that a warmer climate might buy him time, knowing that he probably wouldn't return. But even from Rome, even dying, Parker defended what he and the other members of the Six were doing with Brown. His distance gave him freedom to say publicly what the others couldn't risk saying from American soil. It is always easier to describe a burning building from outside of it.

Revolutionaries

Samuel Gridley Howe had actually fought in multiple revolutions, real ones where regimes fell and people died and the old order got toppled.

Born in Boston, grandson of one of the Sons of Liberty who had dumped tea in Boston Harbor in 1773, Howe sailed for Greece in 1824 at the age of twenty-three to serve as a surgeon in the revolution against the Ottomans. For six years, he didn't just treat wounds — he fought, organized supplies, raised money, and learned what resistance violence actually looked like. He understood refugees and burial parties. When Greece gained independence in 1830, he went to Paris and joined the resistance against the Bourbon restoration. The July Revolution forced Charles X to abdicate in August. Then Poland rose against the Russians. Howe went to Berlin and organized for the revolutionaries in Warsaw before Prussian authorities arrested and imprisoned him. He eventually made his way back to Boston with revolutionary credentials that money couldn't buy and stories that made him legendary in reform circles.

Higginson had assumed that Howe's experience would translate to complete commitment. A man who'd helped liberate Greece, pushed over a French king, and risked Prussian prison for Polish freedom should have no hesitation about arming enslaved people in Virginia. Howe was a Harvard man, educated and connected, but it often seemed that he had left his zeal for revolutionary work in another life, on another continent. Fighting for Greek independence or French freedom or Polish liberty was adventure for a young man on foreign soil. He could return to Boston as a hero, tell stories about toppling

Ottoman rule, build a reputation as a man of action. But he directed his energies to fighting other battles at home, for the blind and others left behind by the expanding wealth of American society. Sometimes it appeared that he was distracted from the core of the fight against slavery, as if it were someone else's revolution, someone else's system, someone else's blood to be spilled.

But Howe made it clear: "No man's freedom was safe until all was safe." Enough of the true revolutionary remained to continue to voice support for the Six and their support of John Brown's plan.

What Howe brought to Brown's work was not just his experience with what resistance violence really meant but also organizational capacity and establishment legitimacy. His revolutionary credentials made him credible to wealthy donors who might otherwise dismiss anti-slavery organizing as impractical idealism. He'd proved that he could coordinate complex operations under dangerous conditions. His connections, his experience, his willingness to be involved — all of it helped create the infrastructure Brown needed.

Franklin Sanborn was the youngest of the Six, barely in his twenties when he first met Brown in 1857. Born in New Hampshire in 1831, fresh out of Harvard College, he'd taken a teaching position at a school in Concord and immediately fell into its intellectual circles: He knew Emerson, was close to Thoreau, absorbed their philosophy about conscience trumping law and individual moral authority superseding state power.

But Sanborn was still finding his philosophical footing. He hadn't developed the moral framework that Parker and Higginson had built to sustain what they were doing. He was following their lead more than charting his own course. That wasn't necessarily a problem — younger men learned from older ones, and Sanborn was smart enough to recognize those who knew what they were doing.

What made Sanborn valuable was his organizational capacity. He became secretary of the Massachusetts State Kansas Committee, which meant that he coordinated everything: recruiting young men from establishment families to go west, organizing weapons shipments, maintaining correspondence networks, tracking who'd contributed what and where the money went. He was the bridge between the world of radical philosophy in Concord parlors and the world of rifles and pikes that Brown inhabited. Tedious work that had to be done right or the entire operation would collapse.

Higginson worked with Sanborn constantly through 1857 and 1858. Sanborn handled logistics while Higginson provided strategic direction and philosophical justification. Sanborn wrote letters, tracked shipments, maintained financial accounts. When Brown needed someone to coordinate recruits in Canada or arrange meetings in Boston, Sanborn did it. When funds needed raising, Sanborn activated his networks and begged his contacts for contributions, with striking success.

Sanborn's Harvard credentials mattered enormously for this work. His position in Concord connected him to literary and reform circles that could provide both money and recruits. His role at a respected school gave him access to young men from establishment families — exactly the demographic that Brown needed to help ensure that his operations would not be dismissed as criminal rebellion by social outcasts.

By 1859, Sanborn had been doing the coordinating work for two years. He knew the details, knew what Brown intended, helped make the plan operational. His position as secretary meant that his name was on everything — correspondence, financial records, coordination details. He apparently believed that Harpers Ferry was doomed to failure. He said so. But he kept working anyway, kept coordinating, kept facilitating. He was committed to the cause even if he hadn't fully developed his own philosophical framework for carrying the moral weight of what they were enabling.

As Thoreau observed of him, "Calmly, so calmly, [he] ignites and throws bomb after bomb."

The Money Men

Gerrit Smith and George Luther Stearns — the two men who actually wrote the checks — came from outside the Harvard circle, and the contrast with the others revealed what different forms of privilege meant for resistance organizing.

Smith was the oldest of the Six, born in 1797, and the wealthiest man most of the others would ever meet. A New York land baron whose father made his fortune partnering with John Jacob Astor in land speculation, Smith had been financing reform causes for decades: newspapers, schools, land grants to Black families. The organized anti-slavery movement that evolved from colonization efforts through the Underground Railroad to outright abolition. The women's rights movement that his cousin, Elizabeth Cady Stanton, led. The entire apparatus of the temperance movement in the United States. When John Brown needed money, Smith provided most of it. Thousands of dollars over multiple years, far more than everyone else combined.

His wealth wasn't just capital — it was calling. Smith believed that his fortune was a divine gift meant to be given away to righteous causes. He'd already demonstrated the scope of that conviction with Timbuctoo: 120,000 acres of Adirondack land divided into forty-acre plots and granted to three thousand free Black men, an attempt to create the property ownership that would meet New York's voting requirements. The experiment failed — most settlers found the conditions too harsh — but it revealed Smith's willingness to use his wealth for radical purposes. Supporting Brown wasn't aberration. It was culmination.

But Smith struggled with an internal conflict between the reformist methods he'd practiced for decades and the violent means Brown demanded. He'd supported moral suasion, political action, Underground Railroad operations — resistance that stayed within legal boundaries or hidden beyond them. Brown wanted invasion and open insurrection. Smith vacillated, moving between supporting peaceful non-resistance and acknowledging that the destruction of slavery might require force. His religious intensity gave him absolute certainty about the righteousness of ending slavery but made the actual violence harder to face. He'd been enthusiastic about financially supporting Brown's efforts with Kansas settlers or Underground Railroad operations. But as Brown's plans evolved toward direct invasion of Virginia to spark slave revolt, Smith became nervous. He told Sanborn that he didn't want to know details, preferred to be kept in the dark about specifics.

When he finally gave Brown hundreds more dollars, knowing what they'd be used for, he crossed his personal Rubicon. But he crossed it averting his eyes, trying not to see where the path led.

Stearns, born in 1809, made his money in manufacturing — linseed oil and lead pipe, the unglamorous commodities of industrial Massachusetts. He became the treasurer for Brown's operations and the conspiracy's quartermaster. He didn't just contribute dollars. He owned the weapons. Two hundred Sharps rifles, Colt pistols — the arsenal that would go to Harpers Ferry belonged to Stearns. He purchased them, stored them, arranged their transport. When Brown needed rifles, Stearns knew where to buy them and how to move them without drawing attention.

Stearns ran the conspiracy like a business operation, treating revolution as a problem of supply and demand. While the others contributed money and talked about principle, Stearns was sourcing weapons, coordinating shipments, managing the practical mechanics of armed insurrection. His opposition to slavery was straightforward Christian conviction — no transcendentalist philosophy, no radical theology, just the basic Protestant certainty that bondage was sin and had to be stopped. What made him valuable wasn't theoretical sophistication but his capacity to translate moral conviction into material support.

His commitment ran through his household. His twelve-year-old son gave pocket money to Brown's cause. Brown wrote the boy back — a long autobiographical letter explaining his life's work, treating a child's donation with the seriousness of an adult contribution. Stearns was raising his family in the conspiracy, teaching his children that funding violent resistance to slavery was normal, righteous, the work good people did.

By 1859, the Six had all committed to supporting Brown's plan to invade Virginia and spark insurrection. They'd reached that commitment through different paths and brought different resources to make it possible. They shared the conclusion that slavery required strategic provocation — violence designed not to win tactically but to force a national crisis the system couldn't contain.

Whether all of them could carry the moral weight of that choice when Brown was captured and the consequences arrived was a question yet to be answered.

The Spectrum of Commitment

By 1859, the question of violence had become a fault line within the anti-slavery movement. But that fracture revealed something essential about how resistance movements escalate: They don't move until the comfortable middle moves. And the comfortable middle doesn't move all at once. It shifts in stages, each position enabling the next, until enough establishment figures have delegitimized the system that the most committed can finally force the crisis.

The Six weren't outliers. They were the vanguard of a broader establishment shift that had been building for a decade. Understanding where others stood on the spectrum — and why some crossed certain lines while stopping short of others — reveals how resistance reaches the threshold where strategic provocation becomes possible.

At the January 1858 Massachusetts Anti-Slavery Society meeting in Boston, Thomas Wentworth Higginson rose to argue that violence in Kansas and on the Senate floor had changed the terms of struggle. The Slave Power had closed every peaceful channel. Force was now necessary.

William Lloyd Garrison "responded with great force." The society's business, he insisted, was not to "construct a political platform" but to "speak the truth." Moral suasion remained the only legitimate weapon. Violence was sinful.

The room divided. Not over whether slavery was evil, but over what resistance could legitimately do about it.

Abby Kelley Foster, born in Pelham in 1811 and as active in the Underground Railroad as she was visible in the anti-slavery movement, tried to hold the increasingly unstable middle ground. She suggested that women could sway public opinion by "telling them truths which they were unwilling to hear," while men might "carry a ballot." It was a revealing position — acknowledging gendered divisions in tactical options while trying to maintain movement unity. But her husband, Stephen, sided with Higginson's approach. By the next year, 1859, Abby came to agree with what Black abolitionists had been saying for years: Moral suasion had failed. From that point on, she stood with Stephen and Higginson at meetings, endorsing resolutions that denounced the Republican Party as "more dangerous to the cause of freedom" than the Democrats due to their refusal to endorse Black political rights in the North.

That meeting revealed how far the establishment middle had already moved. Even the pacifists were disunionists now. Even those who rejected violence had accepted that the Constitution was irredeemable. The spectrum of commitment had shifted dramatically since 1850. The question was how much further it could shift, and who would go all the way.

The Pacifist Disunionists

Garrison remained the movement's most visible pacifist, even as his position grew increasingly untenable. Born in Newburyport in 1805, he had spent three decades building the American Anti-Slavery Society on the foundation of moral suasion. His slogan — "No union with slaveholders" — made him a committed disunionist, but he expected dissolution to be peaceful. He denounced the Constitution as a covenant with death while insisting that moral force alone could dissolve it. He felt morally tainted by residing in the same country as slaveholders yet believed that taint could be cleansed without bloodshed.

When Lysander Spooner proposed helping runaways form insurgent Maroon camps in western Virginia in September 1858 — the first whispers of Brown's resurfacing — Garrison promptly denounced the idea.

Garrison's position represented the floor of establishment antislavery sentiment by 1859: slavery was evil, the Constitution protected it, the Union should dissolve. But violence remained unthinkable. That floor had moved considerably since 1850 — Garrison was a disunionist now, which would have been radical a decade earlier. But he wouldn't move further.

Wendell Phillips occupied similar ground, though with more ambivalence. Born in Boston in 1811, Harvard-educated like Sumner and Parker, Phillips had become Garrison's intellectual equal though they differed on tactics. He had witnessed the attempt to lynch Garrison in Boston, which radicalized him into the movement. Close to both Parker and Higginson, Phillips understood that moral suasion had limits. He told Higginson that he believed "the time [had] come for resisting the U.S. Government in Kansas, & sustaining such resistance everywhere else."

But Phillips stopped short of endorsing violence himself. He maintained faith that the Union's dissolution could be achieved through moral force rather than physical confrontation. It was half a step beyond Garrison — accepting that violent resistance might be justified elsewhere, by others, while declining to participate in or explicitly endorse it. Phillips stood at the edge of one threshold without crossing it. His position showed how far even committed pacifists had moved, and how close they were to accepting what they still officially rejected.

The Converts

Kansas changed minds. The violence in the territories, combined with Brooks's assault on Sumner, moved people who had spent years preaching moral suasion across the first threshold to accepting tactical violence.

Lydia Maria Child, born in Medford in 1802, represents one of the clearest examples. Child had been a committed pacifist, editing the *National Anti-Slavery Standard* as a forum for moral suasion. But after the attack on Sumner and the violence in Kansas, she changed her position on violence as a resistance tool — at least in Kansas.

Writing as Kansas convulsed in 1856, Child reflected, "What a convenient book that Old Testament [was], whenever there is any fighting to be done." When Higginson's Garrisonian friends expressed shock at his course, Child disagreed: "If the heroes of '76 were praiseworthy, the heroes of Kansas will be more praiseworthy for maintaining their rights."

A friend of Higginson's, Child crossed a line that Garrison never would. By 1859, she stood with those who understood that some battles couldn't be won with words alone. She accepted tactical violence. Whether she could accept strategic provocation remained untested.

Lucy Stone took a different path to a similar destination. A dear friend of Higginson's and one of the most brilliant figures in the reform movements, she was a beacon for women's rights and anti-slavery. She had recently married Henry Blackwell while insisting on retaining her birth name — an act of resistance in itself. When Higginson faced possible prison for the Burns rescue, Stone wrote to him that it would best serve "the 'cause' if they should hang you." When Higginson led his Kansas expedition in 1856, Stone remarked to Susan B. Anthony: "Higginson is looking after the interests of Kansas. God bless him too!"

Stone understood that reform movements were interconnected, that the fight for women's rights and the fight against slavery shared common ground in resistance to abusive authority. But she had come to see what Higginson saw: Moral suasion didn't "take hold of the mind of the community," particularly the Northern Black community, which demanded bold action. Like Child, Stone had been moved by events to accept what she once would have rejected.

Wendell Phillips had made a similar journey, though earlier and from a different starting point. On the first anniversary of Thomas Sims's rendition in 1852, Phillips spoke at Boston's Melodeon. A year earlier, three hundred armed guards had marched Sims to the docks at dawn and shipped him back to Georgia, where he was publicly whipped before being sold to Mississippi.

Phillips, the "golden trumpet" of abolition who had spent years preaching moral suasion alongside Garrison, declared: "I acknowledge no allegiance to this government." The Constitution that protected slavery was a covenant with death. The federal government's hunt for fugitives was organized kidnapping. When marshals came for fugitives, Bostonians should stop them. By force if necessary.

This was 1852 — seven years before Harpers Ferry, and two years before Burns. Phillips was already crossing lines that others would take years to reach. The failed Sims rescue had taught him what the Burns rescue would later teach Higginson: Moral suasion was over.

These converts represented the establishment middle in motion. They had accepted tactical violence as a legitimate response to immediate oppression. They provided cover for those willing to go further, creating an environment where armed resistance wasn't dismissed as criminal extremism. But they hadn't yet faced the question of strategic provocation — deliberately initiating violence to force systemic crisis.

The Philosopher

Henry David Thoreau might have traveled the furthest ideological distance. The man who had written *Resistance to Civil Government* as a meditation on the liberty of conscience had become, by the end of the 1850s, one of John Brown's strongest, loudest, and most indefatigable advocates. Though he moved in smaller social circles and lacked the Six's wealth or connections, he possessed moral clarity sharpened to a cutting edge.

After the Burns case, he delivered "Slavery in Massachusetts" at an anti-slavery convention in Framingham. The speech was absolute in its condemnation: Massachusetts had become complicit in slavery, the Constitution was worthless, the government was illegitimate. "My thoughts are murder to the State," Thoreau declared. He meant it.

Kansas and the Sumner assault had changed him, as they had changed so many. By 1859, Thoreau no longer spoke of passive resistance or mere refusal to cooperate with injustice. He spoke of violence as necessary, even righteous, when authority had closed every peaceful channel. If he'd had money, if he'd had any social network to speak of, no one could have matched his commitment to Brown's cause. Without money to contribute, he gave what he had: his voice, his pen, his unwavering defense of Brown's raid when others fled for cover.

Thoreau had crossed the second line: accepting not just tactical violence but strategic provocation. He understood what Brown was attempting — not defensive response but offensive action designed to force crisis. And he endorsed it completely. Like Higginson and Parker, when Brown went to Harpers Ferry, he had been waiting for someone to act on what he'd already concluded was necessary.

The Tactical Nationalists

Douglass and Nell occupied different ground from the Six. They had accepted that violence was necessary, but they understood something the white abolitionists didn't have to think about. Black-initiated strategic provocation would be crushed and used to justify more repression. The system could absorb that. Turner had proved it. What the system couldn't absorb was comfortable establishment figures initiating violence against federal authority.

That was the structural constraint. Not whether Black resistance had the courage or the will; the question was never that. The question was who could make strategic provocation work without inviting massacre. Douglass and Nell would accept violence, support violence, but the provocation itself had to come from outside the demographic the system was designed to crush.

By 1859, Douglass had embraced a concept of direct resistance, repeatedly arguing that if Black abolitionists had come to accept violence as necessary, white abolitionists had no right to condemn their methods. Speaking at a predominantly Black convention at Faneuil Hall in March 1858, Higginson reminded his audience that the first man through the courthouse door in the Burns riot was not himself, "contrary to general supposition," but Lewis Hayden, a Black man. Two months later, while addressing the New York Anti-Slavery Society, Higginson elaborated: "We white Anglo-Saxon Abolitionists are too apt to assume the whole work is ours, and to ignore the great force of the victims of tyranny." He admitted, "For years I was disposed to think that salvation for the slave in this country was to be worked out not by him, but for him. My eyes have been opened, and I see it otherwise now."

"Never in history was there an oppressed people who were set free by others," Higginson added at that May meeting.

Douglass understood this better than anyone. That is one reason why when John Brown outlined his Harpers Ferry plan in August 1859, Frederick Douglass refused to join. By that point, Douglass had publicly stated that slaveholders had "no right to live" and that he would "welcome the intelligence tomorrow, should it come, that the slaves had risen in the South, and that the sable arms which had been engaged in beautifying and adorning the South were engaged in spreading death and devastation there." He understood that violence was necessary and justified. But when Brown explained the specifics — seize the federal arsenal at Harpers Ferry, arm enslaved people, retreat to the mountains for guerrilla war — Douglass told him directly: "You're walking into a perfect steel-trap, and you will never get out alive."

Brown insisted that the plan would work. Douglass knew better. He understood the tactical realities Brown wouldn't accept: Federal troops would arrive quickly, the arsenal couldn't be held, enslaved people wouldn't have time to organize and arm themselves, Brown and everyone with him would die or be captured. He understood the strategic realities, too: that Black participants would be branded criminals and used to justify more violence against Black communities across the South, while white America might — *might* — see Brown's execution differently.

Douglass was proven tactically correct. Harpers Ferry failed completely as a military operation. Every prediction he made came true. But Douglass was also proven wrong strategically, and the reason exposes the core resistance dynamic: Harpers Ferry worked precisely because Brown was white and backed by white establishment figures. Brown got a stage that no Black resister had the chance to stand on. His execution became a martyrdom that transformed Northern opinion.

Douglass's position on the spectrum was unique. He had crossed every ideological threshold — accepting disunionism, tactical violence, even the necessity of strategic provocation. But he understood the structural constraint that white abolitionists didn't face: Black-initiated strategic provocation would be crushed and used to justify more repression. The system could absorb that. What it couldn't absorb was the comfortable establishment initiating violence against federal authority.

The Ambivalent: Unable to Cross

Charles Sumner stood at the center of the resistance movement's contradictions. Born in Boston in 1811, Harvard-educated, he had become the only member of the anti-slavery resistance in the Senate. He had brought the conflict home — almost literally — when he delivered his "Crime Against Kansas" speech and paid for it with Brooks's cane assault on the Senate floor.

Three years later, in 1859, he was still recovering, still suffering the headaches and dizziness that kept him from the Senate floor for long stretches. The beating had made him a martyr to the cause. It should have radicalized him completely.

But where was he on disunion and violence? Sumner occupied uncomfortable ground. When Higginson invited him to the January 1857 disunion convention, Sumner declined. He couldn't embrace the logical conclusion of his own rhetoric. The two spoke in Boston, Sumner promising only to return to Washington to deliver a speech in the Senate so incendiary that it would be "as first proof brandy to molasses and water." Most likely, he added, it would get him shot. "Disunion is not a desire, merely," Higginson replied, "it is the destiny of this nation."

But Sumner wouldn't endorse disunion, couldn't quite accept that the Constitution he had studied at Harvard might be fundamentally irredeemable. He was the most radical Republican in the Senate, yet he maintained faith that the system could be reformed from within. By 1859, that faith looked increasingly naive to those who had already crossed the line into strategic provocation.

Sumner represented the limit of what institutional politics could produce. He had been beaten nearly to death for speaking truth about slavery's violence. But he couldn't make the leap from exposing the system's brutality to accepting that the system itself had to be destroyed. He remained trapped in the logic of reform even after the system had tried to kill him for demanding it.

Julia Ward Howe, married to Samuel Gridley Howe since 1843, occupied similar ambivalent ground. While her husband sat among the Six, organizing Brown's violent plans, Julia remained skeptical of the path they were taking. She was committed to anti-slavery but less willing to embrace the violence her husband was helping to make possible. She would later write "The Battle Hymn of the Republic," transforming anti-slavery resistance into nationalist pageantry — precisely the kind of mythology that Douglass and Nell understood they needed to claim, but that the Six saw as the problem itself.

The ambivalent — Sumner, Julia Ward Howe, and others who couldn't quite cross the final threshold — revealed the limits of establishment commitment. They had been moved by events, had accepted that slavery was evil and the Constitution compromised. But they stopped short of the final conclusion: that only force could break the system and that someone had to be willing to initiate that force.

Their ambivalence, paradoxically, made the Six's work both necessary and possible. Necessary because people like Sumner proved that working within the system wouldn't succeed. Possible because their partial commitment showed how far the establishment middle had moved, creating space for those willing to go all the way.

By 1859, the anti-slavery resistance stood divided not by commitment but by strategy and by what each person's structural position allowed them to risk. The spectrum ran from Garrison's pacifist disunionism through Child and Stone's acceptance of tactical violence, through Thoreau's embrace of strategic provocation, to the Six's willingness to organize and fund it. Douglass stood at the threshold the Six had crossed but made a different calculation based on structural constraints. Sumner and others couldn't cross at all.

The Eve

By the time John Brown came asking for weapons and money in 1858, all six men had reached the same conclusion through different paths: Violence was not just justified but also necessary. The question was whether that intellectual conviction could survive reality.

Higginson and Parker had crossed the line completely. Higginson had led the Burns rescue attempt, taken a saber cut to the face, and accepted violence as a tactical tool to be evaluated on practical rather than moral grounds. Parker, dying of tuberculosis in Rome, had worked through the theology methodically: When systematic oppression cannot be reformed, resistance must escalate. Both men committed without equivocation.

The other four wanted slavery ended and believed that force was necessary but hadn't fully accepted what that meant. Sanborn loved the romance of conspiracy — the coded letters, the clandestine meetings, the drama of resistance. Whether he could face the reality of blood and trials remained untested. Howe, the only one with substantial combat experience, told himself that he was financing a defensive mountain stronghold, not offensive assault. Stearns, the Boston industrialist, convinced himself that he was supporting Brown's broader humanitarian mission while remaining detached from the methods. Smith, the wealthy New York outsider, created elaborate financial distance through intermediaries and business associates, funding Brown while preserving plausible deniability.

Higginson and Parker had accepted that organizing bloodshed made them responsible for it. The other four believed that they could achieve slavery's end through violence without owning the moral weight of the deaths that would follow. That distinction would matter when the consequences arrived.

The Event

On that night in October, John Brown and eighteen men crossed the Potomac River and seized the federal armory at Harpers Ferry. The plan: Take the armory, distribute weapons to the enslaved people who would join them, establish a stronghold in the mountains from which resistance could operate. The raid lasted thirty-six hours.

Five Black men crossed with Brown into Virginia that night — Shields Green, Dangerfield Newby, Lewis Leary, John Copeland, Jr., and Osborne Anderson. They knew what capture meant: not trial and execution, but torture first. They went anyway. Newby carried a letter from his enslaved wife, begging him to buy her and their children's freedom — he'd been trying to raise the money legally. Now he was trying to rescue them by force. He died in the first hours of fighting. Leary died of wounds two days later. Green and Copeland were captured, tried, and hanged. Only Anderson escaped.

Thirteen white men fought alongside them. Two were Brown's sons. Ten died in the fighting or were executed after. By October 18, federal troops under Lieutenant Colonel Robert E. Lee had stormed the engine house where Brown made his last stand. Brown was wounded and captured, his men dead or scattered.

Enslaved people didn't rise up. They couldn't — how were they supposed to know this was real? How could they trust this white man appearing in the night with weapons and wild promises? Brown had courage and guns and absolute conviction. What he didn't have was communications infrastructure, established trust networks, or time to build them. The raid collapsed before most local enslaved people even knew it was happening.

What Did They Know?

Historians have debated for 160 years what exactly the Six knew in advance about Harpers Ferry. Did Brown tell them he planned to seize a federal arsenal? Did they understand the raid would attempt to spark a general slave insurrection? Were they supporting a specific attack or general resistance operations?

We will never know.

After Harpers Ferry, most of them destroyed everything. Letters burned, documents shredded, correspondence carefully erased. Sanborn later claimed that he'd destroyed "all dangerous papers." Howe admitted to burning Brown's letters. Stearns destroyed his records. Smith burned everything connecting him to Brown.

Only Higginson kept his papers. He refused to destroy evidence, refused to run, refused to deny what he'd done. His correspondence survived, giving us fragments of what the others discussed. But those fragments reveal more gaps than certainties.

What we know: Brown met with them repeatedly in 1858 and 1859. They gave him money specifically for weapons. They knew he planned violence in Virginia — multiple letters reference this. They knew the target was federal property. But the specifics of timing, tactics, the full scope of Brown's intentions — these remain uncertain because five of the six ensured that they would remain uncertain.

The destruction of evidence was itself revealing. Whatever they'd known, whatever they'd agreed to organize, most of them couldn't face defending it publicly once Brown was captured. The intellectual commitment to violence as necessary resistance proved very different from the moral weight of actually enabling it.

Higginson stood alone in refusing to hide what he'd done. The others discovered, in those desperate October days of 1859, that supporting revolutionary violence in theory was far easier than owning it in practice.

In the Wake

Word reached Boston within days. Not the full story — telegraph reports were fragmentary, contradictory — but enough. A raid at

Harpers Ferry. John Brown captured. Federal troops involved. Men dead. Brown's papers seized, likely containing correspondence with his supporters.

The Six's responses came fast and revealed everything about who had truly crossed the moral line.

Higginson's reaction was immediate and unequivocal: rescue Brown by force. He began organizing a raid to break Brown out of jail, convinced that a swift strike could succeed. He wrote to the others, urging action, insisting that they couldn't abandon Brown now. "I am always ready to invest money in treason," Higginson declared, "but at present have none to invest." For Higginson, Brown's capture didn't change the moral calculus — it confirmed it. They had made this possible. They had sent Brown to Virginia. Now their duty was clear: Get him out or die trying.

The others weren't ready for Higginson's clarity.

Parker, dying in Rome, couldn't organize a rescue from his sickbed. But he defended Brown publicly and without equivocation. In letters that circulated widely, Parker declared the raid righteous, necessary, justified by slavery's evil. "I think the world will sustain his measure," Parker wrote. He had accepted the moral burden completely. He was dying anyway — tuberculosis would kill him within six months — but more than that, he genuinely believed that Brown had done God's work. Parker's conscience was clear.

The other four collapsed.

Sanborn received the news on October 19 and immediately panicked. Federal marshals would be coming — they had to be. Brown probably had correspondence, documents, evidence. Sanborn had been the secretary, the coordinator. His name was everywhere. Within hours, he fled to Canada.

Stearns followed him north days later. The industrialist who had admired Brown's courage discovered that admiring it and possessing it were different things. Stearns had provided two hundred Sharps rifles, but now that men were dead and federal prosecutors were investigating, he couldn't face the consequences. Canada was safe. Massachusetts wasn't.

Howe didn't flee but began a frantic campaign of distancing. He wrote to newspapers, denying foreknowledge of the raid, insisting he'd only supported Brown's general anti-slavery work, claiming he knew nothing about Harpers Ferry specifically. The man who had fought in the Greek War of Independence couldn't admit that he'd sparked American revolution.

Smith went to pieces completely. On November 7, he was committed to the New York State Lunatic Asylum at Utica. Whether the breakdown was genuine or calculated remains debated. His symptoms included paranoia, delusions, obsessive fear of arrest. What's certain: Smith had funded violence while telling himself he was supporting something else. When the raid failed and the consequences became real and unavoidable, Smith broke.

The spectrum of commitment was now completely visible. Higginson and Parker had crossed the line and could live on the other side of it — could accept that embracing violence meant owning its consequences, could defend their choice without equivocation. The other four discovered they hadn't truly crossed at all. They'd accepted violence while maintaining psychological distance from it. Brown's capture destroyed that distance. The money and the blood became one thing.

They had all said yes to supporting Brown. But only two of them had truly meant it.

The Trial

At his trial in Charles Town, Virginia, Brown refused the insanity defense his lawyers attempted. "I view it with contempt," he told the court. The strategy might have saved his life, but Brown wasn't interested in saving his life. He was interested in making his life mean something.

When allowed to speak before sentencing, he was crystalline:

> I deny everything but what I have all along admitted — the design on my part to free the Slaves. I intended certainly to have made a clean thing of that matter, as I did last winter, when I went into Missouri and took Slaves without the snapping of a gun on either side, moved them through the country, and finally left them in Canada. I designed to have done the same thing again, on a larger scale. That was all I intended.

Then came the line that would echo through history:

> Now, if it is deemed necessary that I should forfeit my life for the furtherance of the ends of justice, and mingle my blood further with the blood of my children and with the blood of millions in this Slave country whose rights are disregarded by wicked, cruel, and unjust enactments, I say, let it be done.

Brown was putting slavery on trial, not defending himself against its charges. He acknowledged what he'd done and declared it righteous. The violence wasn't regrettable — it was necessary. The raid hadn't failed because it was wrong but because it was incomplete. No equivocation. No distance between action and conviction.

The contrast couldn't have been starker. Brown, wounded and facing certain death, was utterly at peace. The Six, safe and free, were falling apart. Brown had crossed the moral line completely and could live with — and die with — what that meant. Most of the Six were discovering that they hadn't truly crossed it at all.

The Public Reckoning

Brown's capture forced everyone who'd taken positions on violence to face what those positions actually meant. Theory was now blood and bodies and a man in chains.

Thoreau moved first. On October 30, less than two weeks after Brown's capture, he delivered "A Plea for Captain John Brown" in Concord. Didn't ask permission of local authority — simply rang the bell himself. The town fathers warned him not to speak. He spoke anyway.

What Thoreau delivered wasn't a plea — it was complete endorsement. "He was like the best of those who stood on Concord Bridge once, on Lexington Common, and on Bunker Hill, only he was firmer and higher principled than any I have chanced to hear of as there."

This was Thoreau demolishing the line he'd crossed years before: "I shall not be forward to think him mistaken in his method who quickest succeeds to liberate the slave. I speak for the slave when I say, that I prefer the philanthropy of Captain Brown to that philanthropy which neither shoots me nor liberates me." Binary choice. Violence that freed or pacifism that left people enslaved. "I think that for once the Sharps' rifles and the revolvers were employed in a righteous cause."

Thoreau gave that speech three times — Concord, Boston, Worcester — each time more defiant. He'd finally met someone who lived the principles he'd only written about.

Emerson followed more carefully. He called Brown "that new saint . . . will make the gallows glorious like the cross." High praise, but never defending the raid itself. The philosopher could admire the martyr without endorsing the method — maintaining the position he'd held before, commenting on meaning rather than committing to action.

Douglass faced the hardest test. Virginia's governor demanded his arrest as coconspirator. He fled to Canada, then England. Critics called him a coward — Brown was willing to die, why wasn't Douglass? The accusation stung because it held truth. Douglass had accepted violence as necessary, met with Brown, encouraged the plan theoretically. But he'd said no to joining because he knew it would fail.

From exile, Douglass defended Brown: "His zeal in the cause of my race was far greater than mine — it was as the burning sun to my taper light — mine was bounded by time, his stretched away to the boundless shores of eternity. I could live for the slave, but he could die for him."

Garrison faced an impossible contradiction. After thirty years of preaching absolute nonviolence, how to defend Brown while condemning violence? At a meeting on December 2 — Brown's execution day — Garrison declared: "Success or failure, Bunker Hill or Harpers Ferry . . . upon the rock of eternal justice stands the immortal patriot."

The man who'd built pacifist abolition discovered that his architecture couldn't hold. His movement was fracturing in real time. People who'd followed his doctrine for decades couldn't maintain that nonviolence was the only moral choice. Garrison himself couldn't, even while desperately trying.

Tubman mourned the failure but never questioned the attempt. "It was not John Brown that died at Charlestown. It was Christ — it was the savior of our people."

The spectrum ran from comfortable condemnation to fierce embrace. What united most was discovering that thirty years of peaceful resistance had brought them here: a man about to hang for trying to end slavery by force. Each had to answer whether they'd defend him, distance themselves, or condemn him.

Only Thoreau endorsed without qualification continuing on the same path. Only Thoreau declared that what it looked like when you stopped talking and started acting was right and necessary. He was now publicly defending armed insurrection, calling weapons righteous, declaring government "demoniacal force" and Brown a better patriot than the founders.

Thoreau erased the line completely, publicly, permanently. When he died in 1862, the violence he'd advocated for in defending Brown's raid was consuming the nation in Civil War.

The Execution

On December 2, 1859, Brown was led to the gallows in Charles Town. As he left the jail, he handed a note to one of his guards: "I John Brown am now quite certain that the crimes of this guilty land will never be purged away but with Blood. I had as I now think vainly flattered myself that without very much bloodshed it might be done."

He mounted the scaffold without assistance, stood calmly while the noose was placed, waited fifteen minutes while final preparations were made. When the trap dropped, he had been completely himself until the end. No apology. No regret. No attempt to claim his actions were anything other than what they were: an armed assault on slavery that had failed tactically but would succeed strategically.

Sixteen months later, the war Brown predicted erupted. Union armies sang "John Brown's Body" as they marched south. On New Year's Day 1863, Lincoln's Emancipation Proclamation turned Brown's vision into federal policy. Everything the Six had planned came to pass.

But vindication is not absolution.

The Legacy

The Six were vindicated almost immediately. Within four years of the Harpers Ferry raid, slavery was dead — destroyed not by moral suasion or political compromise but by blood and iron, exactly as Brown had predicted. The Thirteenth Amendment ended slavery, the Fourteenth nailed the lid on the coffin of the First Republic. Everything the Six had worked for came to pass. It was the end of the resistance: structural change at last.

But vindication is not absolution.

The Six lived with what they had done for the rest of their lives.

Higginson, the only one to cross the moral line completely, acknowledge his role, fully willing to accept the consequences, and never look back, led Black troops in the war — the 1st South Carolina Volunteers, formerly enslaved people fighting for their freedom with rifles in their hands. He had no regrets. In 1859, when Brown was captured, Higginson had wanted to mount a rescue raid. His coconspirators talked him out of it. For the rest of his life, he carried that as his failure, not making Harpers Ferry possible.

Parker died in Rome in May 1860, his body ravaged by tuberculosis, his mind unbroken. His last public act was defending Brown in letters published across America. He had accepted the moral weight and carried it to his grave without equivocation. Parker believed that what he had done was right. The approaching war proved him correct. He died at peace with his choice.

Sanborn lived longest — until 1917, dying at eighty-five, having spent nearly sixty years as a respected teacher and author. But he never quite recovered his composure after fleeing to Canada. He wrote extensively about Brown in his later years, always positioning himself as a supporter, never quite acknowledging that he had run when the federal marshals came. The image of himself diving out a window to avoid arrest must have haunted him. He had supported violence intellectually but discovered, when tested, that he couldn't face its consequences.

Stearns also fled to Canada, returning only when assured of safety. He spent the war years raising Black regiments and funding abolitionist causes — good work, necessary work. But he knew, and his coconspirators knew, that he had hidden when courage required standing. The money he raised for Black soldiers couldn't erase the fact that when John Brown needed defenders, Stearns had sought distance.

Howe returned from his flight in 1861 and dove into war work. The man who had fought for Greek independence couldn't admit that he'd organized American revolution. He never publicly discussed his collapse when Brown was captured, never explained why he had denied everything before the Senate committee while Parker, dying in Rome, was publishing fierce defenses. Howe lived until 1876, respected and honored, carrying his private burden in silence.

Smith's mental collapse remained controversial. Was it genuine — the psychological burden of making killing possible finally breaking him — or calculated, a way to avoid prosecution? His enemies said the latter. His friends insisted the former. Perhaps both were true. The mind has ways of protecting itself from unbearable knowledge. Smith recovered and lived until 1874, continuing his reform work, generous with his money to the end. But something had broken in him in those weeks after Harpers Ferry. He would fund many causes after that, but never again would he support violence.

Decades later, long after the others had scattered or died or buried their involvement, Higginson wrote to the historian Oswald Garrison Villard, who was researching Brown's life. He described members of the Six with biblical precision: "We were the six Peters, five of whom denied their master and one of whom stood by him to the end."

The line was devastating in its clarity. Peter had denied Christ three times before the rooster crowed. Five of the Six had denied John Brown when federal marshals came. Parker had denied Brown by dying in Florence rather than returning to face trial. Sanborn had denied him by diving out a window. Stearns by fleeing to Canada. Howe by testifying before the Senate committee. Smith by collapsing into madness — whether genuine or calculated. Even Higginson, who had wanted to mount a rescue, had denied Brown by letting the others talk him out of it.

They had struck the spark that lit the fire that consumed slavery. They had been right. History had vindicated them. The war came. Slavery died. Everything they had worked for was achieved.

But they had watched a man to whom they provided material support go to the gallows while they hid behind lawyers, fled to Canada, or claimed ignorance.

Brown had understood what would be required from the beginning. That's why, when captured and facing certain execution, he didn't claim insanity. Didn't deny his intentions. Didn't apologize. He put slavery on trial: "I believe that to have interfered as I have done, in behalf of His despised poor, I did no wrong, but right."

He had crossed the moral line completely and could live with — and die with — what that meant.

The others discovered, when the moment came, that they had supported violence as an idea but couldn't bear it as a reality. Even Higginson judged himself a Peter for not attempting to rescue Brown. The gap between intellectual conviction and moral commitment is the difference between writing a check and pulling a trigger, between supplying weapons and accepting responsibility for the dead.

The moral weight of necessary violence cannot be delegated or avoided. You carry it. You carry it even when you're right. You carry it even when history proves you correct. You carry it to your grave.

Dirty Pink Frocks

In 1856, in St. Louis, Higginson had stood in a slave pen watching children in dirty pink frocks preparing themselves for sale. He'd watched a girl — eleven years old — beg to be with her mother. He'd spoken with the slave trader, who seemed to him "a good-natured looking man, not unlike a reputable stable keeper" in New England, conducting his business with perfect matter-of-fact confidence that what he was doing was legal, normal, just commerce.

"The perfectly matter-of-fact character of the transaction, and the circumstance that those before me did not seem exceptionally cruel men," Higginson had reflected, "made the whole thing more terrible." What he had witnessed was "a case, not of special outrage, but of every-day business, which was worse."

Thirty years of speeches and essays hadn't saved those girls. Moral suasion hadn't closed the slave pen. Legislative compromises hadn't stopped the daily business of tearing families apart. Every approved, peaceful channel had been tried, exhausted, blocked by a system designed to make reform impossible.

The question the Six faced — the question that every resistance movement faces when tactical violence fails to break the system —

is whether to cross the line from resistance that works within the system's logic to resistance that deliberately provokes systemic crisis.

Brown understood this. Harpers Ferry wasn't meant to succeed tactically — to hold the arsenal, arm thousands, establish mountain strongholds. It was meant to force the South to reveal slavery's true nature, force the North to see federal complicity, force the nation to confront what it had avoided for decades.

Strategic provocation. Calculated crisis. Accepting that you will cause destruction and death to break a system that cannot be reformed. Accepting that permanent moral weight.

This is what Resistance Principle #8 means: When tactical violence fails to break the system, resistance faces its hardest threshold — escalating to strategic provocation. Deliberately initiating violence not to achieve tactical goals but to force systemic crisis. Accepting permanent moral weight. Revealing who has truly committed completely.

Half measures don't work at this interruption point. You can't organize strategic provocation while maintaining plausible deniability. You can't enable the spark while claiming you didn't want the fire. You can't start a war and then flee when the war comes.

Either cross completely — accept the transformation, own the consequences, carry the weight for life — or don't cross at all.

The Six discovered what every resistance movement learns: Strategic provocation can work. Brown's tactical failure became strategic success. Within eighteen months, the war was raging. Within four years, slavery was dead. Everything they had sought to achieve came to pass.

Higginson understood in 1909, looking back across fifty years, that the cost isn't just the dead in the raid or the war that follows. The cost is what it does to you. The permanent transformation. The Six had helped bring about the freedom of four million people. They had ended the most brutal system of oppression in American history. They had been vindicated by history, celebrated as heroes, proven correct in every prediction.

The slave pen was closed. The system that allowed men to conduct their everyday business of tearing families apart was destroyed.

But Higginson never forgot the plea of the girl in the dirty pink frock to be with her mother, never stopped carrying the weight of what it took to free her, never escaped the knowledge that even being right — even succeeding — doesn't absolve you from the permanent moral burden of choosing to break a system through strategic violence.

That's the test. That's the threshold. That's the interruption point where most resistance movements fail — not because they can't accept violence, but because they can't accept carrying the weight of deliberately provoking systemic crisis.

The Six crossed. History vindicated them. And they carried the weight until they died.

That's Principle #8. That's the price of breaking systems that cannot be reformed. That's what it means to commit completely.

CHAPTER NINE

The Last Battle of the American Revolution

Resistance Principle #9 — Seize the day: When resistance achieves power, use it completely.

WASHINGTON, DC, DECEMBER 1865

The air inside the Capitol was thick and warm, strange for December, as if spring had wandered in by mistake. Washington had never seen a winter like this one — mud instead of frost, magnolias holding on longer than they should, and the smell of coal smoke clinging to everything. Crowds packed into the galleries of the House of Representatives' vast new chamber, restless with rumor: diplomats in dark coats, reporters scribbling in their laps, office seekers leaning over the rail. Citizens had come from every corner of the Union to watch history restart itself. No one knew quite what was about to happen, only that this opening session would decide what victory meant — and for whom.

At noon, the clerk of the House, Edward McPherson, rapped for order. Normally his role was ceremonial, a ritual of continuity. Read the roll. Count the votes. Step aside when the Speaker took the chair. He knew it well. He had even been a member of this House for two terms. But this morning the script had been rewritten.

McPherson's eyes met those of his old friend and mentor, Thaddeus Stevens, seated at the edge of the well. They had spent the past forty-eight hours planning an outcome that would look like boring parliamentary process but would, in fact, change the course of the American republic.

McPherson began.

"Maine . . . Mr. Lynch."

"Present."

"Mr. Blaine."

"Here."

And so on, going down the roll as the old Continental Congress had done — geographically, beginning with the northernmost state and working south.

McPherson then came to the first of the states that had seceded.

"Virginia."

Silence.

"North Carolina."

Silence.

The silence was nothing new. The seats of the rebel states were — in theory — still there, but Congress considered them vacant, so no names were called. During the war, the states' names were called, but no members were recognized.

But this morning there *should* have been something new, something different. The war had been over for months. Robert E. Lee was no longer a revered rebel general but instead the president of a small college in western Virginia. Jefferson Davis was no longer the president of a breakaway republic but imprisoned in a cell in Fort Monroe, Virginia, awaiting trial for treason. Every defeated rebel state had established a new government under President Andrew Johnson's Reconstruction plan, and several of them had sent men to represent them, once more, in the House of Representatives.

And there they were, standing in the House chamber, credentials in hand, waiting to be acknowledged by McPherson. Representatives from Tennessee and Louisiana, from Virginia and Arkansas.

But he ignored them.

"Tennessee."

Horace Maynard stood up. He knew this moment. Although born in Massachusetts and a graduate of Amherst College, Maynard had represented Tennessee in Congress at the beginning of the war. And he had spent the past few years working with Johnson to keep Tennessee in the Union. He was as loyal as they came. He was ready to return to the House. And it's not as if McPherson didn't know him, couldn't recognize him. They had served together in Congress.

But silence.

"Alabama."

Maynard tried to stop McPherson. There must be a mistake.

"I beg to say that in calling the roll of members —"

McPherson cut him off. "The clerk will be compelled to object to any interruption of the call of the roll."

Maynard was bewildered. "Does the clerk decline to hear me?"

"I decline to have any interruption for the call of the roll."

The room stiffened.

McPherson continued to the end. And then a motion was made to move to the election of a Speaker.

But Maynard tried again. "Before that motion is put —"

Thaddeus Stevens's voice cut through the chamber: "I call the gentleman to order."

McPherson followed instantly. Stevens had invoked procedure, the rules by which they operated, the order of the day. Was Maynard part of those rules, in order, or operating outside those rules, out of order?

"The clerk rules, as a matter of order, that he cannot recognize any gentleman whose name is not upon his roll."

And there it was.

James Brooks, a Democrat from New York, shot to his feet with an objection. By what authority had Maynard and the others been struck from the roll? Was Tennessee not in the Union? Had several states been denied their representation in the United States Congress by . . . the clerk of the House of Representatives? If so, Brooks proclaimed, it is a "revolutionary step."

McPherson's answer was mechanical, bloodless. He had acted "according to his understanding of law and duty."

Brooks demanded an explanation.

"It is not necessary," Stevens told him, his voice cold as iron. "We know all." He gestured to the men around him.

Brooks demanded to know when the mystery would be explained.

"I have no obligation to answer the gentleman," Stevens said. Then, after the briefest pause — the pause he was famous for — "I propose to press it . . . at the proper time."

And Stevens would control that time, just as he would control — through the next bill he introduced — when the members from the rebel states would return to Congress.

Laughter erupted. The House knew what had just happened, even if the newspapers would take a day to catch up. In a few measured sentences, Thaddeus Stevens and Edward McPherson had taken hold of the Constitution of the United States, and they weren't going to let anyone else touch it until they were done with it.

Their partner in that work, US Senator Charles Sumner, at that moment rose in the Senate chamber on the opposite side of the Capitol to introduce several bills including a civil rights act, a constitutional amendment guaranteeing equal rights, and Stevens's bill to keep out the former rebels until Congress decided that the war wasn't just over that but that it had been won.

December 4, 1865, was the hinge on which America's resistance history turned.

Had the Southern representatives been seated, they would have joined Northern Democrats to form a new majority — one that could have undone the war's results without firing a shot. The Radicals feared that they might repudiate the Union debt while assuming the Confederate one, legitimizing the rebellion. They could have seized on the loophole in the Thirteenth Amendment — "except as punishment for crime" — to rebuild slavery under a different name. Legislatures in the states reconstructed by Johnson were already showing how: vagrancy laws that criminalized unemployment, labor contracts that chained freedpeople to their former plantations, apprenticeship statutes that tore Black children from their parents and delivered them to white "guardians."

The war had been won on the battlefield, but it was in danger of being lost in Congress.

Stevens and Sumner understood that better than anyone alive. Two days earlier, they had gathered the Republican caucus and laid out the plan. Senators and representatives from the rebel states would not be seated, would not even be recognized. Instead the Joint Committee on

Reconstruction — Stevens's first bill of the 39th Congress — would be created to oversee what happened to the defeated Confederacy and decide when — if ever — those states were fit to rejoin the Union, a new Union, under a new Constitution. And until both chambers of Congress agreed to admit them, no Southern representative would take a seat, regardless of what the president of the United States had to say about it.

That last clause was the lock. It bound the Senate to the House, where Stevens ruled. Sumner knew that the Senate, as always, was the weakest link in the chain of anti-slavery resistance. And he knew that his influence was limited there. As the strongest, loudest voice against slavery and for equality, he had alienated many of his moderate colleagues, and all of the pro-slavery ones. That was fine with Sumner, but it created a problem in how to manage the Senate under Stevens's plan. They had to arrange it so that the Senate couldn't move without Stevens — and they knew exactly how to hold the line against any compromise, in the name of reconciliation, that would undermine every gain for which the dead of the war had paid.

Stevens was seventy-three, frail, carried into the chamber in a sedan chair. Half the members thought he might not live out the session. Born in 1792 during George Washington's presidency, Stevens, like Sumner, had spent half a century fighting slavery through every legal avenue the republic offered, and Slave Power had closed all of them with its control of government. But now the war had broken the machinery itself. The Constitution lay in fragments, and Stevens saw in those fragments the chance to rebuild something new.

Sumner and Stevens knew this was the brief window they'd waited for their entire political lives. Reconstruct the republic so completely that slavery — and the abusive authority it required — could never come back.

By midafternoon, it was done. Stevens had passed his resolution for the Joint Committee on Reconstruction. Outside the chamber, Horace Maynard and the other members from rebel states waited and then stormed away, down Capitol Hill to Pennsylvania Avenue and the White House, locked out of the government their states had once tried to destroy — fuming at the new American order that might take shape without them.

Most resistance stories end at the barricades. The patriots of 1775 pushed abusive authority back to Boston, stopped the Intolerable Acts, held power themselves — then watched nationalists steer that victory toward a federal republic that institutionalized new forms of exclusion and control. Black Loyalists achieved freedom in 1783, escaped the constitutional slavery that metastasized behind them — then spent decades fighting to hold what they'd won in a world organized against them.

Getting inside isn't enough. Winning at the point of provocation isn't enough. Even seizing power temporarily isn't enough. Because the clock starts ticking when you're through the gates, and if you don't use that brief window to rebuild the structure itself — changes that can't be easily undone — then you've won nothing except the right to watch it all get taken back.

The resistance to the First Republic started the moment that republic took shape. Ona Judge recognized what George Washington's Constitution meant when the first Fugitive Slave Act gave him authority reach into states where she'd found freedom. She ran anyway. Others followed — building the Underground Railroad, creating organized networks of defiance against federal power. But the abusive authority kept expanding. The war with Mexico made the problem undeniable even to those who'd tried to ignore it: The Slave Power wasn't a faction within the republic, it *was* the republic. Thoreau saw it. The abolitionists saw it. The comfortable started seeing it.

Recognition wasn't enough. Organization wasn't enough. The Underground Railroad saved individuals but couldn't stop the structure from growing stronger. So the resistance escalated — strategic provocation designed to force the confrontation, to make the system defend itself openly, to strip away any pretense that it could be reformed from within. Harpers Ferry was the spark. The war the slaveholding states started in response finally broke the machinery itself.

That's Resistance Principle #9: Seize the brief window when the structure breaks, and rebuild it before it can reconstitute itself. Don't celebrate the victory. Don't wait for legitimacy. Don't trust that winning the war means keeping what you've won. The comfortable always want reconciliation, a return to normalcy, peace that looks like the old order with new names. Resistance movements face two major interruption points: the first when permitted channels are exhausted and allies withdraw rather than accept unpermitted action, and the second when violence becomes necessary and even more allies resign.

But there's a third interruption — the window after apparent victory, when resistance either seizes power to transform the structure or watches the old authority rebuild itself within the new institutions and erase every gain. The Radicals understood this. They'd seen it before. The patriot resistance had won regime change but lost the negotiation over what that victory meant, accepting the Bill of Rights while surrendering structural change. The Radicals weren't going to make that mistake. They took everything they could get before the window closed.

For a brief window, for the first time in American resistance history, the resisters controlled the government. The anti-slavery resistance movement that began with Ona Judge acting from clandestine networks, that found its intellectual foundation in Thoreau's recognition of systemic failure, that scaled up through the Underground Railroad, that accepted violence at Harpers Ferry — that movement's political wing, the Radical Republicans, now held power.

But to understand what they did — and why it still wasn't enough — we need to see what they were up against.

The First Thirteenth Amendment

MARCH 4, 1861, 5:20 A.M.

Charles Sumner was exhausted. He had been in the new Senate chamber for two days straight. Two all-night sessions, Saturday through

Sunday and into the earliest hour of Monday, debating and voting on version after version of constitutional amendments designed to save the Union by protecting slavery forever.

To save the Union by enshrining slavery, even after seven states had already seceded to defend keeping people as property. Tension filled the Senate's cavernous new home, which was down the hall from the dark, cramped old Senate chamber where Preston Brooks had assaulted Sumner with his cane. The anger, the violence of that assault had made its way down the hall to the Senate's new chamber. Brooks was long gone. He died only eight months after the attack. But his animus survived him. It could be felt in the new galleries surrounding the chamber, from which people could witness the events on the floor. The men and women in attendance did more than watch as the senators debated the amendments; they acted. Three times there were disturbances. Three times the sergeant at arms had to clear the galleries. Three times the doors had to be locked against the public. Once only ladies were permitted to return, but they, too, had to be sent out again.

Sumner sat at his desk. Fifty years old, less than five years from Preston Brooks's cane, carrying permanent damage in his spine. While he'd been in Paris enduring treatments that felt like torture, while he'd been trying to recover enough strength to return to the building where slavery's defenders had beaten him unconscious, his friends had crossed lines across which he could not reach them. Samuel Gridley Howe and Thomas Wentworth Higginson — closest to him among the Six who made Harpers Ferry possible — had been preparing for war.

He wasn't quite a disunionist. The distinction was technical more than philosophical as he became leader of the Conscience Whigs — standing apart from the Cotton Whigs, such as Daniel Webster, who accommodated enslavers. When Higginson invited Sumner to the Worcester Disunion Convention in 1857 — declaring that "disunion is not desire, merely, it is the destiny of this nation" — Sumner declined, too weak still to travel. But he understood what Higginson was proposing: two antagonistic nations cannot remain together. Perhaps the Union itself was in fact the problem. Sumner held no sentimental attachment to the Constitution that protected slavery and empowered slaveholders. His 1845 Fourth of July oration had attacked the "false patriotism that proclaimed 'our country, be she right or wrong,'" the attitude that transformed citizens into "the provokers of war." Like Thaddeus Stevens, he believed that the Constitution was not sacred when it was clearly wrong. If ending slavery required dismantling the constitutional order and reconstructing it, Sumner wouldn't mourn. The question was venue and means, not conviction: whether transformation could come through constitutional politics or required the Constitution's destruction.

His friends had answered that question. Howe had supported Brown. Higginson had organized the conspiracy, had served as point man for the operation, and when it failed had wanted to mount an armed rescue. They had breached the Madison rule — that preserving the Union mattered more than ending slavery — while Sumner was still trying to stand without collapsing. Now they were proven right. Secession — disunion — was coming not from abolitionists but from enslavers who understood exactly what Harpers Ferry had shown to be inevitable.

It would be convenient to draw a clean line from Harpers Ferry to Fort Sumter, to claim that the Six caused the war. Convenient but wrong. The constitutional order had been cracking for years: the Fugitive Slave Act, Dred Scott, Bleeding Kansas, the caning that nearly killed Sumner. What mattered about Harpers Ferry wasn't causation but that it made certain compromises feel impossible to enslavers, even as Congress kept trying them. Brown may have failed tactically, as Frederick Douglass predicted he would, but Brown's execution created a martyrdom that transformed Northern opinion in ways that Black-led resistance — Denmark Vesey, Nat Turner — never would, because the system, with all its embedded racism, had regarded those acts of resistance as slave rebellions to be crushed, dismissed, forgotten. But when establishment figures organized strategic violence against slavery — when Smith and Stearns provided funding, when Sanborn coordinated logistics, when Parker gave theological justification, when Higginson served as organizer, when Emerson and Thoreau and thousands rang church bells the day Brown hanged — the system faced a moral crisis it couldn't control.

The enslaver power understood. Sumner's former Senate colleague, Jefferson Davis of Mississippi, cited Brown's raid as grounds for secession. Southern newspapers called it proof that Republicans would arm slaves and incite race war. Harpers Ferry proved that anti-slavery resistance had crossed the line from opposing slavery to organizing violence against it. That was what mattered to senators watching their colleagues leave the chamber, and to Sumner watching the republic fracture.

Which brought him back to the chamber, to the exhaustion, to the question facing him on that March morning in 1861.

Because the question wasn't whether compromise could preserve the Union. Seven states had already seceded. It was whether complete surrender of everything the anti-slavery resistance had fought for, even as an anti-slavery president entered the White House, would be the sorry, sad conclusion of decades of struggle, strife, and bloodshed — including his own.

Just a few days before President Lincoln's first inauguration, Ohio Congressman Thomas Corwin introduced what would have been the Thirteenth Amendment to the Constitution: "No amendment shall be made to the Constitution which will authorize or give to Congress the power to abolish or interfere, within any State, with the domestic institutions thereof, including that of persons held to labor or service by the laws of said State."

The Madison rule was on the table to become part of the Constitution: accept permanent enslavement to preserve the Union.

William Seward, who had drafted the original amendment, made sure that, like the Constitution itself, the language avoided the word *slavery* — "persons held to labor or service by the laws of said State" — but everyone knew what it meant. The subterfuge, as in 1787, was almost laughable in its translucence. The House had already passed the proposed amendment on February 28, 133–65, barely the two-thirds needed.

Perhaps none of the votes over those days captured the stakes for the resistance more than the version of the amendment George Pugh of Ohio introduced. It was the clearest and maybe most intellectually honest reflection of where the country actually was. It would explicitly enshrine in the Constitution "slavery of the African race," and Congress would not only be barred from interfering with it but also would be bound to protect it. And it took a massive step further: "Persons who are, in whole or in part, of the African race" could never vote or be elected to office in the United States of America.

And in that constitutional amendment, so earnest in its comprehension, so clinical in its application, so revealing in its racism, Sumner on the floor, and the people in the galleries, could see the competing, almost exclusive, visions for the country. Surely, thought some of those looking on, senators could not support such an addition to the Constitution? The vote would surely be lopsided, a ringing defeat. Sumner, though, knew these men: Senator Andrew Johnson of Tennessee, sitting just a few desks away, was an enslaver and a white supremacist. He believed, with the nation's founders, that the Union and slavery were intertwined, indivisible. Pugh's amendment could finally spell that out.

Johnson voted aye. Edward Baker of Oregon voted aye. And the yes votes kept coming.

Sumner voted no. Lyman Trumbull of Illinois (but from Connecticut), a staunch ally of Sumner's, voted no. And Benjamin Wade of Ohio (but from Massachusetts), a close friend of Sumner's, who disliked both Pugh and Lincoln, voted no.

In the end, the nays had it. But fourteen senators — more than a third of the body — voted with Johnson.

Similar amendments kept coming, as Sumner, with Trumbull and Wade, voted against every one of them.

Then, in the dark early hours of March 4, before everyone else who planned to attend the inauguration was even awake, the Senate approached the final question on Corwin's amendment, drafted by Seward, to forever protect slavery, even if the opponents to slavery ever gained the majority in Congress.

The call of the vote began on the language that would forever put beyond reach everything that Sumner had worked, and fought, and suffered for.

It passed 24–12. Andrew Johnson. Edward Baker. Stephen Douglas. And twenty-one more voted for it.

Sumner, Trumbull, Wade, and nine others voted against.

The Senate adopted the first constitutional amendment in fifty-seven years — to bar Congress from ever acting against slavery, even if the opponents to slavery gained a majority.

Just hours later, Abraham Lincoln took the oath as the first anti-slavery president. With Sumner in the audience, Lincoln endorsed the amendment and later sent it to the states for ratification.

Sumner understood what this meant for the anti-slavery resistance. His friends — Howe and Higginson among those who had made Harpers Ferry possible — had believed secession would mean the beginning of slavery's end. The slave states leaving would free the North to finally act. They were wrong. Congress's response to secession was to offer slavery constitutional protection it had never possessed. The Madison rule held: Preserving the Union mattered more than ending slavery. Even now. Even as an anti-slavery president took office — and endorsed it.

The message was clear: Resistance would now have to fight from inside the constitutional system, against the very administration they had worked to elect.

State Suicide

On the day of Fort Sumter's surrender — April 14, 1861 — Charles Sumner went to the White House.

He didn't go to discuss strategy or offer support. He went to remind

Lincoln of history. There were plenty of examples, Sumner told him, from the Revolution and the War of 1812, that the war powers of any executive must include emancipation of the slaves of a military opponent. The British had done it — the Philipsburg Proclamation, Birch's proclamation, the practical policy that brought thousands of Black people to British lines and freedom. It was a military necessity. It was also justice, but Sumner didn't lead with that. He used the practical language of interest — the language that might move a cautious lawyer-president. Emancipation was a weapon. Lincoln should use it.

Lincoln called for seventy-five thousand troops the next day. He did not issue an emancipation proclamation. Four more states — Virginia, Arkansas, Tennessee, North Carolina — joined the Confederacy within weeks. By summer, the war everyone had claimed to want to avoid was fully under way, and the anti-slavery resistance discovered that an anti-slavery president leading a war against slaveholders was not the same thing as a president willing to end slavery.

Sumner kept returning to the White House. Again and again, pressing Lincoln to act, to use the war powers he clearly possessed. But Lincoln would not touch slavery. Not in the border states that remained in the Union — Missouri, Kentucky, Maryland, Delaware — where touching slavery might drive them to secession. Not in the rebel states, where emancipation might undermine his claim that secession was illegal and the Confederate states remained part of the Union. Not anywhere, because the Corwin Amendment was still out there, ratified by Ohio, Maryland, and Illinois, waiting to become part of the Constitution if enough states approved it.

The war, in Lincoln's framing, was about preserving the Union, not ending slavery. When General John C. Frémont issued an emancipation order in Missouri in August 1861, freeing slaves owned by Confederate sympathizers, Lincoln revoked it. Sumner protested. When General David Hunter did the same in South Carolina, Georgia, and Florida in May 1862, Lincoln revoked that, too. Sumner protested again. The pattern was clear: Military necessity could justify suspending habeas corpus, imprisoning suspected Confederate sympathizers without trial, expanding executive power in ways that would have horrified the framers. But it could not justify freeing enslaved people. The Madison rule held even in wartime. Perhaps especially in wartime, when Lincoln needed to keep the border states loyal and leave open the possibility of reconciliation with the rebels.

The anti-slavery resistance watched with mounting fury. They had worked to elect Lincoln. They had accepted the necessity of working within the constitutional system rather than embracing Higginson's disunionism. And now the anti-slavery president was protecting slavery while waging war against slaveholders. The Corwin Amendment proved it: Even with Southern states gone from Congress, even with war declared, the government's first instinct had been to offer slavery permanent constitutional protection in an effort to lure back the secessionist states and avert the Union's permanent destruction.

By February 1862, the war was ten months old. The Union had suffered humiliating defeats — Bull Run in July 1861, Ball's Bluff in October. The Confederacy looked like it might actually win. And Lincoln was still refusing to make the war about slavery, still trying to preserve the possibility of bringing the rebel states back into the Union with slavery intact, still governed by the Constitution that protected the institution.

That's when Sumner stopped asking Lincoln to act and started acting himself. Not because the war was going well but because it was going badly, and Lincoln showed no signs of using it to achieve what the anti-slavery resistance had fought for decades to accomplish. If the president wouldn't breach the constitutional order that protected slavery, Congress would have to do it for him.

Sumner's "state suicide" theory provided the constitutional framework. By attempting secession, Sumner argued, the rebel states had destroyed their own state governments. What remained were not states with rights under the Constitution but territories subject to Congress's plenary territorial authority — the same absolute power that Congress exercised over Western territories before they achieved statehood.

Sumner meant this literally, not as legal metaphor. The rebel states had committed felo-de-se — suicide as states. They had ceased to exist as political entities with constitutional protections. The people who lived there were still citizens, the land was still part of the United States, but the governmental structures that had constitutional standing were gone. Destroyed by the states themselves through their attempted secession. What Congress faced wasn't the question of how to readmit states that had temporarily left the Union. It was the question of how to govern territories that had never legally left but had destroyed their own political existence.

He laid this out in resolutions he introduced to the Senate on February 11, 1862, ten months into the war. The resolutions declared that the seceded states had abdicated all rights under the Constitution, had become felo-de-se, lapsed. Therefore slavery, Sumner argued, as a peculiar local institution without any origin in the Constitution or in natural right, had been dissolved along with the state governments that had protected it.

The phrase *state suicide* startled conservative minds. It went against the idea of historical continuity, the concept of "an indestructible Union of indestructible States." Even moderate Republicans deplored it, regarding it as unconstitutional because it seemed to recognize the validity, or at least the effectiveness, of secession. But Sumner wasn't conceding that secession had been legal. He was arguing that the attempt itself had destroyed what the seceding states were trying to preserve — their status as states with constitutional protections.

This gave Congress absolute power over the rebel states. Not the power to negotiate with sovereign states about terms of readmission, but the power to impose whatever conditions it chose on territories seeking statehood. Congress could require new state constitutions. It could demand ratification of constitutional amendments as a condition of statehood. It could establish military governments, dictate voting requirements, invalidate existing state laws. The normal constitutional protections that states enjoyed didn't apply because there were no states — only territories that Congress could organize however it saw fit.

Thaddeus Stevens had reached the same conclusion as Sumner through a different path, one that showed that the anti-slavery resistance wasn't confined to New England's Harvard-educated reformers and Boston's Conscience Whigs. Stevens came from Pennsylvania iron country, a self-made lawyer who'd defended fugitive slaves since the 1820s, who'd fought to establish public education when his state legislature wanted none of it, who'd built his legal practice on representing the dispossessed. By the time he entered Congress in 1849, he'd already spent decades in the Pennsylvania legislature battling the planter class's constitutional protections.

He understood the Union differently from most of his colleagues. The Union, for Stevens, wasn't the Constitution's machinery or the federal government's structures. It was the Declaration's principles — not what Jefferson intended by "all men are created equal," but what people fighting for freedom and liberty meant by those words. That was the Union: people committed to those principles, beyond the mechanics of the state. The Constitution was simply a tool to serve those principles, to be altered and changed whenever found inconsistent with them. As he would say years later when introducing the Fourteenth Amendment, the framers "had been compelled to postpone the principles of their great Declaration," and now Congress's task was to try "to write the Declaration of Independence's promise of freedom and equality into the Constitution."

By 1862, Stevens believed that the Constitution had "vicious principles incorporated into" its institutions, "palpable incongruities and despotic provisions" that betrayed the Declaration's promise. Now the war had broken that machinery. He wasn't interested in fixing it. He wanted to use the opportunity created when rebel states removed themselves from Congress to rebuild the constitutional order entirely. His theory was simpler and more brutal than Sumner's: The Confederate states were conquered provinces. They had no rights. Congress could do whatever it wanted with them.

Both theories arrived at the same place: The constitutional protections that had shielded slavery were gone. The structure was broken.

Congress had absolute power to rebuild it. The question was whether they would use that power before the window closed, before the old order reconstituted itself, before reconciliation and normalcy reasserted the constitutional machinery that had protected enslaver power for eighty years.

The Problem with Proclamations

Through the winter of 1861–1862, Sumner pressed Lincoln constantly — sometimes several times a week — on the necessity to act against slavery. Lincoln seemed to tolerate Sumner's persistent attempts at persuasion as the political price for keeping the anti-slavery resistance on the side. In December 1861, they had a long discussion. Sumner left believing that "we agreed, or agreed very nearly." That was Lincoln's talent: making everyone feel that they agreed "very nearly." Lincoln told him that the only real difference between them was timing — "a month or six weeks." Sumner took that literally. He promised to keep quiet for six weeks.

Two weeks later, Lincoln reached out again. He had a plan to emancipate slaves in Delaware as a test case. One version would reach total emancipation by 1867. The other by 1893. Lincoln preferred the 1893 version. The anti-slavery resistance stood for immediate, uncompensated abolition, but Sumner went along, conceding that "never should any question of money be allowed to interfere with human freedom."

On March 6, 1862 — almost exactly a year after endorsing the Corwin Amendment — Lincoln sent a message to Congress urging gradual abolition with federal financial support "to compensate for inconveniences public and private, produced by such a change in the system." Sumner was delighted. Here was an American president, for the first time in history, proposing federal support for emancipation. Border state representatives wouldn't even consider it.

On July 4, 1862, Sumner went to the White House twice to press Lincoln on "reconsecrating the day by a decree of emancipation."

Lincoln refused. It was "too big a lick." He was too afraid of pushing border states to secession. And he wasn't sure that he could enforce it anyway.

Lincoln placed a draft of the Emancipation Proclamation before his cabinet on July 22, 1862. He put it away again when warned that he couldn't enforce it. Sumner saw an opportunity. He pushed Lincoln every day to issue the proclamation. Lincoln said no, insisting that he needed a victory first. The Union barely won at Antietam in September — Lee withdrew after what amounted to a draw — and Lincoln used this as his opening to issue a preliminary Emancipation Proclamation five days later: Enslaved people in rebel territory would be freed in just over three months, on January 1, 1863, unless those states returned to the Union before then.

Two months later, Lincoln delivered his annual message to Congress. He called on them to "think anew and act anew," to "disenthrall ourselves" from the past, and what he proposed was anything but. Lincoln asked Congress to pass three constitutional amendments: States abolishing slavery before 1900 would receive federal compensation; enslaved people freed during the war would remain free, with compensation paid to loyal slaveholders; and Congress would fund voluntary colonization of freed Black people outside the United States.

This was the British model from 1833 — compensated emancipation, gradual freedom, stretching the process across decades. States could wait until 1900. Slaveholders would be paid. The formerly enslaved would be shipped out of the country.

The pattern was clear. To Sumner and Stevens, Lincoln's December proposal was proof that he would never go far enough. The Emancipation Proclamation, set to take effect in one month, was a wartime expedient that could be undone. These proposed amendments were retreats to eighteenth-century solutions.

January 1, 1863, came. Lincoln signed the final Emancipation Proclamation. Sumner was there, had pushed for it, understood its necessity. But he also understood its limits because he knew the history. Eighty-seven years earlier, Lord Dunmore had proclaimed freedom for enslaved people who joined British forces. In 1779, Clinton expanded that with the Philipsburg Proclamation. In 1782, Carleton honored it, evacuating thousands of Black loyalists who had claimed freedom. Those proclamations worked — they freed people in the moment, created the largest act of emancipation in North America before the Civil War. But they were wartime measures, not structural transformations. Once the war ended, the proclamation's force ended. The Constitution of 1787 had been written explicitly to prevent what those proclamations threatened.

Lincoln's Emancipation Proclamation was the same kind of instrument — powerful in the moment, vulnerable after the war. It freed enslaved people in rebel territories as a means of weakening the Confederacy. It didn't apply to border states or to areas already under federal control. Its legal authority derived entirely from Lincoln's war powers. The moment the war ended, that authority would end. The proclamation could be challenged in courts, revoked by future presidents, rendered meaningless by negotiated peace.

Lincoln knew this. He consistently favored gradual, compensated emancipation — a negotiated end that would preserve property interests where possible, maintain social order. He looked for middle paths, ways to end slavery without overturning the constitutional order. Even after issuing the proclamation, he continued seeking compromises. The Constitution of the First Republic was designed to prevent radical change, to require compromise, to protect existing interests. Lincoln represented what "normal" politics would produce even in crisis.

The anti-slavery resistance understood that moderation had failed. Frederick Douglass had been arguing this throughout the war. In his 1864 speech "Mission of the War," he made it explicit: "No war but an Abolition war; no peace but an Abolition peace; liberty for all, chains for none." When the Emancipation Proclamation was issued, Douglass celebrated it but immediately recognized its vulnerability. A proclamation could be undone. Only constitutional transformation would last.

Sumner saw what the proclamation actually meant. His state suicide theory had given Congress the constitutional framework to treat rebel states as territories without constitutional standing. Lincoln had issued a proclamation that freed people in those territories while leaving slavery protected everywhere the Constitution still operated normally. It was necessary. It would save lives. It would weaken the Confederacy. But it wouldn't end slavery, and it wouldn't prevent slavery's return if the war ended on terms that preserved the constitutional order.

The change had to be constitutional. Not a proclamation that would expire when the war ended. Not legislation that could be repealed when political winds shifted. Constitutional amendment — embedding abolition so deeply that no future Congress, president, or Supreme Court could undo it. That was the only way to make transformation permanent.

Stevens saw this even more clearly. By 1863, he was pushing not just for constitutional abolition but also for land redistribution, for complete reconstruction of Southern society, for breaking the planter class's power so thoroughly they could never reconstitute the old order. "Forty acres and a mule" wasn't charity. It was strategy — giving freedpeople the economic foundation to defend their freedom, making it impossible for former slaveholders to force them back into bondage through economic coercion.

The Thirteenth Amendment

The path to total abolition required using the suspended moment fully. It also required mobilizing pressure from outside Congress. In May 1863, Elizabeth Cady Stanton and Susan B. Anthony created the Women's National Loyal League and launched a campaign to collect one million signatures on a petition demanding a constitutional amendment for total abolition.

By early 1864, the league had collected one hundred thousand signatures on six thousand petition forms and mailed them to Sumner in a large trunk. On February 9, Sumner presented them to the Senate: "a mighty army, one hundred thousand strong . . . They ask for nothing less than universal emancipation." The speech became known as "The Prayer of One Hundred Thousand."

Sumner introduced his own version of an abolition amendment. Not just ending slavery — establishing what came after. "All persons are equal before the law, so that no person can hold another as a slave." Abolition would mean nothing if Southern states could immediately create new legal structures of subordination. Freedpeople had to have equal standing in law, equal access to courts, equal protection from state power. Otherwise, the constitutional transformation would be incomplete, vulnerable, reversible through state legislation that treated freedpeople as a separate class of persons with diminished rights.

The Judiciary Committee rejected Sumner's proposed amendment. Making all persons "equal before the law," one senator argued, might lead to dangerous consequences such as providing voting rights to women. Instead the committee approved language that echoed the Northwest Ordinance of 1787: "Neither slavery nor involuntary servitude, except as a punishment for crime whereof the party shall have been duly convicted, shall exist within the United States."

Just abolition. No equality. No protection against what would come after. The Senate passed this watered-down version in April 1864. The House didn't. Not enough votes. Lincoln worked behind the scenes through the fall and winter — his reelection in November gave him leverage — and in January 1865, with the war still ongoing and Confederate states still excluded from Congress, the House passed it by two votes.

Total abolition. No gradual phase-out. No compensation for slaveholders. No exceptions for loyal border states. The amendment didn't just free enslaved people in rebel territories as a wartime measure — it abolished the institution entirely, nationwide, permanently, as a matter of constitutional law.

The Constitution of the First Republic had been designed to protect slavery. It had included multiple provisions ensuring slaveholding states' power, had treated enslaved people as three-fifths of a person for purposes of representation while denying them any rights.

The entire constitutional structure had been built to prevent exactly this kind of fundamental transformation.

But the constitutional structure was suspended. The Southern states weren't there to block the measure. Stevens and Sumner pushed it through while they had the chance, using the rupture that secession and war had created.

By December 1865, enough states had ratified the Thirteenth Amendment — including several reconstructed Southern states acting under duress — for it to become law. Douglass had long believed that forces were in operation "which must inevitably work the downfall of slavery." Now it had happened. But he knew, as Sumner knew, as Stevens knew, that this wasn't enough. An amendment abolishing slavery didn't address what came after slavery. It didn't establish what freedpeople's status would be. It didn't prevent Southern states from creating new systems of subordination that would replicate slavery's function if not its name.

The Northwest Ordinance language was finally in the Constitution. Eighty years late. But slavery was only the most visible manifestation of the enslaver power. The constitutional mechanisms that had given slaveholders disproportionate control — the forces that Sumner and Stevens had identified in their theories — remained intact. The three-fifths clause effect was gone, but the language remained. *Dred Scott* remained good law. Nothing prevented rebel states — or any state — from counting freedpeople for representation while denying them the vote, giving former enslavers even more power than before. The fugitive-slave provisions were moot, but nothing prevented Southern states from using their criminal justice systems to re-enslave freedpeople under the "except as a punishment for crime" exception the amendment itself contained.

The Thirteenth Amendment was necessary. But it wasn't sufficient. The window was still open, but it was closing.

The amendment's shortcomings were obvious to those who had the most at stake. The Radicals' Black allies — the heart of the resistance to the First Republic — had not let up during the war years. By war's end, nearly two hundred thousand Black men had served in the Union military. Their service transformed the army's fortunes and, as Lincoln himself acknowledged, made the difference between victory and defeat. As political fighters, they clearly saw themselves as key actors in the new republic, shaping the future of reconstructed Southern states. And that would be as equals, full citizens, not second-class agents with conditional access to the blessings of liberty.

For that they worked with, and pushed forward, Sumner and his Radical compatriots. And here, as had been the case since the dawn of the First Republic, the core of the anti-slavery resistance was revealed. For too long, abolitionists — those intent on ending slavery and leaving it at that — had garnered most of the attention, but the limits of their advocacy became clear at the point of application.

The old question moved to the spotlight. The question that had revealed the emptiness of the founders' anti-slavery protestations: Sure, they'd be happy to end slavery, if only someone would solve the problem of what to do with freed Black people who — they insisted — could never exist alongside white people in America.

For the Radicals, their resistance had not just been about ending slavery but about erasing the power behind it, too, and the capacity for abusing it. In that they differed significantly from the abolitionists. The end of the First Republic would not come by only abolishing slavery but also by granting freed Black people equal rights, protected by the same Constitution that had excluded them so effectively for eighty years.

And that is what the Radicals worked for, against the white establishment that leaned into questions of expediency and practicality to enable reconciliation. For too many, including Lincoln, the Madison rule continued to govern their actions: Before 1861, action against slavery was cautioned because it would threaten the Union; after 1861, action against slavery was cautioned because it would threaten the rebuilding of the Union. But Sumner and the Radicals were increasingly motivated by the same argument that George Mason had made at the Virginia Ratifying Convention in 1788 and echoed by Higginson and the disunionists in 1857: No union with slavery was worth the injustice. They could do better, or at least they should try.

After all, even with the passage of the Thirteenth Amendment, even with Roger Taney now in his grave, the holding of *Dred Scott* was alive and well: The framers' Constitution was only for white people. Lincoln stayed reticent on the point, but Frederick Douglass was crystal-clear and increasingly vocal: Black people would never be free unless they had the means to exercise their own consent among the governed, until they had the vote. Stearns boosted that message every way he could, including by sponsoring speeches by Douglass in Washington and elsewhere.

This was the context when Lincoln pushed for Louisiana's readmission.

Rickety, Unformed, Unfinished

The Thirteenth Amendment's adoption made the Radicals' work harder, not easier. Lincoln, believing his work more or less done, pushed for quick reconciliation. He needed ratification, which meant he needed rebel states to approve it. Louisiana, Arkansas, and Tennessee were under governments that Lincoln had created. And those governments would need to be recognized by Congress for readmission to the Union.

But the Radicals understood that freedom was not enough to ensure liberty for freed Black people. They needed their rights protected. They needed the vote to be meaningful participants in the consent of the governed. Lincoln had never been for that, though he was willing to concede it, at least for better-educated Black men and those who had served in the Union army.

Louisiana would be the test case. Moderate members of Congress thought Lincoln, at the height of his influence, held all the cards. Lincoln "can't be successfully resisted" on Louisiana reentering the Union, one claimed.

But the resistance was ready to get back into the arena, including a familiar face. George Luther Stearns had steered clear of politics since Harpers Ferry, devoting his considerable energy and resources to enlisting Black soldiers in the Union army. He'd been tireless. Commissioned a major, by one count Stearns had raised thirteen thousand Black men to serve. But when he learned that Louisiana might be fully restored, with its congressional representation, and no real change to the culture and society that had rapaciously exercised its outsized clout over the rest of the Union for decades, he saw a threat to everything they had fought and bled for — from Kansas in 1854, to Harpers Ferry in 1859, through Gettysburg in 1863 and the Wilderness in 1864.

So he collaborated with the Radicals to push for their vision of a reformed Union. As his son, who witnessed it, later wrote: "It was now that Charles Sumner proved himself the great statesman, and George L. Stearns was not a foot behind him." The old anti-slavery resistance leaders had not worked together, or even seen each other, for years, "but now they came together and worked hand-in-hand for the common cause. It was like a meeting of old friends."

Lyman Trumbull, who had joined Sumner in opposing the Corwin Amendment four years earlier, huddled with Lincoln to strategize about readmitting Louisiana. The plan was to go around the immovable wall of Thaddeus Stevens by seating Louisiana's senators first, giving Stevens no choice but to accept the representatives in his chamber. Trumbull felt that Sumner could be more easily handled in the Senate. He'd already collected a majority of senators in favor of seating the Louisiana men.

But Sumner saw the threat and all that it meant. Louisiana's unionist constitution, adopted a year before, might have banned slavery, but it refused to allow Black people to vote. *The Liberator* proclaimed the Louisiana constitution better for Black people than the laws of most Northern states. Lincoln agreed. So did many of the old Garrisonian abolitionists, the non-resisters who had always seen incremental progress as victory.

The Radicals thought that was ludicrous. The division that had always existed between the abolitionists and the Radicals now came into sharp relief. The point wasn't whether freedpeople's situation was better than it had been. Almost anything would be better than slavery. The goal was to make sure that Black people had the rights and protections they deserved everywhere — equal, unconditional voting rights, without discrimination at the ballot box. Not just better than before, but equal to all other citizens.

The anti-slavery resistance had seen too much, bled too much, been beaten too much to accept "better than slavery" as the endgame. They were not going to let this chance to remake the Union slip away without seizing every moment. And this one was Sumner's.

But not his alone. Stearns supported Sumner's plan with more than words. He founded a newspaper to spread the message, in ways that the old *Liberator* never could, for this new age. It would carry the message of the Six and their hopes for the country as they fought for it to be born. He simply called it *The Nation*.

Trumbull introduced the bill to seat the men from Louisiana and was not surprised to see Sumner claim the time in opposition. What did spark the senator from Illinois, and then his colleagues, and then rippled all the way down to the White House, was that Sumner did not then sit down. He went on for an hour, and then another, and then another. Gaining the strength of his powerful marathon speeches of the 1850s, Sumner began to thunder, as if Preston Brooks's ghost was standing in front of him. The "pretended" government of Louisiana was "a mere seven-months abortion," he shouted — a government born prematurely and malformed. It was a "criminal conjunction . . . born before its time, rickety, unformed, unfinished." To even think of recognizing it would be "a burden, a reproach, and a wrong."

Benjamin Wade of Ohio then joined him, as he had against the Corwin Amendment. Then James Grimes of Iowa stood up. And then Henry Wilson of Massachusetts, all trading time with Sumner.

The rhetorical resistance went on for three days. Sumner knew the Senate was coming up on adjournment, that the senators wanted to go home, and there was still work that needed to be done before they could. So he pressed on. One witness remembered that in "a feat of human endurance," Sumner "fought that bill with all the weapons of parliamentary warfare."

And he won. Trumbull withdrew the bill, defeated. Lincoln was incandescent with rage. But he had to let that go. He still needed Sumner.

After all, Louisiana would certainly be admitted in the next Congress, and his reconstruction plan would go forward. So Lincoln thought.

The resistance understood differently. They had just demonstrated that they could block Lincoln, that they had the power to prevent the reconstitution of the old order disguised as reconciliation. Stearns's *Nation* would broadcast that message. The anti-slavery resistance that had spent decades operating in clandestine networks, that had been relegated to the margins of constitutional politics, that had finally broken into mainstream politics in the 1850s — that movement now had a political wing in Congress that could stop a president at the height of his power.

The Thirteenth Amendment would abolish slavery. But what came after — who would have rights, who would vote, how the constitutional structure would be rebuilt — that was still being fought over. And the Radicals had just proved they wouldn't surrender that fight to Lincoln's incrementalism or the moderates' desire for quick reconciliation. The window was still open. The question was what they could force through it before it closed.

The Final Shot of the First Republic

Lee surrendered at Appomattox on April 9, 1865. The next day Washington, DC, celebrated — cannon fire, flags flying from the Anacostia to Rock Creek. The evening after that, April 11, thousands of free Black men and women climbed the hill to Arlington House,

Robert E. Lee's house, which had been built by Martha Washington's grandson, George Washington Parke Custis, and filled it with light. Had Ona Judge's children lived, ownership of them would have passed to Custis's daughter, then to her children with Robert E. Lee. Now the house blazed with light held by the people who had transformed the war.

That same evening, Lincoln appeared at a second-floor White House window facing the South Lawn. He wanted to talk about reconstruction. He wanted Sumner to hear it.

Sumner wasn't there. Lincoln had Mary Todd invite him, but Sumner declined. He'd been burned before — invited to the inaugural ball, danced with Mary Todd, woke up to newspapers reporting that he'd softened his opposition to Lincoln's policies. He wouldn't make that mistake twice. By April 1865, Sumner and Lincoln were effectively enemies on reconstruction. Sumner had made it clear that he'd do whatever it took — including three days on his feet filibustering — to prevent anything short of a reformed Union.

But Sumner would learn what Lincoln said that night. Lincoln made the point that rejecting Louisiana's constitution meant rejecting the state's ratification vote for the Thirteenth Amendment. Then he showed that he was willing to concede. He acknowledged that Congress — not the Executive — would determine when rebel states could seat representatives. And he publicly supported giving the vote to "the very intelligent" Black men and those who'd served as soldiers. In four years, Lincoln had moved from endorsing the Corwin Amendment, which would have protected slavery to preserve the Union, to accepting limited Black suffrage.

Sumner was unimpressed. He saw Lincoln the tactician at work. "I fear his policy now," he wrote.

Someone else in the crowd feared it, too. "That means nigger citizenship," John Wilkes Booth told a fellow conspirator. Four days later he fired the last shot of the First Republic into Lincoln's head. Lincoln died the next morning.

A month later, William Lloyd Garrison stood before the American Anti-Slavery Society and proposed that they disband. Slavery was abolished. Their work was done.

Frederick Douglass rose to object. The movement had two goals, he argued: "First, the freedom of the blacks of this country; and, second, the elevation of them." Freedom had been achieved. Elevation had not. Without protection for their rights, freedpeople would face what the Black loyalists had faced — legal freedom in a nation organized to deny them everything else. In a *Dred Scott* nation, nothing prevented new forms of servitude.

The division between abolitionists and Radicals was now in sharp relief. Garrison saw abolition as the endpoint. The Radicals understood that it was the beginning. The enslaver power remained in the Constitution and the culture. The First Republic might have lost slavery, but it hadn't been transformed.

And Andrew Johnson sat in the White House, working to restore exactly what the war had broken.

Johnson's Reconstruction

Johnson was a disaster — wrong person, wrong moment, worst temperament. A Tennessee unionist who'd stayed loyal when his state seceded, added to Lincoln's 1864 ticket for electoral calculation. What the nation got was a rigid white supremacist and an authoritarian who refused to compromise. He'd owned slaves. Accepted emancipation only when forced to, with no change in his fundamental belief that Black people had no place in the republic. "This is a country for white men," he told Missouri's governor, "and by God, as long as I am President, it shall be a government for white men."

Sumner despised him. Later called him "the impersonation of the tyrannical Slave Power." Not the planter class Johnson had once opposed, but the deeper structure — the conviction that republican government required racial hierarchy.

With Lincoln dead, Johnson claimed reconstruction as his personal domain. No role for Congress. Every rebel who took an oath got their political and property rights back immediately. He appointed provisional governors to organize whites-only conventions. The requirements: abolish slavery, acknowledge that secession was illegal, repudiate Confederate war debt. That was it. Four years of civil war, and that was the price of treason.

The results were predictable. The men who'd run the South before 1861 returned to power in 1865 as if the war had been an unfortunate interruption. Confederate officers reclaimed state legislative seats. Confederate generals became governors. And the violence resumed — against freed Black people, to force them back into their "proper" place.

Worse were the Black Codes. Mississippi's, passed in late 1865, required all Black people to carry written employment contracts. Quitting was criminal. Any white person could arrest any Black person. Black children were apprenticed to their former enslavers. This was slavery under a different name, exploiting the Thirteenth Amendment's loophole — "except as punishment for crime."

For Johnson and the former rebels, this was the natural order reasserting itself. For Sumner and the Radicals, it was intolerable. "The same national authority that destroyed slavery must see that this other pretension is not permitted to survive," Sumner wrote.

Johnson declared Reconstruction complete in December 1865 — the rebel states had loyal governments, the Union was whole, and their representatives should be seated.

The Radicals said no.

Seizing the Moment

The exclusion of the newly elected representatives and senators on December 4 gave the Radicals the procedural power they needed. But holding that power meant fighting on treacherous ground. Republicans held the majority, but the Radicals remained what they'd always been: a minority voice within their own coalition, pushing against the same forces of inertia and moderation that had compromised with Slave Power for decades.

Most Republicans would tolerate abolition. Voting rights and legal equality for Black people? That was different. They knew that most white Americans felt the same way. They wanted to work with Johnson, modify his plans, find the middle ground that had always been the death of structural change. The Radicals would have to fight uphill for every inch.

Sumner made extending the Freedmen's Bureau, through a Freedmen's Bureau Bill, his first priority. Education and free speech were essential to establishing equal rights — he'd believed that since his 1845 oration attacking false patriotism. Before the war, shutting down First Amendment protections for Northern speakers and teachers who might spread the truth about slavery had been crucial to maintaining the South's hold on power. Expanding the bureau's authority would give freed people a foundation the old order couldn't easily dismantle.

The harder battle was the Civil Rights Act of 1866. The Thirteenth Amendment wasn't enough. Freedom had to be defined. All persons born in the United States were citizens. All citizens had rights. And crucial to Black activists and the Radicals was no specific reference to Black people. The Thirteenth Amendment had erased the fiction that property could be a person. Given that, citizenship and rights followed for everyone. Let the white supremacists argue otherwise.

Johnson vetoed both the Freedmen's Bureau Bill and the Civil Rights Act. States' rights must be protected, he said. The Civil Rights Act would establish "a perfect equality of the white and colored races . . . by Federal law in every State of the Union." He couldn't allow that. It would destroy the republic as he understood it — a republic that required racial hierarchy to function.

Some moderate Republicans began reconsidering their position. Moderation in the face of Johnson's extremism started looking less like prudence and more like capitulation. But what really shifted the ground wasn't reasoned argument. It was violence — the same mechanism that had broken containment in the 1850s.

In Memphis that spring, discharged Black soldiers clashed with Irish police. Soldiers and police were wounded. Then gangs of police and armed white supremacists set upon South Memphis's Black population in a three-day rampage. Beating, shooting, robbing, raping. When order returned on May 3, forty-six Black men, women, and children were dead. At least seventy-five injured. Every Black church and school in the city destroyed, plus nearly one hundred homes.

The local authorities? They'd either turned a blind eye to the violence or joined it. No attacker was punished. No victim was compensated.

In July, it was New Orleans, the same pattern: white supremacists, local authorities, coordinated violence. Thirty-five Black citizens were killed, more than a hundred wounded. Their crime was gathering to support a constitutional convention that would have given them the vote.

This was the old abusive authority reaching out from Boston and Christiana and Kansas, unchanged except for the names and locations. The political struggles of the 1850s had shown that no compromise was possible with such authority. John Brown had tried to provoke recognition of that. The war should have proved it. But only now was broader public support leaning toward the Radicals.

Even white Americans began seeing what the Radicals had been arguing all along.

The Constitutional Revolution

That summer, Congress passed the Fourteenth Amendment.

It was a whole Constitution in itself, one that would have thrilled the Anti-Federalists and all the Enlightenment thinkers who'd been disappointed by the American Revolution's compromises. It established birthright citizenship and transformed the federal government's nature — from a bastion of centralized authority deployed against the people to the protector of all people's rights. Here was new authority directed against the states, denying them any power to abridge citizens' "privileges and immunities" or deny any person — even non-citizens — "equal protection of the laws."

Sumner had wanted the amendment to go further, to explicitly guarantee and protect Black citizens' voting rights. He'd brought a concept to the discussion that had been swirling through the resistance since before the Constitution closed off the Enlightenment's potential. Drawing on the universality principles that had informed the Declaration of Independence but also on the French Revolution's more honest Declaration of the Rights of Man, from Diderot and Condorcet, he crafted language relying on "equality before the law" — an idea that had informed his perspective since the day he defended a Black child's right to public education in Massachusetts.

In this thinking, Sumner had finally come around to the disunionism of Thoreau and Higginson, even if he wouldn't admit it. The Constitution was not sacred. America should not be forever situated in 1788. He and his contemporaries had gained from experience a better understanding of how to apply Enlightenment ideas. The Constitution should reflect that evolving understanding rather than adhering strictly to 1787's compromises. The amendment should reflect the higher law for which the anti-slavery resistance had reached.

Sumner's version never made it out of committee. Neither did a guarantee of voting rights for Black men. But the amendment did erase the three-fifths clauses and the fugitive-slave clause from the Constitution, and it connected denial of representation to any group of men with a direct reduction in a state's entire representation. In a move that might have impressed even Patrick Henry in 1788, the Fourteenth Amendment gave white supremacists a choice: deny Black men the vote and diminish your state's representation, or accept it and retain your federal political power.

Their choice.

Every Democrat in the House voted against it, along with four Republicans. But it cleared the threshold in both chambers. Stevens was disappointed that the amendment fell short of Sumner's vision to protect Black people's voting rights, but he was resigned to voting for it, acknowledging that "I live among men and not among angels."

With that, the First Republic was dead — at least on paper.

The Campaign

The Fourteenth Amendment became the central issue of the 1866 midterm congressional elections. Johnson embarked on a speaking tour of the North — journalists called it "the swing around the circle" — to urge voters to elect members of Congress committed to his Reconstruction program. He denounced his critics, made wild accusations that the Radicals were plotting to assassinate him. His behavior further undermined public support for his policies, as did the riots in Memphis and New Orleans.

Sumner seized the moment. The fall 1866 congressional elections would determine whether the Radicals' tactics — their exclusion, their priorities, their approach — could be ratified by the American people, the same electorate Johnson thought was with him in wanting to preserve white people's rights over those of freed Black men and women.

He laid out his case in Boston on October 2, 1866, at the Music Hall just off Tremont Street. Sumner commanded the stage that evening before a crowd of about two thousand people. Johnson had sought to restore rebels to power and deny Congress any authority over Reconstruction. The question facing Americans in the coming election was simple: Were they for the president or the people? For the power of one man, or the authority of Congress?

The stakes could not be higher. "We are to secure by counsel what was won by war," he asserted. "Failure now will make the war itself a failure; surrender now will undo all our victories."

> Congress must be sustained in its conflict with the One Man Power, and ex-rebels must not be restored to power. Bearing these two things in mind the way will be easy. The

> constitutional amendment must be adopted. As far as it goes, it is well; but it does not go far enough. More must be done. Impartial suffrage must be established. A homestead must be secured to every freedman . . . If to these is added education, there will be a new order of things, with liberty of the press, liberty of speech and liberty of travel . . . Our present desires may be symbolized by four "E's," standing for Emancipation, Enfranchisement, Equality and Education. Let these be secured and all else will follow.

The goal of the Radicals, as had been the goal of the resistance to the First Republic for eighty years, was "to give to mankind a new definition of republican government." But that was not, and could not be, enough. It was one thing to wipe away abusive authority, another to ensure that it would never return — to use Congress's power to "prevent efforts against the revival of the Rebellion."

In the congressional elections that fall, Republicans opposed to Johnson's policies won a sweeping victory. Nonetheless, at the president's urging, every Southern state but Tennessee refused to ratify the Fourteenth Amendment. The intransigence of Johnson and most of the white South pushed moderate Republicans toward the Radicals.

The Window Closes

Congress passed the Civil Rights Act of 1866 — the first civil rights legislation in American history — over Johnson's veto in April. The vote was 122–41 in the House and 33–15 in the Senate, just one over the threshold needed. From that point forward, the Radicals would run what had become a fight against Johnson for the country's future.

They extended their hard line to the Fourteenth Amendment's ratification, essentially adopting the Madison-Hamilton strategy from 1788 and using it against those same interests: making inclusion in the Union dependent on ratifying the document. As in 1788, it worked.

Enough states ratified to give the Fourteenth Amendment the legitimacy it needed.

In March 1867, over Johnson's veto, Congress adopted the Reconstruction Act, which temporarily divided the South into five military districts and called for creating new state governments with Black men given the right to vote. Thus began the period of Radical Reconstruction, which would last until 1877.

The Radical-led Congress then moved directly against Johnson, impeaching him and coming within one vote of removing him from office. They maintained their grip on power only briefly, to the middle of 1868, when they could hold back no more — with Stevens dead and Sumner ailing — and reconstructed rebel states began returning to Congress, almost immediately changing the dynamic.

Soon those states would reclaim the majority and, as feared, begin rolling back as much as they could, with help from the federal judiciary. The Radicals had anticipated this counter-resistance response, which was why they had spent so much energy pursuing their strategy of exclusion for as long as they could.

The resistance had achieved what seemed impossible: They'd remade the Constitution, killed the First Republic, and established — on paper — a new foundation for equality. But the historical pattern held yet again: American resistance was effective in the moment and vulnerable afterward. The work of interrupting the Radicals' success began immediately.

The Pattern Complete

Stevens died in the summer of 1868, his body lying in state in the rotunda of the Capitol, home to the institution he'd fought to transform. The requiem for him drew thousands, but more telling was what came after: The reconstructed rebel states began returning to Congress, their representatives taking seats alongside the men who'd excluded them three years earlier.

Sumner remained in the Senate, increasingly isolated in his own Republican Party. The wartime coalition that had enabled Radical power fractured once the emergency passed. Northern voters tired of Reconstruction. The Supreme Court began gutting the Fourteenth Amendment — the Slaughterhouse Cases in 1873, *United States v. Cruikshank* in 1876. By 1877, federal troops withdrew from the South. The Compromise of 1877 saw the Republicans trade Reconstruction for control of the White House, when their candidate, Rutherford Hayes, lost the popular vote but was still handed the presidency. Redemption swept through the former Confederacy. The same men who'd led the rebellion returned to power, and the violence that had maintained their world before 1861 resumed.

Sumner died in 1874, never seeing how completely his work would be undone. His final words, according to those at his bedside, were "Don't let the civil rights bill fail." It passed after his death, a symbolic gesture. The Supreme Court struck it down eight years later.

The pattern of resistance gains becoming vulnerable afterward may have held yet again, but the Radicals had done something unprecedented in the entire history covered in this book: They'd breached the barricades and used power to remake the structure. Not just pass laws that could be repealed. Not just win elections that could be reversed. They'd transformed the Constitution itself.

CONCLUSION

The American Way of Resistance

Nine chapters. Two centuries. One undeniable fact: American resistance to abusive authority achieved the greatest advances for liberty in the nation's history.

Not through patience. Not through working within the system. Not through trusting that the arc of history bends toward justice on its own. Through people who recognized that those holding power were abusing it, understood where and when permitted channels had failed, and forced change against institutions designed to prevent it.

Slavery ended because resistance made it end. The Constitution got transformed — birthright citizenship, equal protection, voting rights regardless of race — because the Radical Republicans seized a moment of crisis and used power completely while they had it. Women won suffrage because the anti-slavery resistance created constitutional tools and tactical knowledge that carried forward through generations. Every significant expansion of rights in American history came from resistance forcing authority to answer.

That's the American way of resistance. It works. It has always worked — in the moment. The question now is whether we can recognize and remember how it actually worked, or whether we'll let patriot mythology forever bury those lessons under sanitized versions that contain rather than enable opposition.

American institutions were designed to interrupt successful resistance and roll back whatever changes resistance achieves. The pattern has repeated for two centuries with mechanical precision. The interruption points are real. The rollback mechanisms function exactly as designed. Understanding that matters because it tells you what you're actually facing when you confront abusive authority.

But understanding the pattern isn't the same as accepting defeat. It's recognizing the terrain so you can operate within it effectively. The

American way of resistance navigated that terrain and achieved structural transformation — often temporarily, vulnerably, but actually. The people who did it weren't exceptional. They were ordinary people who recognized specific roles that resistance required and filled them.

What Resistance Requires

When you face abusive authority, resistance needs people who can think clearly about what's actually happening. Not react emotionally, not accept the framing authority offers, but articulate why the abuse is illegitimate and what principle is being violated. That's what Thoreau did — he inherited from his grandmother's family a commitment to liberty of conscience so clear it survived two generations, and he articulated it in ways that traveled globally for a century. *Civil Disobedience* didn't stop the Mexican War or free enslaved people, but it gave resistance movements worldwide the ideological foundation they needed to distinguish between legitimate authority and abusive authority that has forfeited legitimacy.

Ideas matter. Not as abstractions but as ground to defend. When you can articulate in one sentence what you're fighting for — not what you're against, what you're *for* — you can recognize when you've abandoned your principle or when someone's trying to redirect you. You can tell the difference between genuine progress and empty accommodation. That role doesn't require dramatic action. It requires clarity that survives pressure, confusion, and the inevitable attempts to make you doubt your own perception of reality.

Resistance also needs people who can read power dynamics accurately and act on them strategically. Nancy Dixon didn't wait for the patriots to live up to their rhetoric about liberty. She didn't petition for gradual reform or trust that moral suasion would eventually work. She watched, listened, identified that the British-versus-patriot conflict created an opening, and moved decisively to claim actual freedom for herself and her daughter. That's strategic pragmatism — trusting interests rather than intentions, using conflicts between powers to create space for action, delivering concrete results rather than symbolic gestures.

The test isn't whether your allies are morally pure, it's whether their interests align with yours in this specific moment and whether that alignment creates tactical opportunities you can exploit before they close. Strategic pragmatism produces results. Nancy and thousands like her didn't just resist — they won. They achieved permanent freedom. Not someday, not after more appeals to conscience, but actually. They got free, stayed free, built lives in freedom. That's what matters.

When systematic oppression operates at scale, resistance needs people who can build sophisticated infrastructure. Individual courage can't defeat federal machinery deployed to crush it. The Underground Railroad demonstrated what organized networks can achieve — tens of thousands moved to freedom through systems so disciplined that their methods remain partially hidden 170 years later. That required specialization of roles, compartmentalized knowledge, operational security that protected the network even when individuals got prosecuted.

Building infrastructure means accepting that you're part of something larger than dramatic individual action. You might never get credit. You might do unglamorous work maintaining systems rather than executing rescues. But organized networks can sustain resistance that individual heroism cannot. They can withstand prosecution, infiltration, sustained government pressure. They can operate for years, deliver results, force authority to pay costs it cannot sustain. That's effectiveness over authenticity, results over recognition.

Resistance needs people who can persist. Ona Judge's escape from the Washingtons was one night in 1796. Her resistance lasted fifty-four years — until her death in 1848, still free, still refusing to validate the lie that she was property. That night required courage. The decades that followed required something harder: the persistence to never surrender her freedom and the resilience to survive every attempt to take it back. Washington deployed federal officials, hired slave catchers, sent his nephew on a kidnapping mission. For the rest of his life, he never stopped trying to reclaim her. Ona had to remain vigilant for fifty-four years. Every knock on the door could mean capture. She lived in poverty, was widowed young, lost children. And through it all she maintained her resistance — never wavering, never accepting that maybe it would be easier to go back.

Most resistance movements fail not because they lack brave people willing to take dramatic action but because they lack people capable of sustaining resistance when it becomes grinding, unglamorous endurance. Authority's strategy is attrition — outlast the resisters, make resistance so costly over time that people eventually give up. Persistence breaks that strategy. Each year Ona remained free was another year proving the system could be defied. Her persistence was her victory. When she finally told her story to abolitionists in the 1840s — still free, still defiant — she became living proof that one woman's refusal to quit could outlast the most powerful man in America and the government he helped create.

When all peaceful avenues have been closed and authority is already deploying violence systematically, resistance needs people who can accept what stopping that authority actually requires. Not philosophically justify violence, but accept that nothing is off the table when the choice is between making authority stop or accepting that it will continue. Samuel Adams sending Crispus Attucks into a Boston street. Captain Parker leading men onto Lexington Green. Daniel Shays at the Springfield arsenal. Thomas Wentworth Higginson at a Boston courthouse. Harriet Tubman in Chesapeake nights. John Brown at Harpers Ferry.

They understood that abusive authority is like a ball rolling downhill, unstoppable unless someone steps in front of it. They understood that violence was already being deployed against them — systematically, legally, lethally — and that every permitted channel had been deliberately closed. So they accepted what was necessary. Not because it was preferable, but because it was the only option left. The Six enabled John Brown, made him possible, intellectually convinced that stopping slavery required what it required. When consequences arrived, four of six discovered they'd only approached the line, unable to actually accept what stopping slavery demanded. Only Higginson and Parker had crossed completely. That's the test — not whether you can theorize about necessity, but whether you can accept it and act on it when the moment comes.

Finally, when resistance achieves power — through crisis, through institutional collapse, through war — it needs people who can use that power completely before the window closes. The Radical Republicans understood they had maybe five years to transform the constitutional order before Southern states returned and Northern voters moved on. So they kept rebellious states out of Congress, forced through amendments while the South couldn't block them, used military occupation to enforce change, impeached a president who tried to stop them. They operated outside normal constitutional bounds because they recognized the moment wouldn't last. They were right. By 1877 federal troops withdrew. By 1883 the Supreme Court was gutting the Fourteenth Amendment. But those amendments stayed in the Constitution, dormant for decades, waiting to be revived when the next resistance movement needed them.

Seizing the moment means acting with complete clarity about what structural transformation requires and using whatever power you have completely — even when that means breaking rules and forcing changes that seem illegitimate to those benefiting from the old order. Hesitation guarantees that abusive authority will return and adapt. The Radical Republicans' achievement demonstrates both the power and the limitation of this role: They transformed the Constitution more completely than any resistance movement before or since, and it still wasn't enough to prevent rollback. But without their willingness to seize power when they had it, there would have been nothing to roll back, no constitutional foundation for the Civil Rights Movement to revive seventy years later.

Why We've Forgotten

Resisters, filling these roles, achieved the greatest liberty advances in American history. So why don't we remember how American resistance actually operated?

Because modern patriot mythology is more powerful than ever at obscuring those lessons. The mythology celebrates the founding as a moment of inspired wisdom, renders the Constitution sacred rather than interested, insists that fundamental questions were answered in 1787 and everything since has been working out the details. It lionizes patient reformers, peaceful protesters, noble losers who fought the good fight within permitted channels. It transforms actual resisters into sanitized versions that fit the mythology — Thoreau becomes a quirky hermit rather than a diagnostician of abusive authority; the Underground Railroad becomes humanitarian charity rather than sophisticated criminal infrastructure; the abolitionists become moral voices rather than people who concluded that violence was necessary.

The effect is containment. When you teach people that resistance means working within the system, respecting institutional norms, trusting that patient reform eventually produces change — you've taught them not to resist. You've taught them to stop at the first interruption point, to accept procedural reforms as victories, to mistake accommodation for transformation. That's what patriot mythology does. It doesn't suppress resistance through overt force. It contains resistance by making people internalize deference to institutions, by making escalation feel like betraying American identity rather than challenging abusive authority that has captured American institutions.

And it's gotten more sophisticated. The founding generation became demigods within fifty years. Now we're 250 years out and the mythology has metastasized into something even more effective at interrupting resistance. Every permitted channel for change gets celebrated as proof that the system works — even when those channels produce no structural transformation. Every resistance movement that forces change gets rewritten as vindication of American ideals rather than challenge to American institutions. The pattern repeats, and we forget that it's repeated because the mythology erases how resistance actually worked and replaces it with stories about inevitable progress and patient reform.

That forgetting has costs. When you don't know how resistance actually achieved liberty gains, you can't recognize when you're being played. You can't tell the difference between genuine resistance and performance that serves someone else's pursuit of power. You accept symbolic victories that preserve fundamental arrangements. You wait for perfect conditions instead of forcing fights you can't win but that extract concessions for future use. You exhaust yourself in dramatic moments rather than building infrastructure for endurance. You debate whether violence is ever justified while carefully avoiding whether you can accept what stopping abusive authority actually requires. You waste power when you achieve it by respecting norms designed to protect the old order.

The American Way Forward

So when you're staring at your Instagram feed feeling doom about the state of things, when you're at another rally wondering what any of this achieves, when you're asking yourself what to do — the American way of resistance offers actual methodology, not inspiration.

It tells you that abusive authority gets challenged by people filling specific roles that resistance requires. You don't need to be exceptional. You need to recognize which role matches where you are and what you can do. Can you think clearly and articulate principles when everyone around you is accepting lies? Can you read power dynamics and act strategically on conflicts between authorities? Can you build infrastructure or maintain it? Can you persist through years of grinding resistance when progress isn't visible? Can you accept what's necessary when authority is already deploying violence and has closed all other avenues? Can you seize power completely when the moment arrives?

The American way of resistance also tells you what you're facing. The interruption points are real — the moments when you must escalate beyond permitted channels, when you must accept that nothing is off the table. American political culture has been engineered to make crossing those thresholds feel like betrayal rather than necessity. When most resistance movements stop at the first interruption, that's the system functioning as designed. Understanding that won't make crossing easier, but it will stop you from believing that something's wrong with you when the crossing feels impossible. It's supposed to feel impossible. That's the point.

And the American way of resistance tells you that even when you navigate both interruptions and achieve structural transformation, American institutions will adapt to roll back those gains. The mechanisms are sophisticated, they appear democratic, and they function with mechanical precision. The Radical Republicans achieved more than any resistance movement in American history and still couldn't prevent rollback within twenty years. That's not a reason to give up. It's a reason to understand the terrain. Gains are always temporary. Defense is permanent. The constitutional tools the Anti-Federalists forced into existence in 1791 became weapons the Radical Republicans deployed in 1868 that the Civil Rights Movement revived in the 1960s. That's how resistance carries forward — not through continuous possession of power, but through forcing changes that future resistance can build on.

None of this promises success. The pattern is clear: American resistance has been consistently effective in the moment and consistently vulnerable afterward because American institutions were designed to produce exactly that outcome. But "vulnerable afterward" doesn't mean "achieved nothing." It means the achievements require defense, that rollback is systematic and not accidental, that resistance is never finished.

The American way of resistance produced the greatest advances for liberty in the nation's history. Slavery ended. The Constitution got transformed. Rights were expanded. Not because the system worked as designed, but because resistance forced the system to work differently than designed — temporarily, vulnerably, but actually. Those weren't gifts from enlightened authority. They were victories forced by people who recognized abusive authority, concluded that permitted channels had failed, and acted.

That's what this history teaches. Not how to be inspired by noble resisters, but how resistance actually operated when it achieved results. Not promises that resistance will succeed, but clarity about what resistance faces and what roles it requires. Not mythology about patient reform and inevitable progress, but evidence about how Americans forced change against institutions built to prevent it.

Authority in a republic exists only on loan from the governed. When it turns against them, when it serves narrow interests rather than the people who grant it legitimacy, when it demands complicity in obvious injustice, resistance isn't rebellion against American ideals, it's their defense. And their duty.

The American way of resistance has always been there. It achieved extraordinary things. We just forgot how it actually worked because patriot mythology buried those lessons under stories that contain rather than enable opposition.

Now you know how it actually worked. Now you can recognize which role matches where you are. Now you can see the interruption points coming and understand why crossing them feels impossible — because they're designed to feel that way. Now you can operate within terrain that systematically contains resistance while understanding that resistance within that terrain still achieved the greatest liberty gains in American history.

That's usable history. Not for inspiration but for instruction about how power actually works and what people without it have actually done when those holding it abused it.

Nine movements. Two centuries. The American way of resistance.

It worked before. It can work again. If we remember how it actually worked.

EPILOGUE

The Return of the First Republic

On January 6, 2021, the First Republic reasserted itself.

A sitting president incited a mob to attack Congress and prevent certification of an election he'd lost. Insurrectionists broke into the Capitol, hunted legislators, erected a gallows, and chanted for the vice president's execution. For several hours, armed men carrying Confederate flags — the banner of the slaveholders' rebellion — controlled the building where the Second Republic had been born.

This wasn't democratic breakdown. This was the founders' framework operating exactly as designed.

The insurrectionists understood the Constitution better than its liberal defenders. They'd studied the founders' design, identified its vulnerabilities, exploited them systematically: the Electoral College's arcane procedures creating opportunities for subversion, state certification processes manipulable by loyalist officials, the vice president's ambiguous role, mob violence when institutional channels failed. They used the tools the founders created to protect property and prevent popular majorities from seizing power.

The Constitution had no answer to a sitting president inciting a mob as part of an attempt to stay in office after he'd lost reelection, because it was never designed to. The founders created mechanisms to enable minority rule, to protect property from democratic majorities, to prevent the people from controlling government. When a president attempted to keep power through those mechanisms, backed by a minority willing to use violence, the system did what it was designed to do: and the attempt almost worked.

The moment demanded recognition that the founders' framework enables authoritarianism. That the vulnerabilities weren't bugs but features. That defending democracy required transforming or abandoning the constitutional structure itself.

President Biden's response was a speech.

Biden's Speech: Liberal Nationalism's Obituary

Speaking from the Capitol on the first anniversary of the January 6 assault, Biden invoked the founders, quoted the Constitution, appealed to "the soul of the nation" and "our better angels." He treated January 6 as moral crisis — a test of American character requiring renewed commitment to founding principles. No proposals for constitutional reform. No structural changes to prevent the next attempt. No acknowledgment that the founders' design had created the conditions for what happened.

The speech was written in large part by Jon Meacham, presidential historian and purveyor of founding mythology to Democratic elites. Meacham's career consists of selling politicians the comforting lie that the founders already solved democracy's problems, that wisdom lies in recovering their vision rather than imagining something new. His books present American history as cycles of falling short of ideals and redeeming ourselves through appeals to founding principles — acknowledge the darkness, find the light, believe in American resilience.

Biden didn't respond structurally because everything in the formation of his understanding of American history and politics taught him that the Constitution is sacred, the founders wise, the system self-correcting. He's the perfected product of what this book has called liberal nationalism: a political tradition so committed to constitutional reverence that it cannot respond structurally even when the Constitution demonstrably enables democratic collapse, even when democracy's survival demands transformation.

The result: no constitutional change. Congress passed the Electoral Count Reform Act in 2022 — legislative tweaking of an 1887 statute, not a constitutional amendment. The vulnerabilities that the insurrection exploited remained embedded in the constitutional structure. The Electoral College's anti-democratic design, the presidency's pardon power scope, the Senate's minority rule mechanisms, the lack of clear processes for removing presidents who attempt coups — all remain untouched.

This is containment perfected. Even literal insurrection — the clearest possible demonstration that the founders' framework enables rather than prevents authoritarianism — produced no transformation because the political culture has made constitutional reform unthinkable.

And then the restoration began in earnest.

The Restoration

When Trump returned to power, the First Republic's restoration accelerated. The administration framed itself explicitly as recovering founding principles, issuing executive orders to restore "truth and sanity to American history" by eliminating what it characterized as efforts to "undermine the remarkable achievements of the United States by casting its founding principles and historical milestones in a negative light."

This isn't euphemism. It's accurate description of the project: restoring the First Republic — the founders' actual design before resistance movements forced its partial transformation.

The First Republic was designed by and for white male property owners. It protected slavery as a constitutional right. It denied women legal personhood. It treated Native Americans as foreign nations to be conquered or removed. It created instruments — the Electoral College, the Senate, lifetime judicial appointments, the pardon power — specifically designed to prevent popular majorities from controlling government or redistributing property.

The restoration proceeds meticulously. Heritage Foundation's Project 2025 provides the blueprint: dismantling the administrative state, reclassifying civil servants as political appointees removable at will, concentrating power in the Executive Branch, using originalism to eliminate rights achieved through interpretation rather than explicit amendment. The Supreme Court, with its conservative supermajority secured through the founders' mechanisms, enables each step.

Presidential immunity for official acts. Elimination of federal agency authority. Gutting of voting rights protections. Reversal of reproductive rights because they are not explicitly contained in the Constitution.

The restorationists are systematically destroying everything that American resistance achieved since 1790, using the founders' own tools. Not by repealing the Thirteenth, Fourteenth, and Fifteenth Amendments — that's unnecessary. They're rendering those amendments inoperative while leaving them on the books, exactly as the Lost Cause did after Reconstruction: making the amendments' promises meaningless through judicial interpretation, administrative refusal to enforce, legislative blocking, and cultural reconstruction that makes the original exclusions seem natural again.

The Voting Rights Act gutted. Affirmative action eliminated. Reproductive rights abolished through *Dobbs*, returning authority to states. LGBTQ+ protections rolled back. Labor power decimated. Regulatory agencies captured or destroyed. Civil rights enforcement disappeared. Each achieved through the constitutional system working as designed: courts interpreting the Constitution to narrow rights, executives refusing to enforce laws, legislatures blocking reforms, and the founders' mechanisms preventing popular majorities from responding.

This is the First Republic restored. And liberal nationalism has no answer except appeals to the same founding framework that enables the restoration.

The New Moral Suasionists

By the late twentieth century, constitutional reverence had produced a particular pathology: the liberal nationalist belief that eloquent speeches about founding principles can defeat people who are using the founders' actual framework.

Ken Burns is the high priest of this liberal nationalist tradition. For forty years he's been teaching Americans that their history is a series of sins redeemed by the American spirit. Darkness followed by light. Problems the project eventually solves, but never resolves. Acknowledge the horror, mourn it beautifully, then locate the saving grace that proves everything's basically fine.

His 2025 *The American Revolution* is the purest representation yet of this practice. The final episode opens with a historian offering what Burns apparently considers a thesis: "I think that to believe in America, rooted in the American Revolution, is to believe in possibility. That to me is the extraordinary thing about the patriot side of the fight. I think everybody on every side, including people who were denied even the ownership of themselves, had the sense of possibility worth fighting for." This is liberal nationalist history: rhetoric that sounds profound until you ask what it means. It doesn't say anything. It just asserts.

Burns scourges the founders for their sins, then anoints their legacy against Trump. Why should Americans inherit from the founders a commitment to ideals they clearly did not share? Liberal nationalists can't ask, because the answer ends the project. So, they give you "possibility." They give you the feeling of reckoning without the reckoning.

Burns taught Americans to feel their history. Aaron Sorkin taught them to perform it. His show *The West Wing* made the formula weekly television; the right words substitute for structural change; the system works if you staff it with people who love it enough and have a big enough vocabulary. But fictional president Jed Bartlet never actually changes much. He gives phenomenal speeches, faces chronically low approval ratings, never wins a House majority — and the show frames all of this as noble soldiering rather than failure. In Sorkin's universe, manner matters more than outcome. Attitude over transformation. Apolitical politics dressed up as idealism.

Lin-Manuel Miranda's *Hamilton* completed the circuit: Burns's historical piety plus Sorkin's faith in rhetoric. Diverse actors play enslavers. The founding feels progressive. Veneration stays intact. You leave humming about immigrant hustle and not thinking about what Hamilton actually built.

This was the training ground for a generation of establishment foot soldiers. Obama staffers talked openly about their *West Wing* obsession. The show teaches that opposition operates in good faith, that the right arguments persuade, that loving the institutions hard enough will save them. The establishment foot soldiers got steamrolled by a Republican movement that understood power: controlling institutions beats winning debates; the founders' framework enables minority rule; constitutional veneration is useful precisely because it stops the other side from seeking reform.

Jon Meacham is the type specimen. He has asserted that "patriotism is allegiance to an idea" while "nationalism" is allegiance to your own kind. Trump is a nationalist. Biden is a patriot. The distinction means nothing — both worship the founders, just from different angles — but it reveals the dead end. Liberal nationalists keep responding to the First Republic's restoration by invoking founding principles. As if eloquent appeals to mythology could defeat people deploying the founders' actual machinery.

Thoreau would recognize liberal nationalists instantly: People who oppose injustice in theory but won't resist in practice, who believe that if you just appeal to authority correctly, authority will reform itself, who treat working within the system as the only legitimate action, even when the system is designed to prevent the change they claim to want.

The new moral suasionists: Still waiting for the speech that changes everything — and never lands.

Where American Resistance Stands

American resistance finds itself trapped between two forces that both worship the founders, unable to move beyond either because the political culture has made structural transformation unthinkable.

The restoration project wants to recover the First Republic — the founders' actual design, the constitutional order that explicitly excluded most people and built mechanisms to keep them excluded. The restorationists venerate the founders because the founders created the framework they're using.

Liberal nationalism wants to redeem the First Republic — to make the founders' ideals real despite the founders' having built structures that prevented fulfillment. They venerate the founders because they believe that founding principles, properly applied, can save democracy.

American resistance — the tradition that forced slavery's end, secured women's suffrage, broke Jim Crow, expanded rights to excluded populations — tries to move beyond the First Republic entirely. To acknowledge that the founders created structures designed to prevent democracy, that the Constitution requires transformation rather than interpretation, that appealing to founding principles means appealing to the framework that enables oppression.

But this position proves nearly impossible to articulate because both dominant political traditions treat the founders' framework as sacred. Suggesting that the Constitution itself is the problem, that the founders' design enables authoritarianism, that structural transformation requires breaking with founding mythology — all of this remains outside legitimate discourse. The person who says such things gets dismissed as extreme, unrealistic, un-American.

The result: Resistance movements emerge, organize, mobilize millions, articulate clear demands — and achieve nothing structural.

Mass mobilization occurs, demonstrates public support for change, generates enormous energy — and hits the first interruption point immediately. Protest becomes the endpoint rather than resistance's beginning. People march, make signs, chant slogans, feel they've done something, go home. Institutions remain unchanged. Power adapts, absorbs the energy, continues operating.

The Women's March in 2017 brought millions into the streets. The George Floyd protests in 2020 brought tens of millions. The "No Kings" protests after the Supreme Court's immunity decision demonstrated widespread public understanding that the Court had created an executive above the law. Each time: impressive organization, real energy, justified anger. Each time: The administration, the institutions, the system continued exactly as before. No constitutional amendments proposed. No structural transformation achieved.

Meanwhile, the restoration proceeds, understanding what liberal nationalists refuse to acknowledge: Controlling institutions matters more than winning arguments; the founders' framework enables minority rule; constitutional veneration prevents structural reform.

The Pattern Established

Every major resistance movement since 1920 has hit the same wall.

The last full victory — the one that actually changed the Constitution and forced permanent transformation — was the Nineteenth Amendment in 1920. Alice Paul understood that working within permitted channels had failed for seventy years, that appealing to authority produced nothing, that transformation required making continued resistance unbearable. The suffragists picketed the White House during war, accepted arrest, endured force-feeding, compelled a constitutional amendment that couldn't be reversed when power shifted.

Nothing like that has happened since.

After 1920, resistance operated entirely within containment. Protest as endpoint. Legislation rather than amendment. Court interpretation rather than constitutional transformation. Faith that the system would save itself if pressured correctly. Trust that authority would reform if appealed to with the right words. Belief that the founders' framework could be redeemed rather than transformed.

The labor movement won collective bargaining, minimum wage, Social Security through legislation — the National Labor Relations Act, Fair Labor Standards Act, Social Security Act. Real achievements that transformed millions of lives, but through legislation, not constitutional amendments. When political winds shifted, protections weakened through new legislation, hostile interpretation of regulations and of the law, administrative neglect. The Taft-Hartley Act rolled back labor power in 1947. Right-to-work laws spread. Union density collapsed from more than 30 percent in the 1950s to under 11 percent today.

The Civil Rights Movement achieved extraordinary gains — destroyed legal segregation, secured voting rights, established federal civil rights protection, transformed American culture's explicit racism into something requiring rhetorical disguise. The movement broke containment at critical moments, accepted that people would die — and people did die — forced transformation through organized resistance that made maintaining Jim Crow unbearable.

But the victories came through legislation and court interpretation: the Civil Rights Act, Voting Rights Act, Fair Housing Act, *Brown v. Board*, and finally unlocking the Fourteenth Amendment's potential. Not constitutional amendment. Which meant the gains remained vulnerable.

The pattern that destroyed the Second Republic after 1877 repeated itself. Not immediately — the victories were too complete, the transformation too profound. But systematically, over decades, through methods that left civil rights laws on the books while rendering them increasingly inoperative. *Milliken* gutted school desegregation. *Washington v. Davis* made proving discrimination nearly impossible. *Shelby County* eviscerated the Voting Rights Act's preclearance requirements. Within hours of that decision, states began implementing voting restrictions that would have been illegal the day before.

This was the constitutional system working as designed. The founders created lifetime judicial appointments to insulate judges from democratic pressure; gave the Supreme Court authority to interpret the Constitution, knowing that interpretation could change; designed the Senate to over-represent conservative states controlling judicial appointments. The Civil Rights Movement achieved victories within this framework — and that framework made those victories reversible.

Constitutional Storytelling's Collapse

The Equal Rights Amendment should have passed. It had overwhelming public support. Passed Congress in 1972 with bipartisan votes. Thirty-five states ratified it within three years — three short of the required thirty-eight. And simple language: "Equality of rights under the law shall not be denied or abridged by the United States or by any State on account of sex."

It failed because the political culture wouldn't allow constitutional change. Americans had been taught to revere the Constitution as near perfect, to fear fundamental alteration, to see amendment as radical. Even reform with majority support, clear language, and obvious justice couldn't overcome internalized belief that the Constitution shouldn't be changed.

Without constitutional protection, women's rights advocates couldn't simply identify rights and add them through amendment. The political system wouldn't permit it. So they played a different, more dangerous game: constitutional storytelling.

Rights had to be discovered through interpretation, through fictive twisting of language never intended to include them, written by men who didn't believe women should vote, own property independently, or serve on juries. Constitutional storytelling required convincing judges that eighteenth- and nineteenth-century language meant things its authors never imagined.

Roe v. Wade was this game's product. The court found an implied right to privacy in the Fourteenth Amendment's Due Process Clause — a clause written in 1868 by men who never contemplated abortion rights, and ratified by states that criminalized abortion. Justice Harry Blackmun's majority opinion constructed elaborate frameworks connecting penumbras and emanations to build a right the text never explicitly mentioned. Constitutional storytelling: taking language meant for one purpose and persuading five justices that it meant something else.

For fifty years, it worked. Reproductive rights advocates treated *Roe* as settled precedent, building strategy around court access and judicial appointments rather than constitutional amendment. Resistance working entirely within containment — trusting that constitutional storytelling could substitute for structural change, that the right interpretation could be as secure as explicit text.

But constitutional storytelling is as dangerous as it seems. All that's required to erase such rights is a new story and new referees to say they like that story better.

That's *Dobbs*. Justice Samuel Alito's majority opinion embraced originalism — constitutional meaning determined by what the founders and the Reconstruction Congress intended. Since the men who wrote the Fourteenth Amendment never contemplated abortion as a constitutional right, and since abortion was criminalized when the amendment was ratified, no such right existed. The Constitution's text hadn't changed. Only which story the court's majority found persuasive.

Rights created through constitutional storytelling are permanent only as long as five justices agree with the story. And the restoration has spent forty years ensuring the right five justices sit on the court.

The Second Republic's Pattern

This pattern was established 150 years ago when the Second Republic was born and then destroyed.

The Thirteenth, Fourteenth, and Fifteenth Amendments represented genuine structural change — constitutional transformation the founders would have rejected as destroying their design. The Radical Republicans forced this through, moved beyond permitted channels during war, accepted that hundreds of thousands would die, used military occupation to force Southern states to ratify amendments as readmission conditions. Resistance that broke through both interruption points and achieved permanent structural change.

For a brief moment, it worked. Black men voted, held office, built political power. The Second Republic represented the first time that

American democracy actually attempted including the people the founders systematically excluded.

Then it was systematically destroyed. The Supreme Court gutted the Fourteenth Amendment in Slaughterhouse and *Cruikshank*. White terrorist organizations used violence. Northern Republicans abandoned the project when politically inconvenient. The Compromise of 1877 withdrew federal troops in exchange for Hayes's presidency.

But the most effective mechanism was cultural. The Lost Cause wasn't just Southern nostalgia — it was a deliberate political project to reconstitute white supremacy as American identity. Through monuments, textbooks, films, literature, heritage organizations, it rewrote the Civil War as a tragic conflict between honorable men rather than a war to preserve slavery. It transformed Confederate generals into American heroes. It recast Reconstruction as corrupt failure rather than democratic experiment destroyed by terrorism. Most important, it positioned the Constitution's original design — the founders' accommodation of slavery, their fear of democracy, their mechanisms protecting property over people — as a natural and proper order that Reconstruction had temporarily disrupted.

This established the pattern: Structural change achieved through constitutional amendment could be eviscerated without repealing the amendment, simply by making it inoperative through judicial interpretation, legislative neglect, administrative failure to enforce, and cultural reconstruction making original exclusions seem natural again.

The pattern has repeated for 150 years. And now the First Republic is being restored using the same methods.

The Patriot Myth: Containment Perfected

But something changed after World War II. Containment became not just effective but nearly total, embedded so deeply that even recognizing it as containment became difficult.

During World War II, the government faced a mobilization crisis. The Office of War Information, established in 1942, manufactured a solution: a national story powerful enough to override lived experience — the Revolution as eternal struggle for liberty, the founders as visionary geniuses, the Constitution as a near-perfect framework requiring only faithful application.

The campaign was supposed to end in 1945. It didn't. The newly created Department of Defense recognized how effective cultural mobilization had been and repurposed it for the Cold War. The target shifted from fascism to communism, but the mechanism remained: aggressive cultural production of American exceptionalism, teaching reverence for the founders' framework, positioning constitutional critique as dangerous and possibly un-American.

This created something unprecedented: a political culture in which even discussing constitutional reform became nearly impossible. The founders had to be geniuses. The Constitution had to be perfect or near perfect. The founding institutions had to be sacred. Questioning these premises became, quite literally, outside legitimate discourse.

The Patriot Myth didn't just make Americans reluctant to change the Constitution, it made them unable to imagine that change was necessary. The system's failures weren't evidence that the founders' design was flawed — they were evidence that Americans had strayed from the founders' wisdom. Problems were personal (bad leaders) or temporary (current crisis) or cultural (loss of values), never structural. The framework itself remained beyond question.

This was containment perfected. Not through violent repression — though that remained available — but through internalized reverence. Americans were trained to see legitimacy only in working within the system the founders created, on terms they established, through institutions they designed.

The Question

American resistance is left facing a question it hasn't confronted since 1920: Can the pattern be broken?

For more than a century, every resistance movement has achieved gains within containment and watched those gains erode or get reversed. The only mechanism that ever produced permanent structural change — constitutional amendment — has become impossible. Not difficult; impossible. The political culture will not allow it.

As the First Republic's restoration proceeds, using the founders' framework exactly as designed, liberal nationalism responds with appeals to that same framework. Speeches invoking founding principles. Faith that institutions will save themselves. Trust that authority will reform if appealed to correctly. Belief that the system works if staffed by people who love it enough.

Meanwhile, the restoration captures institutions, understanding what liberal nationalists refuse to acknowledge: that controlling institutions matters more than winning arguments, that the founders' framework enables minority rule, that constitutional veneration is useful only insofar as it prevents structural reform.

Breaking the pattern would require several things that currently seem impossible:

It would require recognizing that the Constitution itself is the problem, not its interpretation. That the founders created structures designed to prevent democracy, protect property, enable minority rule, resist transformation. That reverence for the founding framework enables authoritarianism rather than prevents it. That the Anti-Federalists were right.

It would require abandoning liberal nationalism's faith that the system saves itself, that appeals to founding principles persuade authority to reform, that working within permitted channels produces transformation, that speeches matter, that Sorkin was right about how American politics work.

It would require accepting what suffragists like Alice Paul and leaders of the Civil Rights Movement understood: Resistance requires moving beyond permitted channels, breaking laws that protect abusive authority, making normal functioning impossible until demands are met, accepting that people will die as consequences of forcing change.

It would require pursuing constitutional amendment rather than interpretation — actual transformation rather than discovering new meanings in old language. Making rights explicit and permanent rather than dependent on five justices maintaining particular interpretations.

Most fundamentally, it would require cultural transformation as profound as the Office of War Information accomplished: replacing constitutional reverence with constitutional critique, replacing faith in the founders with recognition that they created structures enabling the very tyranny they claimed to prevent, replacing the Patriot Myth with honest acknowledgment that the founding framework requires transformation rather than redemption.

None of this seems likely. The cultural containment is too complete. Liberal nationalism is too dominant. The Patriot Myth is too deeply embedded. Constitutional amendment is too unthinkable. Moving beyond permitted channels is too extreme.

And so the pattern continues. Resistance emerges, organizes, mobilizes, achieves temporary gains through permitted channels, watches those gains erode when power shifts. The First Republic continues its restoration using the founders' framework. Liberal nationalists continue responding with appeals to that same framework. And American resistance remains trapped between two forms of constitutional worship, unable to imagine the structural transformation survival requires.

The resistance history of the United States continues. The patterns persist. The interruption points hold. Containment is complete.

The last full victory — constitutional transformation that restructured power, not merely refined it — was 1920. More than a century ago.

Whether Americans can break free of the founders' framework, or whether — as the Anti-Federalists warned in 1787 — the Constitution the founders created was designed to fail to protect the democratic majority exactly this way, and is now doing so precisely as intended, remains to be seen. But the trajectory is clear, and the time for transformation grows shorter as the restoration proceeds.

A Resistance History Toolkit

Patterns Across Time

The nine principles presented here aren't rules. They're patterns that emerge across centuries of Americans confronting abusive authority. Each one is grounded in specific historical moments when people faced impossible choices: submit or resist, compromise or fight, accept gradual reform or force transformation.

What makes these patterns useful is that they help you see what's actually happening around you — and to you. History doesn't repeat, but power does. The specific abuses change, but the patterns of how authority abuses itself, and how people resist, remain consistent.

Each principle represents a critical juncture where resistance movements succeed or fail, advance or get interrupted. They're arranged roughly in the order resistance typically encounters them: first learning to distinguish genuine resistance from performance, then building from individual acts to organized networks, then facing the question of violence, and finally — rarely — seizing power to transform structures.

You don't need all nine at once. You need the one that matches where you are and what you're facing. The history behind each isn't decorative — it's diagnostic. Understanding how resistance actually worked helps you recognize when you're being played, when you're fooling yourself, when tactics can't work, and when the moment for action has arrived and won't last.

Principle #1: Beware False Prophets — Learn to Recognize False Resistance

Real resistance challenges abusive authority. False resistance exploits popular anger to gain power.

The skill you need: Ask three questions whenever someone claims to lead "the people" against oppression:

1. **Who benefits if they win?** Does victory expand who holds power or just change which narrow group controls it? Bacon's victory would have meant more genocide and his own ascent. Metacomet's resistance aimed to preserve his people's existence.
2. **Who pays the price?** Genuine resistance puts the resisters at risk. False resistance scapegoats the vulnerable. Bacon sent others to slaughter Indigenous peoples while positioning himself for power. Metacomet and his warriors risked — and lost — everything.
3. **What authority are they actually challenging?** Real resistance confronts the system of abuse itself. False resistance demands a larger share within that same system. Bacon wanted more colonial power, just distributed differently. Metacomet fought against the colonial project entirely.

Why this matters now: Popular anger is real, powerful, and easily redirected. Someone will always emerge to channel that anger — claiming to speak for "the people," wrapping themselves in resistance rhetoric, promising to fight "elites" or "corruption" or "tyranny." The question is whether they're challenging the abuse of authority or just angling for their own turn at the controls.

The warning: Many resistance movements have been captured midflight by ambitious operators who saw an opportunity. The anger was genuine, the grievances real, but the outcome served someone else's pursuit of power. Don't let your resistance become someone else's ladder. Stay focused on the actual abuse of authority you're confronting, and be honest about identifying when leaders are serving themselves rather than the cause.

The test: If their victory means you're still not free — just serving a different master — it's not resistance. It's a power grab wearing resistance clothing.

Principle #2: More Weight — Refuse to Validate the Lie

The most dangerous abusive authority doesn't just demand obedience — it claims the power to define reality itself. It insists on controlling what is true, what is real, what is legitimate. Your commitment to truth, even when it costs you everything, is the foundation of all resistance.

The skill you need: Recognize when authority is demanding control over reality itself, then refuse to surrender your grip on what you know to be true.

The dynamic: Salem's court didn't just punish witches — it claimed the authority to determine who was a witch based on invisible, unprovable "evidence" that only the accusers could see. The enslavers' republic didn't just hold people in bondage — it insisted that Black people *were* property, that this was a fact of nature, that anyone who said otherwise was delusional or dangerous.

These systems require you to accept their version of reality. Not just to obey it, but to internalize it. To see what they say you should see. To unsee what they say doesn't exist. To call truth "lies" and lies "truth." When authority controls the narrative, it controls everything — because if it can make you doubt your own perception of reality, it can make you doubt your right to resist.

The first step in building resistance: Before you can organize opposition, before you can refuse unjust laws, before you can build networks or take action, you have to establish what is true. The Unconfessed didn't have power, didn't have weapons, didn't have influence. What they had was an unshakable commitment to truth: *I am not a witch. I will not say I am. You cannot make me call this lie the truth.*

That commitment is the bedrock. Everything else builds on it.

Why this matters now: You live in an era of competing realities, where powerful forces insist you accept their version of events, their framing of problems, their definition of what's possible. They don't just want compliance — they want you to *believe*. To see the world through their lens. To accept their narrative as the only legitimate one.

The moment you surrender your commitment to truth — when you start repeating things you know aren't true, when you accept obvious lies as "complicated," when you let authority define reality for you — you've given up the ground on which all resistance stands.

The warning: Maintaining your grip on truth has costs. It isolates you from those who've accepted the lie. It marks you as difficult, unreasonable, a troublemaker. The Unconfessed were called stubborn, wicked, possessed. You might be called worse. Authority will pressure you to "be reasonable," to "see both sides," to accept that maybe your perception of reality isn't the only valid one.

But there's a difference between genuine uncertainty and forced surrender. When you *know* something is true and authority demands you say it isn't — that's not complexity. That's a loyalty test.

The test: Can you hold on to what you know to be true when everyone around you is accepting the lie? Can you refuse to call reality by the wrong name, even when the cost is high? Can you say, "This is a lie," when authority insists it's truth?

The power: When authority builds itself on lies, your refusal to validate those lies is an act of structural resistance. You're not just protecting your own conscience, you're also denying the system the complicity it needs to function. Each person who refuses makes the lie harder to sustain.

The Unconfessed couldn't stop the trials, couldn't save themselves, couldn't overthrow the court. But their commitment to truth — maintained until death — added weight that eventually broke the system. The lies couldn't hold against people who refused to call them true.

This is where resistance begins: with an unshakable commitment to truth, even when truth has no power. Especially then.

Principle #3: My Enemy's Enemy — Your Ally Doesn't Have to Be Pure

Resistance doesn't require morally perfect allies. It requires clear-eyed assessment of whose interests align with yours in this moment, and the courage to leverage that alignment for concrete results.

The skill you need: Learn to read power dynamics accurately, identify conflicts between authorities, and exploit those conflicts to create space for resistance — without mistaking temporary allies for permanent friends.

The dynamic: Nancy Dixon didn't need the British to be morally superior to the patriots. She needed them to be in conflict with the patriots. That conflict created an opening. The British weren't offering freedom out of benevolence — they were offering it to weaken their enemy. Nancy understood this perfectly. She didn't trust British virtue; she trusted British self-interest pointed in a direction she could use.

The Black loyalists as a whole demonstrated this principle at scale. They didn't wait for the patriots to live up to their rhetoric about liberty. They didn't petition for gradual reform. They read the strategic situation, identified which power was more likely to deliver actual freedom (however cynical the motivation), and moved decisively to claim it.

Why this matters now: Waiting for morally pure allies means waiting forever. Waiting for authority to reform itself out of enlightened self-interest means dying in chains. The world doesn't work that way. Power conflicts with power, and those conflicts create openings. Your job is to identify those openings and move through them before they close.

This doesn't mean allying with anyone for any reason. It means being ruthlessly clear about what you're trying to achieve and which conflicts between existing powers create space for you to achieve it. Nancy's goal was freedom — permanent, actual, lived freedom for herself and her daughter. The British-versus-patriot conflict created a path to that freedom. She took it.

The warning: Strategic pragmatism is not the same as naive trust. Nancy didn't believe British propaganda about liberty. She watched, listened, tested, and verified. She built networks within the Black community to share intelligence about what was really happening versus what was being promised. She prepared for betrayal — because allies motivated by self-interest will betray you the moment their interests shift.

And here's the harder warning: Your community might judge you for this. They might call you a traitor, a sellout, someone who sided with "the enemy." The patriots certainly did — they branded Black loyalists as traitors to American liberty, never mind that American liberty meant their continued enslavement. You have to be willing to bear that judgment while staying focused on results.

The test: Can you distinguish between an ally's motivations and the results they can deliver? Can you work with someone whose values you don't share if their interests temporarily align with yours? Can you maintain clear boundaries — using the alliance without being used by it?

Most important: Can you deliver actual freedom, not just symbolic gestures or promised reforms?

The power: Strategic pragmatism produces results. Nancy Dixon and thousands like her didn't just resist — they won. They achieved actual, permanent freedom. Not someday. Not after more petitions. Not after the patriots had a change of heart. They got free, built lives, raised children in freedom, and created communities that proved Black people were fully capable of self-governance.

The patriots offered rhetoric. The British offered ships to Canada. Nancy chose ships. That's strategic pragmatism — and it worked.

The caution for resistance movements: This principle also warns resistance movements about their own vulnerability. Just as you can use conflicts between authorities, those authorities can use conflicts within resistance movements. Someone will always emerge claiming to be your ally, offering resources or support, while actually serving their own interests. The test is the same: Does this alliance move you toward concrete freedom, or does it redirect your resistance toward someone else's goals?

Stay focused on results. Trust interests, not intentions. And never mistake a temporary ally for a permanent friend.

Principle #4: Force the Fight, Even When You're Losing

Don't wait for perfect conditions or overwhelming strength. Force abusive authority to respond, to slow down, to pay a price. Even when you're outmatched, engagement creates opportunities that passivity never will.

The skill you need: Recognize when authority is trying to rush through changes that will be difficult to undo, then force them to fight for every inch — adjusting your tactics with each setback, extracting whatever concessions you can, understanding that partial victories now can become foundations for total victories later.

The dynamic: The nationalists at Philadelphia in 1787 had stacked the deck. They exceeded their mandate, operated in secrecy, and produced a constitution that concentrated power in ways the Revolution had supposedly fought against. Then they rushed it through ratification before opposition could organize — demanding quick votes, limiting debate, claiming any delay would mean chaos.

The Anti-Federalists were caught off guard, disorganized, fighting against momentum and establishment power. By every measure, they should have accepted defeat and moved on. The Constitution was going to be ratified. The nationalist vision was going to win.

But they forced the fight anyway.

The progression: At each state ratifying convention, they pushed. They lost in Pennsylvania, but they learned. They lost in Massachusetts, but they extracted the first promise of amendments. They lost in Virginia, but Madison had to publicly commit to a Bill of Rights to win his own election. They didn't get what they wanted — a second constitutional convention, fundamental restructuring of federal power — but they made the nationalists pay for every victory.

And here's the crucial point: Madison didn't want a Bill of Rights. He thought it was unnecessary, even dangerous. He fought it, delayed it, tried to kill it with procedure. But the Anti-Federalists had forced him into a corner where his political survival depended on delivering amendments. So he did — while controlling the process to minimize the damage to his constitutional structure.

Why this matters now: You will face moments when authority has seemingly won. The law has passed. The policy is implemented. The structure is in place. The establishment tells you the fight is over, it's time to move on, pragmatism demands acceptance.

Force the fight anyway.

Make them defend what they've done. Make them explain it. Make them pay a political price. Extract whatever concessions you can — knowing they won't give you what you really want, but understanding that concessions can become tools.

The long game: The Bill of Rights seemed limited when ratified. It didn't apply to state governments. It didn't free enslaved people. It didn't fundamentally redistribute power. Madison and the nationalists could live with it because it didn't threaten their constitutional structure.

But seventy-eight years later, the Fourteenth Amendment nationalized those rights, making them binding on states. Suddenly those "limited" protections became the constitutional foundation for challenging state oppression. The Anti-Federalists' forced concessions became weapons they never lived to see deployed.

Frederick Douglass understood this: "The Constitution is a GLORIOUS LIBERTY DOCUMENT" — not because of what the framers intended, but because the Anti-Federalists had forced amendments into it that could be used against the very system that produced them.

The warning: Forcing the fight when you're losing is exhausting and often thankless. You'll be told you're being unreasonable, that you should accept reality, that you're making things worse with your obstinacy. The Anti-Federalists were dismissed as cranks and alarmists. Madison gets credit for "their" Bill of Rights in every history textbook.

You might not get credit. You might not see victory in your lifetime. But forced concessions can become the basis for future freedom.

The test: Can you fight when you're losing? Can you extract concessions when total victory is impossible? Can you recognize that making authority pay a price — even a small one — changes the landscape for future resistance?

Can you plant seeds knowing someone else will harvest them?

The tactical principle: Each defeat should teach you something. The Anti-Federalists got more sophisticated at each convention, learned what arguments worked, where the pressure points were, which delegates were persuadable. They lost battles but built capacity.

Adjust. Learn. Force the next fight smarter than you forced the last one. Don't accept that the moment has passed — create new moments by refusing to let authority consolidate its victory without cost.

The power: Even when you lose, you can force authority to reveal itself, to spend political capital, to make promises it must later keep or break publicly. You can create tactical openings. You can establish precedents — even compromised ones — that future resisters can expand.

The Anti-Federalists didn't stop the Constitution. But they forced into it the very amendments that would later be used to challenge Jim Crow, expand civil rights, and protect individual liberty against state power. They lost the battle and won wars they never knew would be fought.

That's the power of forcing the fight even when you're losing: You change what's possible for everyone who comes after.

Principle #5: Resistance Is a Lifetime, Not a Moment

The dramatic act of defiance — the escape, the refusal, the confrontation — is just the beginning. Real resistance requires persistence to keep pursuing your goal and resilience to withstand the inevitable counterattacks without breaking.

The skill you need: Build the capacity for sustained resistance over years or decades, not just the courage for one brave moment. Learn to recover from setbacks, adapt to new threats, and maintain your commitment when the cost keeps rising.

The dynamic: Ona Judge's escape from the Washingtons was one night in May 1796. Her resistance lasted fifty-four years — until her death in 1848, still free, still defiant, still refusing to validate the lie that she was property.

That night in Philadelphia required courage. The decades that followed required something harder: the persistence to never give up her freedom and the resilience to survive every attempt to take it back.

Washington deployed federal officials, hired slave catchers, sent his nephew on a kidnapping mission. He used the law, ignored the law, threatened, bribed, and hunted. For the rest of his life, he never stopped trying to reclaim her. After his death, Martha continued the pursuit. After Martha's death, the Custis heirs remained a threat.

Ona had to remain vigilant for fifty-four years. Every knock on the door could be a slave catcher. Every stranger could be a spy. Every rumor of a ship from Virginia meant danger. She lived in poverty, was widowed young, lost children. And through it all, she had to maintain her resistance — never wavering, never surrendering, never accepting that maybe it would be easier to go back.

Why this matters now: Resistance movements often focus on the dramatic moment — the protest, the walkout, the confrontation. Those moments matter. But authority's first response to resistance is to wait you out. They know most people can sustain defiance for days or weeks, not years. They know life gets in the way — you need a job, you have a family, you get tired.

Their strategy is attrition. Outlast the resisters. Make resistance so costly over time that people eventually give up and go back to "normal." This works remarkably well, because most people underestimate what sustained resistance requires.

The twin pillars: *Persistence* means keeping your eyes on the goal even when progress seems impossible. Ona's goal was simple: Stay free. For fifty-four years, she persisted in that goal. Washington offered forgiveness, promised she could return to a "comfortable" life in slavery. She refused. Always refused. The goal never changed.

Resilience means recovering from the blows that will inevitably land. Whipple blocked her marriage. Bassett tracked her down. She lost her husband, lost her children, lived in poverty. Each blow could have broken her resistance. Instead, she adapted, recovered, and continued. She moved when she had to, hid when necessary, built new support networks when old ones failed.

The warning: This is the hardest principle, because it demands the most. A moment of courage you can summon when adrenaline runs high. A lifetime of resistance requires something deeper — an unshakable core that sustains you when no one is watching, when the world has moved on, when you're exhausted and alone.

Many resistance movements fail not because they lack brave people willing to take dramatic action, but because they lack people capable of sustaining resistance when it becomes mundane, grinding, unglamorous work.

You have to build your life around resistance — not as a phase you're going through, but as a permanent condition. That means accepting costs most people won't pay: isolation, poverty, constant vigilance, sacrificed opportunities.

The test: Can you maintain resistance when it's no longer exciting? When years pass without visible progress? When the cost keeps accumulating and the reward seems distant or impossible?

Can you recover from defeats without abandoning the fight? When authority lands a blow — and it will land many — can you absorb it, adapt, and continue?

Most important: Can you resist as a way of life, not just as a moment of defiance?

The power: Sustained resistance breaks authority in ways dramatic action never can. Washington couldn't break Ona because she simply would not stop resisting. For fifty-four years, she denied him — and the entire enslavers' republic — the authority to define her as property.

Each year she remained free was another year proving that the system could be defied. Each decade was another demonstration that one woman's persistence could outlast the most powerful man in America and the government he helped create.

When she finally told her story to abolitionists in the 1840s — still free, still defiant — she became living proof that resistance could succeed. Not because she'd overthrown the system, but because she'd survived it. Her persistence was her victory.

The caution for resistance movements: Build for the long haul from the beginning. Don't assume that momentum will carry you through. Create support structures that can sustain resisters over years: mutual aid, shared resources, emotional support networks, ways to recover from defeats without collapsing.

Celebrate the dramatic moments, but honor the people who show up decade after decade, doing unglamorous work, maintaining resistance when no one's watching.

Because authority is counting on you getting tired. Your persistence — your refusal to quit no matter how long it takes — is what they can't plan for, can't budget for, can't outlast.

Principle #6: Ideas Matter — Know What You're Fighting For, Not Just What You're Against

Resistance without a clear ideological foundation is easily redirected, co-opted, or exhausted. You need an unshakable principle that defines what you're defending — something that gives resistance its shape, direction, and staying power.

The skill you need: Articulate the positive principle you're fighting for, not just the abuses you're fighting against. Know the moral ground you're defending so clearly that you can recognize when you've abandoned it, when someone's trying to redirect you, or when victory has actually been achieved.

The dynamic: Thoreau inherited from his grandmother Mary Jones and her family a principle so clear that it could survive two generations: liberty of conscience. Not as an abstraction, but as a lived commitment. The Joneses refused to surrender their conscience to patriot committees demanding loyalty oaths. They went to jail, lost their property, scattered across the Atlantic world — all to defend one principle: *No authority has the right to command your conscience.*

That wasn't a reaction against one bad law or one corrupt official. It was a positive assertion about human dignity and moral autonomy that could be applied to any authority, in any era. When Thoreau sat in jail in 1846, he wasn't just protesting the Mexican War or the Fugitive Slave Act. He was defending the same principle his family had defended seventy years earlier: *When government demands you violate your conscience, your first duty is to refuse.*

This clarity is what made *Civil Disobedience* the ideological foundation for resistance movements worldwide. Thoreau didn't just say, "Slavery is wrong," or "This war is unjust." He articulated *why* individual conscience must refuse unjust authority and *when* that refusal becomes a moral obligation.

Why this matters now: It's easy to know what you're against. The list of grievances writes itself — injustice is everywhere, abuses are obvious, everyone can point to what's wrong. But being against something isn't enough to sustain resistance.

Without a clear principle of what you're *for,* resistance becomes reactive — you're always responding to the latest outrage, always chasing the next fight, never building toward anything coherent. You can be redirected by anyone who offers you a new enemy. You can be satisfied with symbolic victories that don't actually advance your cause. You can't tell the difference between genuine progress and empty reform.

Worse, without a positive principle, you can't recognize when your resistance has been captured. Someone can redirect your anger toward their preferred target, use your energy for their purposes, and you won't even notice — because you were never clear about what you were actually fighting for.

The ideological foundation Thoreau provided: Authority in a republic exists only on loan from the governed. When that authority is abused — when it turns against the people, serves narrow interests, demands violations of conscience — the compact is broken. At that moment, the governed have not just a right but a *duty* to refuse.

This isn't about improving bad laws or reforming corrupt institutions. When the system itself is organized for injustice — when the Constitution protects slavery, when the government wages wars of conquest, when the machinery of state demands you become an agent of wrong — then working within that system is complicity.

Your conscience is the ground you defend. "The only obligation which I have a right to assume is to do at any time what I think right." That's the positive principle. Not just "resist bad government" but "defend the sovereignty of individual conscience against any authority that demands its surrender."

The global effect: Gandhi read Thoreau and found the ideological foundation for satyagraha — soul-force, truth-force. Martin Luther King, Jr., read Thoreau and found the moral justification for civil disobedience that could be explained in churches and courtrooms. Anti-colonial movements, Eastern Bloc dissidents, pro-democracy activists — all drew on Thoreau's articulation of when and why individual conscience must refuse state authority.

Not because Thoreau invented resistance — people had been resisting for millennia — but because he gave resistance its clearest ideological expression in the American context, one that proved portable to other struggles.

The warning: Ideas matter more than anything. Get the principle wrong and everything that follows is compromised. The patriots of 1775 fought for "liberty" but couldn't articulate what that meant beyond "freedom from British rule." The men of 1787 captured that revolution precisely because the patriots had no positive principle to defend — just a negative one about what they were against.

When you know *what you're fighting for,* you can recognize betrayal. The Anti-Federalists knew — they were fighting for liberty of conscience, limited government, protection of individual rights against centralized power. When they lost the fight for a second constitutional convention, they could still extract amendments that embodied their principles. Madison thought he was giving them scraps. They knew they were planting seeds.

The test: Can you articulate, in one clear sentence, what you're fighting for? Not what you're against — what you're *for*. What positive principle are you defending?

If you can't answer that clearly, you don't have a foundation. You have anger, justified anger, but anger alone gets redirected, co-opted, or exhausted.

Thoreau's answer: I'm fighting for the sovereignty of individual conscience against any authority that demands its surrender.

What's yours?

The power: A clear ideological foundation does several things simultaneously:

It gives resistance *direction* — you know what victory looks like because you know what principle you're defending.

It gives resistance *coherence* — you can distinguish between tactics that advance your principle and tactics that betray it.

It gives resistance *staying power* — when the immediate fight is lost, the principle survives and can be applied to the next fight.

It gives resistance *portability* — others facing different abuses of authority can adopt your principle and apply it to their circumstances.

Most important, it gives resistance *legitimacy* — you're not just angry or reactive, you're defending something fundamental about human dignity that transcends the specific abuse of the moment.

The caution for resistance movements: Spend time articulating your positive principle early. Don't just react to abuses; define what you're defending. Test that principle: Does it hold across different circumstances? Can it distinguish between genuine victories and hollow compromises? Will it guide you when tactics fail and you need to adapt?

The movements that last, that achieve transformation rather than just temporary change, are movements that know what they're fighting for. Everything else is just channeled anger waiting to be redirected by the next ambitious operator.

Ideas matter. Get them right. They're the foundation everything else builds on.

Principle #7: Forge the Chain — Build the Infrastructure; Individual Courage Isn't Enough

When authority criminalizes conscience at scale, individual acts of defiance must evolve into sophisticated, organized networks. The more total the system of oppression, the more disciplined the resistance infrastructure required to defeat it.

The skill you need: Learn to build and protect clandestine networks that can operate under sustained government pressure — specialization of roles, compartmentalization of knowledge, operational security that protects both the network and the people it serves.

The dynamic: Before 1850, the Underground Railroad was mostly individual conscience responding to individual need. A fugitive appeared at your door. You hid them for a night. They moved on. You could honestly say you hadn't "harbored" anyone — they just passed through. It was humanitarian aid, reactive and scattered.

The Fugitive Slave Act of 1850 changed everything. Now every citizen was deputized as a potential slave catcher. Commissioners earned more for ruling against freedom than for it. The entire machinery of the federal government became an engine of slave catching. Suddenly, individual acts of conscience weren't enough. The opposition had to become organized, systematic, and sophisticated — or it would fail.

The transformation: Within weeks of the act's passage, vigilance committees formed in every major Northern city. But these weren't just mutual aid societies — they were resistance infrastructure with specialized roles:

Legal teams filed writs, mounted defenses, used procedure as a weapon. *Intelligence networks* tracked slave catchers, monitored ships and hotels, spread warnings. *Safe houses* created routes stretching to the Canadian border, each link knowing only the next. *Finance committees* raised thousands of dollars for operations, bribes, legal fees. *Security forces* protected fugitives by force when necessary. *Communication systems* used church bells, coded letters, trusted intermediaries.

This wasn't improvisation. This was organizational discipline that would impress any intelligence service.

The crucial element — compartmentalization: The network's greatest strength was what members *didn't* know. Morris knew the legal strategies but not the safe house locations. Hayden knew his fortress on Beacon Hill but not the routes north. Conductors knew the next station but nothing beyond it.

This protected the network. When federal prosecutors arrested Morris, he couldn't reveal routes he didn't know. When they questioned Hayden, he couldn't name contacts he'd never met. The government couldn't roll up the entire infrastructure because no single arrest exposed all the connections.

Even today, after 170 years of historical research, we still don't know precisely how the Underground Railroad coordinated operations across hundreds of miles. That enduring secrecy isn't a gap in the historical record — it's proof of operational discipline so complete, it protected its methods into perpetuity.

Why this matters now: You cannot defeat systematic oppression with scattered individual acts, no matter how courageous. When authority deploys its full machinery — legal, financial, military, surveillance — against you, individual resistance gets crushed.

The response must be organizational: specialized roles so people can develop expertise, compartmentalized knowledge so no single capture breaks the network, operational security so the infrastructure survives prosecution.

This is the hardest transition for resistance movements to make. Individual acts feel authentic, spontaneous, pure. Organizations feel bureaucratic, hierarchical, compromised. But spontaneity doesn't survive federal prosecution. Purity doesn't move thousands of people to freedom.

The test of effectiveness: The Underground Railroad moved tens of thousands to Canada — permanent, actual, concrete freedom beyond the reach of American law. Not symbolic gestures. Not consciousness-raising. Not martyrdom. *Results.*

Robert Morris stood trial twice. Both times, hung juries. Lewis Hayden faced charges. Acquitted. The government indicted dozens.

Secured almost no convictions. Why? Because the network had built community protection into its operations — juries wouldn't convict, witnesses wouldn't testify, entire towns mobilized to sabotage prosecutions.

By 1860, the Fugitive Slave Act was effectively nullified in the North, not because it was repealed, but because organized resistance made it unenforceable.

The sanctuary principle: But none of this works without somewhere to go. The Underground Railroad succeeded because Canada existed — a place where American law had no power, where freedom was real and permanent, where the British flag meant protection.

This is crucial: Resistance networks that just move people around within the same hostile system aren't liberation — they're relocation. The network needed an actual terminus beyond authority's reach. That's what Canada provided, what made the entire infrastructure possible.

The warning: Building organized resistance infrastructure is dangerous and demanding. It requires *trust* in people you might not know well; *discipline* to follow operational security even when it seems paranoid; *patience* to build systems slowly rather than act impulsively; *sacrifice* of individual glory for collective effectiveness; and *long-term thinking* that accepts short-term constraints for long-term capacity.

Many resistance movements fail this transition. They stay spontaneous too long, prioritizing authenticity over effectiveness. Or they organize badly, creating hierarchies that betray the cause. Or they sacrifice security for visibility, making themselves easy targets.

The Underground Railroad survived because it never forgot its purpose: get people to freedom. Everything else — credit, recognition, ideological purity — was secondary to results.

The test: Can you sublimate individual action to organizational discipline? Can you accept a specialized role instead of doing everything yourself? Can you maintain operational security even when it means not knowing what's happening beyond your piece?

Can you build systems that will survive your own arrest or death?

Most important: Can you deliver concrete results, not just dramatic resistance?

The power: Organized networks can sustain resistance that individual courage cannot. They can withstand prosecution, infiltration, propaganda, and sustained government pressure. They can operate for years or decades, moving thousands to freedom, forcing authority to pay costs it cannot sustain.

The Shadrach Minkins rescue wasn't one brave act — it was a network executing a plan. Within hours of his arrest, the alarm spread through church bells. Within days, he was moving through tested routes. Within two weeks, he was in Montreal, permanently beyond federal reach.

That's what organized infrastructure delivers: systematic success at scale.

The caution for resistance movements: Don't romanticize spontaneity. Don't mistake visibility for effectiveness. Don't sacrifice operational security for moral purity or public credit.

Build the infrastructure methodically. Specialize roles. Compartmentalize knowledge. Protect the network above all else. Measure success in results — lives saved, people freed, concrete victories — not in dramatic moments or public recognition.

The Underground Railroad's greatest monument isn't in any museum. It's in the operational methods that remain hidden, protecting the possibility that such networks could function again whenever authority makes resistance necessary.

Principle #8: Arming the Hosts of Freedom — Whatever It Takes

When systematic oppression cannot be reformed or evaded through any peaceful means, resistance faces its hardest test: whether to accept that whatever tools are necessary to push back abuse become the ones for the job. This isn't about whether such tools are justified — it's about whether you can carry the permanent moral weight of that choice.

The skill you need: Recognize when the secret script has reached its limits, every peaceful channel has been deliberately closed, and resistance must choose between accepting what's necessary or accepting perpetual oppression. Then — and this is the hard part — either commit completely or don't cross the line at all. Half measures don't work.

The dynamic: For thirty years, American resistance to slavery operated through the secret script — the Underground Railroad saving lives in darkness, Garrison burning constitutions but not buildings, Douglass thundering against injustice while stopping short of calling for direct confrontation with armed authority. This secret resistance maintained moral clarity by avoiding the tools that would bring the worst consequences.

But by 1856, the secret script had reached its limits. The Underground Railroad had saved thousands while millions remained enslaved. Moral suasion had persuaded the convinced while enslavers consolidated power. Political action was blocked by constitutional structures designed to protect slavery. A senator was beaten nearly to death on the Senate floor. Federal armies deployed to capture individual fugitives. Pro-slavery forces executed free-state settlers in Kansas.

Every peaceful channel for systematic change had been deliberately, violently closed.

The interruption point: Higginson, Parker, Smith, Sanborn, Stearns, and Howe had all worked through the Underground Railroad. This was about whether to force a public confrontation with armed authority that would inevitably result in harm, even death. Not targeting killing necessarily, but accepting destruction as the price of direct challenge to power that would yield only to force.

As Albert Camus wrote about resistance to Nazi occupation, this is "calculated culpability" — accepting that your actions will cause destruction while never becoming comfortable with that fact. The moment resistance becomes casual about the consequences of necessary action, it loses its moral authority.

Why this matters now: You will face moments when every peaceful option has been exhausted or deliberately blocked. When moral appeals mean nothing. When political channels are corrupted. When legal challenges are denied. When the system has made reform structurally impossible. At that point, resistance faces the question: Accept what's necessary, or accept that oppression will continue.

This is the hardest choice resistance ever makes. Most movements end here, unable to cross this line. And that's not necessarily wrong — there's integrity in maintaining the refusal of certain tools even when it means accepting continued oppression. What lacks integrity is pretending you can support such action while keeping your hands clean, enable the consequences while maintaining innocence, cross the line halfway.

The spectrum of commitment: The Six's different responses reveal who had truly crossed the moral line and who had only approached it.

Complete commitment: Thomas Wentworth Higginson and Theodore Parker had genuinely reconciled themselves to what confronting armed authority required. They had organized support, mobilized their networks, used every resource at their disposal to make Brown's challenge possible. When Brown was captured, Higginson wanted to rescue him by force. Parker, dying in Rome, publicly defended Brown. They could defend the action because they had already accepted its moral weight. Their consciences were clear.

Intellectual acceptance without moral commitment: Franklin Sanborn and George Luther Stearns fled to Canada when federal marshals came. They had supported the action intellectually, had helped organize and enable it, but they discovered that building the infrastructure for confrontation and living with the consequences were different things.

Complete collapse: Gerrit Smith, who had provided substantial resources and mobilized his considerable influence to make Brown's work possible, suffered what appeared to be a mental breakdown and was hospitalized. Whether genuine or calculated to avoid prosecution, the collapse revealed someone who couldn't face what he had enabled.

Equivocation: Samuel Gridley Howe denied, rationalized, claimed he hadn't known the specific plans. He would help organize and enable the action but not defend it.

John Brown's clarity: Brown himself provided the starkest contrast.

Wounded, facing certain execution, he didn't claim insanity, didn't deny his intentions, didn't apologize. He put slavery on trial: "I believe that to have interfered as I have done, in behalf of His despised poor, I did no wrong, but right."

He had crossed the moral line completely. He could live with — and die with — what that meant.

The test: Can you accept that choosing this path will permanently transform you? Can you carry the moral weight not just for a moment of crisis but for the rest of your life? Can you organize action that causes destruction and own that you enabled it? Can you mobilize networks and resources for confrontation and accept responsibility for the consequences?

Most important: Can you make the choice completely, or will you flee, collapse, or equivocate when reality arrives?

The warning: You can't organize resistance that causes destruction and keep your conscience clean. You can't mobilize networks, provide resources, enable confrontation with armed authority, and claim innocence when consequences arrive. You can't build the infrastructure for action through layers of intermediaries and avoid moral responsibility. The Six tried to create distance — organizing through proxies, using coded language, maintaining plausible deniability. Brown's capture collapsed all that distance. They had to choose: own what they had enabled or disown it.

Half measures don't work at this interruption point. Either accept that systematic oppression justifies using whatever tools work or acknowledge that you're choosing to let oppression continue rather than pay the moral price of ending it. Both choices have integrity. What lacks integrity is trying to have it both ways.

The permanent weight: The Six lived with it for fifty years. They were vindicated by history — the war came, slavery died, they became heroes. But vindication is not absolution. In 1909, the surviving members reflected on what they had done. Higginson's confession: "We do not deserve remembering. Although there was no Judas among us, there were six Peters, all who denied John Brown at least once."

Six Peters. Six denials. They had organized the networks, mobilized the resources, activated their circles, built the infrastructure that made Brown's challenge possible. They had also sent a good man to the gallows while, with the exception of Higginson, they hid behind lawyers or fled to Canada. History's judgment couldn't ease the private reckoning.

The power — and the cost: The action worked. Not tactically — Brown's raid failed completely. But strategically, it achieved everything Brown intended. It forced the South to reveal slavery's violence. Forced the North to see federal complicity. Forced the nation to confront what it had avoided for decades. Within eighteen months, the war was raging. Within four years, slavery was dead.

They had been right that these tools were necessary. They had been right to enable Brown. But being right doesn't erase the moral weight. You can be justified, successful, vindicated by history — and still carry the burden forever.

The principle: American resistance has always accepted that whatever tools push back abuse are the ones for the job. If the stakes are high enough, nothing stays off the table — not just money, but organizing capacity, influence, networks, everything. You can be uncomfortable with what's necessary and still accept that it's necessary.

The double standard must be rejected: We celebrate these tools when they create our power, condemn them when they challenge it. Samuel Adams organizing confrontation with armed authority — strategic genius. John Brown and those who enabled him doing the same — dangerous extremists. Patriots mobilizing networks to seize the Lexington arsenal — glorious founding. Shays organizing farmers to seize Massachusetts courthouses — criminal insurrection. Same tools, same organizing, same claim that abusive authority justifies resistance.

When systematic oppression closes all peaceful avenues, resistance must choose completely. Either cross the line fully — accept the transformation, own the consequences, carry the weight — or don't cross at all. You either become someone who can live with what you've enabled or acknowledge that you're not willing to pay that price.

Higginson, Parker, Smith, Sanborn, Stearns, and Howe discovered what every resistance movement learns: This moral weight can't be delegated, insulated, or avoided. It must be carried. Those who can carry it become the sharp edge of resistance. Those who can't reveal the gap between intellectual conviction and moral commitment.

Both responses are human. Both deserve understanding. But only complete commitment — accepting the permanent transformation — can make resistance effective when all peaceful avenues are closed.

Principle #9: Seize the Day — When Resistance Achieves Power, Use It

When resistance finally seizes power, it must act with ruthless clarity and speed to transform the structures that enabled oppression. Hesitation, compromise, or faith that the moment will hold — these guarantee that abusive authority will return. Use power completely while you have it, even if that means breaking the very system you're trying to remake.

The skill you need: Recognize when resistance has achieved a fleeting moment of genuine power, understand exactly what structural transformation victory requires, and execute that transformation before the window closes — even when it means operating outside constitutional norms, breaking institutional rules, or forcing through changes that seem illegitimate to those who benefit from the old order.

The dynamic: For seventy years, the cry had been that however evil slavery was, preserving the Union mattered more. Compromise after compromise — Missouri, 1820; the gag rule, 1836; the Fugitive Slave Act, 1850 — all justified by the need to hold the nation together. The Constitution's slavery clauses were untouchable because touching them might dissolve the Union.

The Radical Republicans said: No. Ending slavery matters more than preserving the Union as it exists. If the Union must be broken to end slavery, break it. If the Constitution must be violated to achieve freedom, violate it. They were resistance insurgents who had spent decades in the wilderness of opposition, and when the Civil War finally gave them power, they seized it with both hands.

Flipping the script: This was Madison's logic turned inside out. The nationalists had always argued that the Constitution's survival trumped moral objections to its compromises. The Radical Republicans recognized that the Civil War had shattered that logic. The Constitution was already broken — the Southern states had seceded, the federal government was at war with its own citizens, the entire structure was in crisis.

So they exploited that crisis. They kept the rebellious states out of Congress — states that had seceded to preserve slavery would now be excluded until they accepted slavery's destruction. They forced through the Thirteenth Amendment while the South couldn't vote against it. Then, when Southern states tried to return to the Union with Black Codes that re-created slavery in everything but name, the Radicals said: No. You don't get back in until you accept the Fourteenth Amendment. And the Fifteenth.

This was constitutional hardball that bordered on — maybe crossed into — illegitimate force. But the Radicals understood something crucial: Their moment wouldn't last. Once Southern states returned to full representation, once Northern voters tired of Reconstruction, once the political coalition that had won the war fractured over other issues, the window would close. They had five years, maybe ten if they were lucky, to transform the constitutional order so fundamentally that slavery could never return.

Whatever it takes: The Radical Republicans were clear-eyed about what they were doing. Thaddeus Stevens, their leader in the House, didn't pretend occupied Southern states had "republican governments" as the Constitution required. He called them "conquered provinces" subject to congressional authority. Charles Sumner didn't argue that the Fourteenth Amendment fit neatly into constitutional procedures. He argued that it was revolutionary reconstruction of the entire federal system.

They understood that achieving resistance victory — not just winning the war, but fundamentally remaking the republic — required operating outside normal constitutional bounds. So they:

- Kept Southern states excluded from Congress for years, denying them representation
- Required Southern states to ratify amendments as a condition of readmission — essentially forcing constitutional changes at gunpoint
- Divided the South into military districts under federal occupation
- Used federal troops to enforce Black voting rights and protect Black officeholders
- Impeached a president (Andrew Johnson) who tried to stop them

None of this was "normal" constitutional politics. It was resistance using power to transform the system that had enabled oppression.

Why this matters now: When resistance movements finally achieve power — through election, revolution, constitutional crisis, or institutional collapse — they face a choice. They can operate within the old rules, respect institutional norms, seek consensus with those who benefited from the old order. Or they can recognize that the moment is fleeting and use power completely to transform structures before it's taken away.

The Radical Republicans chose transformation. And they were right to, because the moment didn't last. By 1877, federal troops withdrew from the South. By 1883, the Supreme Court was gutting the Fourteenth Amendment. By 1896, *Plessy v. Ferguson* declared "separate but equal" constitutional. The counter-resistance had returned, and it would take another century to force the Fourteenth Amendment to deliver what the Radicals had promised.

But — and this matters — the Radicals had embedded constitutional transformation so deep that it could eventually be revived. They didn't just pass laws that could be repealed. They amended the Constitution itself. They created federal powers that, dormant for decades, could later be activated. They planted seeds that would take a hundred years to grow, but they grew.

The test: Can you recognize when resistance has its moment of power? Can you identify exactly what structural changes victory requires? Can you execute those changes with speed and ruthlessness, knowing that you might have months or years, not decades?

Most important: Can you operate outside institutional norms when those norms were designed to protect the old order? Can you break rules, force votes, exclude opponents, use whatever constitutional leverage you have — even when critics call it illegitimate?

The warning: This is dangerous. Using power ruthlessly to transform structures can create backlash that destroys everything you've built. The Radical Republicans' aggressive Reconstruction helped fuel Southern "redemption" and a century of Jim Crow. Their unwillingness to redistribute land or create permanent federal protection for Black rights meant that their constitutional victories could be hollowed out over time.

But the alternative — respecting institutional norms, seeking consensus, moving slowly — guarantees that resistance never achieves structural transformation. The moment passes. The old order reasserts itself. You get symbolic victories, policy changes that can be reversed, laws that can be repealed. But you don't get constitutional transformation.

The calculation: The Radical Republicans understood that moments of genuine power are rare and brief. When the South seceded, it created a constitutional crisis that temporarily broke the old rules. When the North won the war, it created military occupation that temporarily prevented Southern states from blocking change. That window might last five years. Maybe ten.

In that window, they had to:

- End slavery permanently (Thirteenth Amendment)
- Establish birthright citizenship and equal protection (Fourteenth Amendment)
- Guarantee voting rights regardless of race (Fifteenth Amendment)

- Create federal enforcement mechanisms
- Remake Southern state governments
- Establish precedents for federal power over states

They did all of it. Not perfectly. Not permanently, as it turned out. But they did it, knowing that if they failed to act decisively, the moment would pass and slavery would return in different forms.

The long view: Thaddeus Stevens was seventy-three when the Fourteenth Amendment was ratified. He knew he wouldn't live to see whether Reconstruction succeeded. Charles Sumner was beaten nearly to death on the Senate floor in 1856 for opposing slavery. Twenty years later, he was dying, still fighting to protect Black rights, knowing the cause was already being betrayed.

They knew the moment wouldn't last. They knew their work would be undone. They did it anyway, because embedding constitutional transformation — even transformation that would be betrayed — was better than accepting that the old order would simply continue.

The principle: When resistance finally achieves power, it must act with complete clarity about what victory requires and complete ruthlessness in executing that transformation. The moment won't last. Abusive authority will return, will adapt, will find new ways to reassert itself. Your job isn't to hold power forever — it's to transform structures so fundamentally that even when power is lost, the transformation can't be completely undone.

This means:

- Knowing exactly what constitutional/structural changes victory requires
- Acting immediately when the moment arrives, not waiting for perfect conditions
- Using whatever power you have completely, without hesitation
- Breaking institutional norms designed to protect the old order

- Accepting that you'll be called illegitimate, tyrannical, revolutionary
- Understanding that even partial transformation is better than none

The Radical Republicans forced the rebellious states to accept constitutional amendments that destroyed the legal foundation of slavery and created the possibility — not the reality, but the possibility — of genuine equality. It took another century to activate that possibility. But they planted it in the Constitution when they had the chance, knowing the window would close.

The eternal return of abusive authority: The Radicals also understood something darker: Abusive authority always returns. The enslavers' republic would become Jim Crow. Jim Crow would become mass incarceration. Each iteration would exploit whatever openings the constitutional order allowed. That's why transformation had to be structural, not just political. Laws can be repealed. Policies can be reversed. But constitutional amendments, federal powers, citizenship guarantees — these are harder to undo.

Not impossible. The Supreme Court gutted the Fourteenth Amendment for decades. But it couldn't erase it. And when the Civil Rights Movement came, that amendment was still there, waiting to be revived and enforced.

The moment: There's a reason this is the final principle. Most resistance movements never get here. They're crushed before achieving power, or they achieve power but can't hold it long enough to matter, or they hold power but lack the clarity or ruthlessness to use it for transformation.

The Radical Republicans had all three: They achieved power through the crisis of civil war, they held it long enough to force through constitutional amendments, and they had the clarity and ruthlessness to break norms and force change.

They still lost. Reconstruction failed. The old order returned in new forms. But they transformed the Constitution permanently, creating tools that future resistance could use.

That's what seizing the moment means: not guaranteeing permanent victory but instead making transformation possible for those who come after.

Recognition and Action

You're living through these principles right now.

Somewhere, someone is performing resistance while serving their own power grab (Principle #1). Authority is demanding that you call lies truth (Principle #2). A resistance movement is waiting for perfect allies instead of using imperfect ones (Principle #3). Activists are accepting symbolic gestures instead of forcing structural change (Principle #4). Someone who took a brave stand is giving up because they didn't build for the long haul (Principle #5). A movement is fracturing because it never articulated what it's actually fighting for (Principle #6). Individual courage is being crushed because it never evolved into organized infrastructure (Principle #7). People are debating whether violence is ever justified while carefully avoiding whether they could carry its weight (Principle #8). And somewhere, someone just won power and is about to waste it by respecting norms designed to protect the old order (Principle #9).

These patterns are active. The question is whether you can see them.

The greatest trick abusive authority ever pulled was convincing people that resistance is either impossible or belongs to the past — that the dramatic moments of history were unique, unrepeatable, the work of exceptional people in exceptional times. This is a lie designed to keep you passive. The people in this book weren't exceptional. They were ordinary people who recognized patterns, made hard choices, and acted.

You can, too.

These principles won't tell you what cause to serve — that's your decision. But they will help you recognize when you're being manipulated by false prophets, when you're surrendering truth to authority's lies, when you're wasting time on tactics that can't work, when the moment for action has arrived, and when power must be used before it's lost.

The history in this book isn't about the past. It's about the patterns that repeat whenever authority abuses itself and people decide whether to submit or resist. Those patterns are playing out around you right now. The only question is whether you're ready to see them — and what you'll do when you do.

Resistance isn't a departure from American ideals. It's their defense. And their duty.

Acknowledgments

This was not an easy book to write. It rolled through issues, ideas, and histories that should take years to explore and explain, not months. It unravels emotions and beliefs that leave almost everyone unsettled — the conclusions don't let you off the hook. And all of that is true even if the author has, essentially, been working in and through resistance history for an entire career.

But until early in 2025, there was no such thing as resistance history, not as a subject with its own dynamics. We had to build it as we went, buffeted every day by the changing world around us. We drew from the scholarship of resistance, the social dynamics of protest, the principles of restorative justice, and the practice of public history, all to understand what people without power did when people with power turned it against them. That required a new way of looking at the past and its relationship to the present, one that interrogates the very purpose of history but can hold its own weight. When I was approached to write this book, we had to wrestle with fundamental questions. What is resistance? What is it as a noun, a verb, an idea, a practice? What is it in the world and what has it been at home? We had to answer those questions before we could begin to apply what the answers taught us.

For all of those who have traveled and continue to travel that resistance history road with me, I am grateful. They are online, in communities that push back with a force and an intelligence that sustains this work. And they are right in front of us, in classrooms and coffee shops, when I am stopped on the street. They have made resistance history something that belongs to everyone who has taken it up as a necessary conversation. Even an intervention.

But while I cannot mention all of them, there are a few who deserve particular notice.

That has to begin with my editor at Steerforth, Chip Fleischer. Not out of any nod to publishing niceties. Anyone who knows me knows that abiding by niceties is somewhat low on my priority list. But naming him serves a larger purpose, reminding me of the absurdity of one name on the cover of a book like this. This is as much Chip's book as it is mine. Resistance history might have been the work of my career, but Chip articulated it first as an idea and presented it to me, then worked with me, not for me, as we struggled with and through it over the course of this project. With every chapter I wrote and then erased. With everything I couldn't quite explain well enough but had to be satisfied that it was still a contribution. And with accepting that this was the beginning of something, not the end. He has kept it grounded and centered on our moment, even as I moved around the world, and up and down our history, in pursuit of all of these answers. To give any thanks to him as an editor stretches that label — editor — into meaninglessness. He's been a guide and a mentor through a storm, even as it continues to rage.

Similarly, my agent, Rachelle Gardner, has become, in many ways, a life coach for me. She saw who I am, what my work is, and what this book does, and has never once asked for any of that to become safer or, worse, more convenient.

And then there are the others who have thrown themselves into this work, foremost among them the greatest surprise of this project: the community at the Center for American Studies at the University of Southern Denmark. Putting into action what my grandmother once said, that "no one ever stopped their house from burning down from inside the house," they gave me a place, and the space, to do this work — to think more, and push further, than staying at home would have allowed. And then they — the faculty, the students, the administration — went beyond, doing the tough work of understanding not just the history, but what it demands of us.

Chief among them have been my anchors, Anders Bo Rasmussen and Thomas Ærvold Bjerre, who helped me untangle the thorniest resistance questions — not just the historical ones, but the moral ones. To them, and to Per Krogh Hansen, JØrn BrØndal, Niels Bjerre-Poulsen, the legendary David Nye, and our honorary colleague, Stephen Kantrowitz, and everyone else on our hallway, I am grateful. And a special nod to the people who literally made our lives in Denmark possible: Maria Holleman, Catherine Nguyen, and, it must be said, Majken Brandt, who ensured that every single morning — without fail — began with coffee, pastries, and kindness to a worse-for-wear American scholar.

There are the institutions that supported much of this work along the way, not least of which have been the Walden Woods Project and its curator emeritus, Jeffrey Cramer (who kindly reviewed the Thoreau chapter); the Houghton Library and University Archives at Harvard; the Lewis Walpole Library at Yale; the John Carter Brown Library at Brown; the Huntington Library; the International Center for Jefferson Studies at Monticello; and the United Empire Loyalists' Association of Canada.

And the scholars and public historians who shaped individual chapters deserve more than a passing mention. A.J. Mercer in Salem, whose perspective on what it takes to make 1692 real for audiences has been invaluable. At Colonial Williamsburg, Abigail Schumann — a gifted playwright, actor, and historian who has forgotten more about that time and place than I will ever know — gave Nancy Dixon the intelligence, texture, and emotional depth I managed to share here. Bill Weldon, who made me a public historian and remains a polestar, is chief among those at Williamsburg who shaped my perspective, alongside an incomparable frontline interpreter team who never stopped challenging my thinking. Bob Gross, whose scholarship runs through so much of this book, and David Wood at the Concord Museum kept me honest about Thoreau and revolutionary Concord over weekly drinks at the Concord Inn. And Marsha Warfield, who was, and continues to be, a necessary check on the sense and sensibility of what escalation demands and what it costs.

And those, both near and far, who have made all of this possible in ways only they will understand: David C. King, Rick Steves, Frank

Cogliano, Phyllis Hecht, Stephanie Joynes, Christa Dierksheide, Mandy Ranslow, Bonnie Schepers, Jennipher Tucy, Erin McClure Schmitz, Allison Schaum, Joan and Harvey Bines, Carolyn and Jon Wilson, Nina Schutzman and Matt Clark, Shantal Riley and Nick Parker, Susie Tweed and Mike Proscia, and, through decades of this, Jason Daniel Mathews.

But then there are those closest, who have weathered this with me, who are my nearest family: Jack Greene and Amy Turner Bushnell, and Peter Onuf, to whom this book is dedicated, even though the shortcomings in the work do not reflect their influence. Peter read this book as he has read all my work; his interventions alone would make for a better, more reflective work on their own. The chapter on the Bill of Rights, which began its life as the prologue, bears those shortcomings most visibly — much more work needs to be done on it, and whatever it becomes will owe more to Peter than to me. And Fran and Dave Hanyok, and Anthony Soucar and Peter Gemei, who add a layer of meaning to this they will never know.

In the end, the main question of resistance, of risk, of striving for something better, begins and ends not in *what* we do it for, but in *who* we do it for. And therein lies my all, my North Stars, Emily and Kai. Every word on every page. Every idea. Every breath.